Pebbles of the Holy Stream

One man's journey through the three great streams of faith into one mighty river

ROBERT E. CARL

BALBOA.
PRESS
A DIVISION OF HAY HOUSE

Balboa Press books may be ordered through booksellers or by contacting:

Balboa Press
A Division of Hay House
1663 Liberty Drive
Bloomington, IN 47403
www.balboapress.com
1 (877) 407-4847

Because of the dynamic nature of the Internet, any web addresses or links contained in this book may have changed since publication and may no longer be valid. The views expressed in this work are solely those of the author and do not necessarily reflect the views of the publisher, and the publisher hereby disclaims any responsibility for them.

The author of this book does not dispense medical advice or prescribe the use of any technique as a form of treatment for physical, emotional, or medical problems without the advice of a physician, either directly or indirectly. The intent of the author is only to offer information of a general nature to help you in your quest for emotional and spiritual well-being. In the event you use any of the information in this book for yourself, which is your constitutional right, the author and the publisher assume no responsibility for your actions.

Any people depicted in stock imagery provided by Thinkstock are models, and such images are being used for illustrative purposes only. Certain stock imagery © Thinkstock.

Cover design by Barbara VanRossum.

Print information available on the last page.

ISBN: 978-1-5043-5317-5 (sc)
ISBN: 978-1-5043-5319-9 (hc)
ISBN: 978-1-5043-5318-2 (e)

Library of Congress Control Number: 2016905680

Balboa Press rev. date: 4/26/2016

"And the Sabbath rang slowly
In the pebbles of the holy stream"
From "Fern Hill" by Dylan Thomas

Contents

Part I The Evangelical Stream

Part II The Charismatic Stream

Part III The Liturgical Sacramental Stream

Foreward

DURING THE JESUS MOVEMENT AND THE Charismatic Movement of the early 1970s there was a tremendous renewal of evangelism and a genuine spiritual awakening that swept the entire country. Churches experiencing this renewal grew with special events, miracle crusades, healing services and outreaches. Whole denominations seemed to embrace renewal ministries like Cursillo, Faith Alive and Emmaus Road. Interest in missions increased as ministries like Youth With A Mission trained scores of young people and sent them around the globe, and Teen Challenge reached young gang members and addicts. Healing Evangelists and Teaching Ministries were in full bloom. Television evangelists and Christian Broadcasting reached new vistas previously not thought possible. The Full Gospel Business Men's Fellowship and its associate organization, Aglow, were holding chapter meetings and international conventions and reaching the professional community with the gospel message.

Those of us who came to faith during this wonderful time of spiritual refreshing rode the wave of renewal. We attended prayer meetings, fellowship groups and healing services almost nightly. The cassette tape was a new medium that found its niche in the Charismatic Movement. When we weren't in a meeting or a service, we were listening to any number of great Bible teachers on our cassette tape players.

In all this frenzied activity, an underlying desire existed to rediscover the Church of the Book of Acts. The 'home church' movement was in full swing and many of the Bible studies and home prayer meetings soon began to take on the structure of a small church. The appointing of elders soon led to the more formalized rise of the so-called 'Discipleship Movement' or the 'Shepherding Movement'. Watchman Nee's wonderful books on church order became the blueprint for reestablishing the biblical model of the early church.

Unfortunately, most of us never understood that we didn't need to reinvent the wheel in order to find the apostolic order of the early church. We also didn't understand that there existed a great deal of historical information about the early church in the New Testament and in extra-biblical sources. We didn't know about the Apostolic Fathers and the later Church Fathers—most of us acted like the Church started at the Protestant Reformation or the Azusa Street Revival. We tended to transpose our own 'counter-cultural' experience onto the Christian community that we saw in the Book of Acts. The result was a vision of something that never really existed.

While we likely could not have articulated what we imagined, we tended to picture those early Christians as: meeting in homes, like we did; sitting cross-legged in a circle, like we did; clapping their hands and singing scripture songs, like we did; choosing elders from the 'older' men, like we did; and doing everything else just the way we did. In other words, in our minds we created a church in our own image and likeness. Some people even went so far as to sell all that they had and live together in Christian communities—assuming that that was what they did in the Book of Acts. Our experience defined *their* experience, and we created a stilted vision of what we imagined life in the early apostolic church looked like.

Our desire was correct; our longing for biblical authenticity was admirable. Our longing for something deeper, something more meaningful, something more in keeping with our newly found faith and passion, was good and right. But unfortunately, for many people it often ended in spiritual disaster. Many people who were involved in the Discipleship or Shepherding movement found it ultimately to be repressive and smothering. Almost all the attempts at Christian community ended in disappointment, betrayal or worse.

Most of the groups and ministries that survived did so by adding structure and organization. This may sound like a normal next step, but for those who had transitioned from the free-spirited counter-culture it was somehow disheartening. To compound the problem, these organizations tended to borrow or imitate the governmental structure of their parent organizations or other churches and rather than re-discover the life and structure of the early church, perpetuate the reactionary mistakes of the Reformation or the ongoing problems of the historic churches. The same issue of defining the early church by our own experience, rather than allowing the early church to define our Christian experience, continued just as it had from the beginning of the Renewal.

Rob Carl's new book is much more than a story about one man's spiritual odyssey. He has captured the journey of a whole Christian generation. While his story is certainly unique in many ways, in many ways it is not. Those of us who experienced the Jesus Movement or the Charismatic Movement can identify with Rob's circuitous meanderings through spiritual deserts and spiritual mountaintops. His story will resonate with those who have made a similar journey, but also anyone who is still searching for the authentic, biblical and ancient expression of radical Christianity.

A great many people who made this journey through the wonderful, and yet sometimes chaotic and disillusioning, spiritual awakening know what a rollercoaster ride it was. Yet, God never intended it to be that way. The ups and downs, the disappointment of failed leaders, the repressive spiritual abuse and the disillusionment in the Church itself, are entirely of man's making, not God's. Jesus established His church on the foundation of the Apostles and Prophets with Himself as the chief cornerstone. Time would fail me to discuss the historical, theological and ecclesiological causes of these failures, but suffice it to say that many people from these days of the Renewal have found the stability and strength God intended for his Church in the structure and order of the historic church of Apostolic times—in other words the church that Christ and his Apostles established.

Rob Carl's journey into the historic faith from the tempest of the counter-culture, and riding the rollercoaster of the Renewal Movement, was not a rejection of all of the wonderful truths of the Charismatic revival—rather, it was (and is for most of us who share this experience) a homecoming. We did not have to repudiate any of the precious orthodox biblical truths or experiences of our Christian odyssey, because what we have discovered is that the early church had the same beliefs and experiences. It was fully liturgical (just like the

Jewish Temple and Synagogue where Jesus and the disciples worshipped) it was fully evangelical (believing the Scriptures and preach repentance and reconciliation with God) and it was fully charismatic (with signs and wonders accompanying the ministry of the early church). In short, the church was and is supposed to be everything that we experienced and so much more.

Jesus spoke of the householder who brought out treasures new and old. Rob Carl is a faithful 'householder' as he recounts his journey through the new treasures of the Charismatic Renewal, but also shares the ancient treasures of the authentic early church. For those who can relate to Rob's experiences *Pebbles of the Holy Stream* will be heartening confirmation that they are not alone. For those who have shared parts of this journey, Rob's story will open new vistas and hopefully challenge you to new heights. It is my hope that the Holy Spirit will use *Pebbles of the Holy Stream* to bless you and bring you new insights, and to know that God has been with you and directing your path even through the darkest times of your own spiritual odyssey.

Rev. Dr. Martin Eppard
Rector, Church of the Good Shepherd
Baltimore, MD

Introduction

*T*HIS IS MY STORY, AND I AM NOBODY. I AM NOT A rock-star, I am not a Hollywood movie star, and I am not a politician. I haven't accomplished great feats, like climbing mountains, winning in the Olympics, nor have I been awarded a Nobel prize. I am just a man who has seen the Lord working in my life, leading me and guiding me, in spite of me. Leading me and guiding me not in the way most people think of. I prayed in my youth, "Lord, get me where you want me to be no matter what it takes." His response was, "Be careful what you pray. You might not like it." My life has been riddled with mistakes and errors and the more I have tried to get it right the worse it has gotten. Just when I thought the Lord was moving me in a direction, the doors have closed and windows shut. But this is a book about what has happened along the way. It is a book about how the Lord has made the way, His way and His purpose.

I once thought to have a goal that you can achieve is the way to live your life. Just when I thought I had gotten it right, something stood in the way and took me in another direction. "In their hearts humans plan their course, but the LORD establishes their steps" (Pro. 16:9 NIV). It has taken me a long time to learn that He is more concerned with our obedience than our achievements. The achievements and successes may make me feel good and look good. But He doesn't care about how I look and feel. He doesn't care how many people I get in my church, he doesn't care how many I bring to the Lord, and he doesn't care how many people I pray for get healed. No, achievements are narcissistic *me*–centered, and if I have learned anything it is that He wants to be at the center, He *has to be* the center of our lives. Oh, I can tell myself that "I am only doing it for Him," but He knows better, and He wants me to know that He knows! No, if I am truly going to find myself *where He wants me to be no matter what it takes,* I will find that I am no longer there or anywhere, that I have lost myself in Him. The problem is there is just too much of me. And there always has been too much of me. Even if I make losing myself in Him the goal, there is too much of me and my efforts in it.

At one time I thought I could measure my spiritual progress by how much I had given up. The more I gave up the more self-assured I felt. I cut my hair, took off my jeans and put on corduroys with a cardigan sweater. I gave away my accumulated record collection and my stereo. I was doing so good at giving things up, I thought I could become the next St. Frances of Assisi. I began to look down on all those who did not give up as much as I had. They just were not as spiritual as I was. My Bible went with me everywhere and grew in size so it could be recognized a block away. Even my speech became King James. Oh, I was so holy! I was so proud of how holy I had become. That's when failure first hit me. So I decided I would die to self. I found it can't be done without me trying to take credit for it along the way. Someone has said that if you try to crucify yourself, you will only succeed in getting the job partly done.

Once you have nailed your feet and one hand, you will still have one hand free.

I once thought I had found the key to getting where the Lord wanted me to be. It was in Acts 14:22 when St. Paul said, "We must go through many tribulations to enter the kingdom of God." So I figured I *had* to go through trials and tribulations to get to where I was going. I began to embrace them and thank God for them. I even prayed for them. When I did, the more they piled on. I found myself in a ministry with opposition to my leadership. I found myself in a marriage that opposed, or at least, did not reflect the faith I imposed on it. It nearly crushed me as I waded into resentment and drove deeper into depression. So I said, "Lord, you have never tested me in my finances, why don't you change directions?" I remarried. She a woman with three kids; I adopted them and sent them to a Christian School, suddenly there never was enough money. Then I said, "Lord the financial thing didn't help much why not my health." Then my health faded with a concussion that created Hypoglycemia, which caused me to have "gray outs." For two years I found myself almost passing out as I sat at my desk or on my way home from work. Once, I even crawled out of my car and up the steps of my home.

And all along, my goal seemed to be getting further and further away from the shore. And the harder I tried to look right on the outside, the more I failed on the inside. So I stopped praying for tribulation and temptation, it would come anyway without my help. I said to myself, "I'll just remain faithful to my vision and calling." A deep sensing in me said I couldn't keep it up, there were just too many obstacles in the way that kept bumping me off the path. The further I got away from the direction I thought the Lord was taking me, the more I thought time was my enemy. I had seen that many who started well didn't end well. So I prayed, "When I am old Lord, keep me in the faith, I pray that I may never fall away or grow indifferent to you." I am glad I prayed that because now I am old and the Lord has kept me. And when I look back on my life, as I have done in this book, I see that the boulders that fell in my way had purpose. The purpose was to direct me to get me where he wants me to be. His purpose was in the process, not the place. And when I look back on those boulders, they somehow seem smaller than they did at the time they were blocking my way. I now see that they have only been Pebbles of the Holy Stream.

Prelude

As I lay face down and my arms stretched out in the shape of a man being crucified, my nose buried in the red commercial church carpet, the cross I was warned not to wear was pinned in the hallow of my chest. Fear trembled through my body as I thought about what was going on. This is what I had wanted for God only knows when but now that it was finally happening dread, apprehension, and the fear of falling into absolute failure had me in its grips. Doubt, deep seated upon the platelets of my mind was trying to drown me and it was succeeding as my breath faded. Time seemed to stop in the moment drawing me back into a cavalcade of events from the past to what brought me here, I would be forced to examine it all...

This Book is Dedicated to
Meg Carl and our Wonderful Children
Wendy, Jesse and Tara

Part I
The Evangelical Stream

"I urge you to be saved. This Christ desires."
– St. Clement of Alexandria

1
Groan in the Wind

WHEN THE WIND BLEW, THE ROADS CLOSED. THE air became a wall of sand impossible to see through. Only the foolhardy ventured beyond its prison walls, then to find themselves captive to gritty teeth, clouded lungs and closed, caked tear ducts. Restlessness, call it youth, has a way of obstructing judgment, creating misguided venture and giving way to planned disaster. A debacle like an explosion in a mine of which only its owner knew diamonds existed. I had lit the fuse not because I was the miner but because it was there, waiting to happen. And now it was in this place that I found myself looking for escape. Like Othello, whose name my home had embraced, I listened to what I had thought was truth, not knowing what I had believed was lies. I had longed for another life than my own, and I envisioned one in the image of peace, love and rock 'n roll, the alternative society which had crumbled from within causing one to grasp for a foothold in the shifting foundation of narcissistic mud. Here I had found myself recently released from prison, for possession of marijuana, standing on the street corners of Spokane trying to peddle someone else's dope.

Everywhere we went, there were longhaired freaky people,

like us, standing on the same corners rejecting our wares, interjecting theirs. It was here that there was this one girl with long, dark brown poufy hair like it had just been washed without conditioner, wearing patched jeans and a T-shirt draped with a plaid shirt two sizes too big. What got me was the glow in her eyes and the smile on her face and the tendentious way she spoke to me. I wanted to run from her, but something wouldn't let me.

"Do you know Jesus?" she asked.

I must have looked puzzled, because she seemed to clarify the question, "Are you a Christian?" I thought I was a Christian, after all I had been taught in school that this was a Christian nation and I was born here, so I had to be, didn't I? My mind flooded with thought, in an instant.

When I was six years old, I went to a Baptist church and everyone had to wear their clothes backward. I was so uncomfortable the way my pants felt, it was hard to walk or sit down. Worse yet, I found out that most of the other kids hadn't participated that acutely and if they did participate at all, they only had their shirts on backward. But that was me, I always had to do things exact to feel I had succeeded, otherwise I wouldn't even try. There rarely was any middle ground and certainly no gray areas. It was called "backward" day because the point, I believe, was that most of us need to get our lives turned around. All I knew was I couldn't wait to get out of there and get my pants turned around.

Then when I was twelve, my parents got a visit from the local Lutheran pastor. My dad said he liked him because he would have a beer with him. My mom liked him because he was Lutheran, and she was Norwegian (on her father's side). The next thing you know we were in the Lutheran Church. This was the first and only time I remember the whole family attending church together, with any regularity. We went to catechism and got to keep the little book. My dad got a bigger book called the New English Bible, but he wasn't much on reading. I had a Bible, some neighbors my mom had called "religious", had asked if they could give it to me when they first saw me as a baby in the bassinette. I couldn't read it of course, but I asked my mother to read it to me when I got older; she tried but neither one of us could understand it. It had a lot of thees and thous in it.

When I got older, thirteen I think, I decided I would rewrite it, to make it more understandable, you know take all "the thees and thous" out of it. That was kind of a novel idea at the time and the book was big so I didn't get very far, besides the thees and thous made it sound holy and maybe we weren't suppose to understand it. Mom said it was a holy book and we needed to treat it with respect, so I was careful not to put it on the floor. I also was careful not to show her the crayon additions I had put in it before I understood how holy it was.

We also got to keep the little white cloths they had used to wipe off the water from our foreheads when my whole family had gone up to the altar in that Lutheran church to receive the sacrament of baptism. After that we never went to church much again, I think that beer drinking pastor had left.

My mind went on, back to when I was in the county jail awaiting trial at the age of eighteen for the illegal possession of marijuana. I had found a book positioned under a leg of the bed to keep it from rocking, it was called *Good News for Modern Man*. I felt strangely warm and kind of high when I read it, it made me want to pray and talk about it to my cellmate. And then there were those jailhouse preachers who came on Sunday to preach hell fire and condemnation and ask us to come to the altar to lay our lives down and repent of our sinful ways. There were bars and no altar that I could see. I had got saved each time they came. I raised my hand and they prayed for me. I needed all the help I could get. I was in jail and facing a maximum of twenty years. (Possession at this time in Maryland was still a felony. What I didn't know at the time was that state legislators had already voted to make it a misdemeanor, which would go into effect two months after I was convicted for being a felon.) That's what I got for throwing myself on the courts mercy without a lawyer and pleading guilty. I had been asked by a secret admirer who called me and said her friend had just gotten back from Nam and wanted some good weed if I could help her help him. I being the kind of guy who was always willing to be helpful, gave a lid to her friend. He paid me back (after I argued with him that he didn't need to after what he had just been through being in Viet Nam and all) for what I had spent, $5.00, and turned out to be a rookie policeman with a fake mustache he kept pushing back against his lip, undercover, hungry for publicity. He got it and so did I, eighteen months!

But I wasn't getting what my pursuant was doing, who was still standing with me on the corner, when my mind had wandered.

"Come on let's go," said a friend who had come with me, as he gave me a gentle tug, "she's a Jesus Freak."

"Yeah, I am a Christian," I had found my lips saying.

"Do you read the Bible," she implored holding a big black book out at me as if it were a platter.

"Yeah, we read it. We get stoned and read Revelation," I said trying to sound cool yet increasingly feeling awkward and stupid. I moved stumbling away from her as she followed.

"Look there is a coffee house just down the street and a great band is going to be playing tonight, Wilson McKinley, why don't you come," she requested.

"Yeah, yeah maybe we'll do that, I am with a bunch of guys. I'll see if they might want to do that," I said trying to placate her and make my exit gracefully.

"Jesus loves you," were her final words to me as I waved, turned and walked away. Those words echoed in my head, how could he "love me". Love was the buzz word of the day; "Peace and Love" were going to change the world. In fact it was so real to us that some simply called it "The Movement". *The Beatles* sang about it, and we were all about it at our festivals, we even had a summer of love – "if you're going to San Francisco be sure to wear some flowers in your hair..." huh?

Needless to say we felt a lot of "love" for the Jesus People as we were leaving Spokane with more drugs and less money in our pockets than we had hoped to come back with. The trip back to Othello took about an hour and a half and the conversation was riddled with how we could eliminate the Jesus People. They were sending astronauts to the moon in those days, and we thought they could probably find room for some long-haired freaky people with Bibles, or as someone even suggested we could just all get some guns and blow their heads off – "all you need is love" the radio played. Love, there was that word again, Jesus loved me – what did that mean? When we got home Keith, who was my sister's boyfriend and the one who was really peddling the dope, had bought it and wanted our help to "unload it" (of course being the helpful person that I was) I had agreed until I got bummed out over the talk about blowing people's heads off and all. So I decided I would just go for a walk when Keith came running after me and grabbed my arm and said, "Where are you going?"

"We have a lot of drugs why don't we just do them up?"

I pulled away. "Na, I'm not in the mood," I said truthfully.

Then he said with a knowing look, as the grin got wider and more sarcastic, "I bet I know where you are going."

"You're going to see that Jesus Freak, Steve," he added grabbing me again.

Steve had been a friend of mine, back when we both worked in a local restaurant. He was a wonderful guitar player and could play more like Jimi Hendrix than anyone I had ever known. But he had always been a depressed, melancholy person who liked being alone. Recently, he had written me a letter; in it he had explained how he had turned his life over to the Lord Jesus and how the Lord had placed me upon his heart. He wrote that God had a plan for my life if I only would give Him a chance. Up to that point I hadn't thought about it. Steve Anderson had recently become a Christian, and he was inviting me to get to know the Lord as well.

Keith grabbed me again, harder, which made me mad and glared at me and said, "I did my Jesus thing in California last year and there is nothing to it."

I jerked away and said, "I think I will go see Steve." I turned and headed down the street.

That was one of the last times I talked to Keith. He was found weeks later with a bullet in his head. He was trying to score some grass and for two hundred dollars he had been killed, shot in the back of the head execution style. I have often thought about that portion of scripture from 1 John 5:16 "... *There is a sin leading to death.*" And that sin is when we reach the place where we completely reject the Holy Spirit's work in our lives to lead us to God through the acceptance of Jesus Christ. Keith had certainly made his decisive rejection; there was no need for his name to remain in the Fathers book of life.

2
If It's the Last Thing

OTHELLO WASN'T A BAD PLACE, IT WAS JUST small; the most populated the town ever got was about 5,000, but that was counting the farmers, migrant laborers and probably a few of the cattle in the stockyards by the railroad tracks at the end of Main Street. The sign at the east entrance of town said Ot**hell**o population 2,269. Some vandal had crossed out the letters "o-t-o" so it spelled "hell", but it wasn't that bad except in the summer when the temperatures could reach 114° without much humidity. It was located in the semi-arid area of the Columbia Basin and was a product of the U.S. Bureau of Reclamation, which was formed in 1902 to bring water to the arid areas of the United States, the Columbia Plato being one of those areas. But that area saw none of the dream until after much debate and the work was begun on the Grand Coulee Dam in 1933, which at the time would hold the title of the largest dam in the world for years to come. The Bureau would draw up canals of water from the dam through the desert, filled with loess soil[1] covered with sage brush, tumble weeds, and small cacti would bloom. The area would become one of the largest producers of potatoes, corn and sugar beets. And, the dam would produce enough hydro-electricity to power a good portion of the west coast. This is how I got there. No, they didn't find me in some sand dune huddled up next to some horn toads and rattle snakes, but my father who had been a Sea Bee in the Navy went to work for the government right after being discharged.

My mother grew up on the White Swan reservation not because she was an Indian, but because she was poor. She was on what they called in those days: "Relief." Today we would call it welfare. She grew-up resenting the "well-to-do" as she called them, she would always find something wrong with them and "their nose in the air" as she described them. I think she did this, not because she was mistreated, but she struggled with her own inferiority complex. Her criticism of the upper middle class or the wealthy was to protect herself from those feelings. She told me she would get a new dress for school from the government relief and go to school feeling good about her new clothes only to find three other girls with the same dress. It was like wearing a sign on her back, "look at me I am a low class poverty-stricken waif."

Her mother, who was Scottish by way of England, worked every hour of the day to provide for her two girls and her alcoholic Norwegian husband who would come home after a long, hard day of chasing women and drinking and then beat her. My mother, who adored her father, was taken aside by him after her mother had told him to leave and asked her what she wanted him to do. Being a child of eight to ten years old, she made the decision she would never quite get over, she told him he should leave.

He moved back to South Dakota never to return. Grandma would remarry into a family whose last name was Carl, his first name was Fred. He was the older brother of my Father's dad whose name was George. Fred already had been married before and had a large family, so my mom and her sister never really felt accepted. In fact, the way my mom told it she was treated like the stepchild, which, of course, she was. When she moved out, she said they stole her toy dolls and some clothes. She never ever had much, so to have it stolen was very painful, especially by those who had taken her place in her mother's life. My grandmother succumbed to the poverty syndrome. After the death of Fred, she lived with many different men and drank a lot. I had little, if any, respect for her when I was a preteen and young teen. Now my heart goes out to her and the pain she must have lived with. I later tried to talk to her about the Lord, but she couldn't understand that Jesus loved her. For one thing, her parents, the Nesmith's, were "Adventists", she would tell me. At this time, the Seventh Day Adventists were very legalistic and strict to the max. I'm convinced this was her greatest obstacle to understanding grace.

She finally met a guy who was several years younger than her and lived with him. To me Bob was just another one of her men that she "shacked up" with. Mom always said Bob was good to her. He finally married her and wanted us to call him grandpa, but I couldn't bring myself to do it, he wasn't my grandpa, Fred was the last grandpa I knew in her house and even he wasn't really my grandpa, he was actually my great uncle on my father's side. She went blind and I still tried to bring her to the Lord and she may have finally prayed "The Prayer" with me, we'll see if she made it in the kingdom to come. The Lord has a funny way of getting around our distain, and in spite of us, reaching the lost where they are.

Mom met my Dad and was married while he was still in the Navy. I have a picture of their wedding day, and he is in his uniform. Dad had been engaged to another woman who jilted him while he was away in the South Pacific, her name was Betty as well, and, in fact, he had a tattoo on his arm with her name on it in a ribbon. Mom made Dad block out her name when he married her. He said but your name is Betty too, yeah she replied, that wasn't put there for me. Mom had lived with his sister when there was no room with her stepdad Fred. That is how he met her. She then moved in with his mom, dad and sister and brother for a time until he got out of the Navy and after that moved to an apartment above a country store on the reservation. I know this because as we drove by he pointed at it he very proudly proclaimed, "There over that store is where you were made." I got a picture in my mind of my mother, covered in flour pounding away at some dough shaping me, not that she loved to bake. Now if Fred was my Dad's uncle and my Mom's stepdad that made my mother my cousin by marriage.

She told me, after I had given my life to the Lord, that I wasn't her first pregnancy, she had had a miscarriage. And when she got pregnant with me she said she prayed and said, "Lord if you let me keep this one – I'll give him to you." I think the Lord likes to answer these kinds of prayers from a mother's heart. They moved to a veteran's relief camp near Ephrata, Washington. Mom started having labor pains a month early – not sure why— and someone, probably my grandmother took her to the nearest hospital which was in Soap Lake,[2] McKay Memorial Hospital. It was early in the morning and my uncle had to go to the relief camp to get my Dad who was so rattled, he ran out of the house with one shoe on and no car keys locking himself out of the house.

My uncle who was younger had to boost my dad through

a window so he could start over again. No doubt this boost reminded him of the time when he and my dad were living at home and my grandmother who was no skinny-minnie caught the chimney on fire and told my dad and his brother Uncle Red (actually Harvey) to get on the roof and run a hose down the chimney and put out the fire. While my Dad went looking for the ladder and hose, my grandmother was so excited she grabbed my uncle, picked him up and threw him on the roof with all that adrenaline running through her veins. Uncle Red, at first, just clung to the roof's edge and stared at her in horror while she flung the hose at him and told him to get his butt moving.

The doctor was impatient and didn't care for false alarms so he induced labor and took forceps, attached them to my soft skull and turned me and pulled me out at 6:02 in the morning. When they handed me to my mother, she took one look at me and began to cry, she knew instinctively that I was born with a problem. The doctor argued with her for a few minutes and then the nurse said, "Doctor, look at his skin and the color of his face; he is struggling to breath." Not only was I jaundice, but because I was premature I had a collapsed lung. I had to be kept in an incubator. My mother didn't get to hold me again or take me home for two months until my lungs had fully developed. I can't imagine what my mother went through during this time, but you can bet there were a lot of prayers.

Snakes and Runaways

The first place I remember living with my parents was a USBR camp called Royal Camp (not to be confused with Royal City which would come around later). Royal Camp would serve those who worked on the crews for bringing water to this area of the desert. We lived in a Quonset hut just about in the middle of the camp, which was made up of three or four streets. There was a brick office building, three streets of Quonset huts and one horseshoe shaped street with small houses with asbestos siding where the crew chiefs and higher ups got to live. My mom called them the "well-to-do" in the camps. Because it was a small camp, families became very close, my parents played cards with friends, and my mom would visit neighbors during the day.

I can remember my mom introducing me to her friends and new neighbors, and they would always make over me like: "What a handsome boy, or what a polite boy." My mom had taught me my manners well, "please and thank you misses so-and-so". I heard it so much that I began to think of myself as "hot stuff". It began to come out in ways of obstinacy and defiance. My mother introduced me by my name, Robert. But people always wanted to call me Bobbie or Bob. I would promptly correct them, "My name is not Bob it is Robert!" To me it sounded like being called "Bloob" or something icky – anyway it wasn't my name, I was Robert and you had better get it right. It would be a couple years later that a cute little girl in another camp would start calling me Rob and for some strange reason I liked how it sounded coming from her, that, I would allow.

Oftentimes, when the jobs were completed the people were moved to another camp together. So we would become like family. One such family was the Freedmans, another was the Ipsons. My dad was known to everyone as "Red" for the color of his hair. His brother, his mom who was half Irish on her mom's side (the Brown's) and mixed German on her father's side (the Hiatt's) all had red hair. She was a stout woman who loved to cook and clean, I loved to go to her house for the holidays! Grandpa was dark haired — jet black, and spoke French so we always thought he was French. But his dad, my great-grandpa, told the family that the name had changed when they came to America by way of Quebec, the name was Carles or Carlos (I never could get it straight). When he got to America, the Census Bureau listed his name as "Carl" born in Ireland, he married a French-Canadian woman and that's how Grandpa learned to speak it. My whole family: my dad and brother and two sisters had red hair. We had some hairy arguments in our house – (more on that later). I think you can see why with so much fighting Irish in us!

Back to the camp: Dad and Carl Freedman built a chicken coop at the camp and we had fresh eggs and good chicken dinners until the chicken coop burnt down just after a family with a wild boy several years older than me moved in, his name was Donnie Rale. (Whenever something bad happened like a break-in at headquarters, Donnie got the blame).

My sister Pamela was born while we were living at the camp, I was two and a half at the time she was born. I had to be a couple of years older when something terrible happened. I remember my mom putting Pam and I down for a nap and telling me she was going to have a cup of coffee with a friend who lived in the nice houses about a half a block away. She asked me if I knew where it was and I said, "Is it the green one?" and she said yes, and she told me to come get her if sissy woke up before she got back. I awoke from my nap with Pam screaming, and I wandered from my room just as the front door shut and someone ran out as I was rubbing my eyes. I could see blood on the floor coming from the room where sissy's crib was kept and a sight stick on the floor (my Dad's crew were surveyors and used these sticks to mark out the area they were outlining). It had blood on it. I walked to the green house to get mom, it seeming like such a long ways away, not knowing for sure where I was going because the houses all looked the same, then I remembered "green". When I got there, I knocked for what seemed like forever, I remember Mom looked uncomfortable to see me, so I hesitated to speak. She said, "Robert what are you doing here?" I am sure she didn't mean it to sound that way but it made me think I was in trouble so I hesitated again, then I said "Sissy had blood on her," and everyone gasped and mom got up and ran to the house leaving me to follow a long ways back. It seems to me Donnie's name came up. All I know is, he wasn't seen on the playground anymore and the family moved away. Mom never left us alone like that again. When Dad got home from work, I heard him yelling while I hid under the covers of my bed trying not to hear.

Royal was an interesting place in many ways not only for the community but for the country which in the desert has its own beauty. When the winds came up, the dust storms were terrible and the tumble weeds would come rolling down the streets. But then there were the snakes, rattle snakes and bull snakes mostly. One day I left the playground and came home to find a large snake curled up in the corner of our front porch. I quickly ran in the house yelling for Mom who reassured me that the snake was a bull snake, and we liked them because they ate rattle snakes. She called Booney, who was like the camp carpenter. He came right away and got the snake. It was nothing for us to go to the playground and find a snake curled up under the monkey bars. Some of the kids used sticks to poke at them. I'd just go home and matter-of-factly tell Mom there was another snake.

I was always hardheaded and strong-willed, which would develop into immaturity and get me in a lot a trouble. Case in point, one time my mother had boiled a pot on the electric stove though it was off, and it hadn't cooled down yet. I held my hand over it, and she looked at me and firmly said, "Robert, don't touch that stove, it's hot." I looked at her defiantly and proceeded to flatten my hand across the red hot burner. I screamed as she came running and put something on my severely blistered hand. Another time I decided I was going to run away from home because I didn't like her disciplining me for some reason. I could see mischief in my mother's eyes when I made the pronouncement. So I pulled out my dad's overnight bag he had left over from the Navy. She asked me what I was going to pack. First went in it my Teddy bear and I thought that was enough, but she asked me, "Aren't you going to need some clean clothes to wear?"

I hadn't thought about that, but I acted like it was my idea, so I emptied my sock drawer into the bag.

"How about underwear," she said.

I said, "Yeah okay." So I put in one pair of underwear.

She asked me if I would need more than that. I very assuredly said no. She said, "What about a tooth brush or soap and wash cloth?"

I said I wouldn't need any of that since she wouldn't be around to tell me to brush my teeth and wash my hands and face.

As I was going out the door she asked, "Where are you going to run away to?"

I hadn't thought about that either! I just thought about the "running away" part and hadn't considered the "going to" part. It was then the idea popped into my head, "I am going to live with Grandma."

Grandma lived about eighty-five miles away in Moxee City, near Yakima.

"How are you going to get there?"

"I will get Daddy to drive me."

"But Daddy is at work, he can't drive you."

Well, then I decided, I would walk. Moxee was at least a two hour drive in those days.

Mom said she was going to be very sad not to have me anymore, but if I wanted to go then "good-bye".

"Bye," I said feeling proud of myself. That would show her! But, I no sooner started down the steps when regret started creeping in. In my mind I could see my mother crying and crying because I was gone. But I left anyway; I started walking down the street. I wasn't sure how to get to Grandmas, but I thought I knew the way out of the camp.

The camp was surrounded by prairie cattle and so there was a mote, fence and a cattle guard to keep the cows out of the camp. The cattle guard had to be crossed because it was on the road out of the camp. There was also a rail gate that swung across the road and was locked at night. I was hoping it would be open and it was. Then I started across the cattle guard. The cattle guard was made up of round rails with two to three inch gaps between them. The whole thing was about ten feet wide over the road, this was to prevent the cattle hooves from being able to walk across into the camp. What I didn't know is that it was also hard to walk across if you had small feet. As I started to cross, my feet slipped off the well worn rails, smooth and slick, and my little leg got caught in the gap between them and dangled above the mote below, where there were always snakes. I looked for them to jump up and get me, but I didn't see any. I would no sooner get my leg out, and I would slip again and got it caught in the next rail. I was getting frustrated. This could take all night! I would have to go back home and wait for Daddy to get home so he could help me run away.

I got to my front door, which was never locked and tried the knob and it wouldn't turn. So I started knocking, but nobody came, so I started hollering Mommy, MOMMY, **MOMMY!** Finally someone came.

"Who is it," she said through the door.

"It's me Robert."

"I don't know any Robert," she said matter-of-factly.

"I live here," I was in a panic.

"I don't have a little boy living here anymore. He ran away."

That did it, I started sobbing. "But I'm your little boy and I WANT to live here."

She opened the door. "Do you promise not to run away anymore?"

"I do, Mommy." And I buried myself in her arms, with tears streaming down my cheeks.

That was not to be the last time I would run-away, but the next time would be years later.

Horn Toads and Missiles

Royal Camp was early in my life, but I still remember so much about it like the time my Dad went to Moses Lake to buy a new sleeping bag and came home with a box with a glass front on it. He put this tall antenna up next to the Quonset hut, and we turned off all the lights and suddenly there were people moving and talking on this thing called a television. Because of the winds, Dad always had to run outside and turn the pole so we could get the picture back, which would often just show snow or an Indian in the center of a bull's-eye.

We had a lot of creatures join us in our Quonset hut. Sometimes birds would get in and mom would have to wait for dad to get home to chase them out with a broom. Sometimes Dad would bring home his lunchbox full of sand and buried in it would be a horn toad, which looked a lot like a tiny fat little dinosaur. And we had a lot of mice. We had one mouse who would come out every night to watch TV with us, Mom and Dad would stomp their feet and try to shoo him away, but he would turn and look at us as if to say, "Hey, keep it down can't you see I am trying to watch TV here."

Royal Camp in 1961 would become one of the six or seven areas in the west where the government would place Titan 11 missile silos pointed at Russia. We were not far from the Saddle Mountains and a few miles from Radar Hill. On the other side of the mountains was the Columbia River, where it made a big bend. And on the other side of the river was a secret government facility called the Hanford Project established in 1943. Only seven years before I was born, it was a part of the <u>Manhattan Project</u>, it was there they made the Atomic Bomb.

We had to cross the mountains (actually bare hills) to get to Grandma's house and on the highway there were warning signs telling us we were in a restricted area "No stopping allowed" with red lights on them. If they were blinking you would have to turn around. I only remember the red lights blinking once or twice, this meant that there had been a spill of radioactive material at Hanford. Now years later the whole area is contaminated and a project of ongoing restoration.

3
Flying High

WHEN I WAS FIVE WE MOVED TO THE TOWN OF Warden, Washington. Warden had been settled in the late 1800s by immigrants of Russian-German (Bessarabian) ancestry who homesteaded in the area and farmed dryland wheat. Prior to this, the area had been inhabited by local Native American Salish tribes that had contact with the early Spanish and British traders.[3] Warden was a German word which meant "worthy" or "treasured". It was neither.

Although the dryland farming known as Horse Haven Hills near Walla Walla was one of the most beautiful places I had ever seen, (it was where there truly were "amber waves of grain") in the middle of those fields were always ghost farms. Places where the hopes and dreams of immigrants had dried up and died leaving sun bleached homes and broken windmills.

My mother wanted to make sure I started school in September, though my birthday was past the due date to start first grade. They told her that it would be better to let me wait either until the beginning of the year when they were going to try a new thing called "kindergarten" or next September when I would be six. My mother was always pushing me ahead, she said I would be fine, after all, I had started talking at six months and walking at nine. Looking back on this move, I can now understand why they wanted me to wait, and how that would have helped me succeed in the long run. Most of the kids had been six for months, some were seven. Many came from farms where they had to grow up faster by helping out on the farms, feeding the livestock, chickens, pigs and cows and gathering eggs – doing chores before school. They were strong, smart and taller than me. I was small, skinny, sickly and very shy.

What I liked about school the most was recess. And because I was the new kid in town and very shy, I had a tendency to only have best friends. Those, I would single out. I didn't fit in with groups. I never played sports much mainly because I was the last to be picked and then I would be left on the bench or put in outfield. I was terribly uncoordinated and lacking in confidence.

Because I had asthma, I always felt different. In those days there was not much you could do for asthma. In fact, most doctors and teachers thought it was a psychological problem. My mom tried everything from putting a pan of steaming water in front of me with a towel over my head to putting Vicks Vaporub on my chest to help me breath. We know now that only makes matters worse. I was highly allergic to animal dander. So that meant I couldn't hang out with the farm kids (or any kids that had pets) who would come to school with fresh dander on their clothes having hugged or fed them before they got there. Later my parents purchased a mask made out of plastic with a foam filter for me to wear when I went out of the house – that did not last too long. It only added to my sense of being a freak.

First grade was not too bad. But I couldn't ever get away

with anything good or bad. Someone asked me a question who was sitting right behind me and because I wanted to be helpful, I turned to ask what I could do for them. That is when the teacher caught me and brought me forward and made me sit on a stool with a rag tied around my mouth for talking in class. That wasn't as bad as some of the other kids though, one had to wear a dunce cap (yeah they really used to do that) for doing something wrong and one she made sit in the closet with the door closed. So I didn't feel too bad. I can say it didn't do a lot for my self-esteem having all the kids laughing at me with a rag tied around my mouth covering half my face.

Moving to Warden meant moving out of the Quonset hut into a real house with two big willow trees in the front yard that you could climb to the top of and a big hedge of lilac bushes between my house and Jerri Snyder's next door. She was another cute girl I liked back then who had moved from Royal Camp. We mostly fought about to whom the lilac bushes belonged. Terrie Duncan lived behind us. She came over to play one day, and she decided we would be boyfriend and girlfriend. That meant, she informed me, we would have to kiss. I don't think I had ever kissed before. I had been kissed by my grandmother (the Scottish / English one) who smelt like alcohol and of course my Mom. I liked the idea of kissing Terrie. Just as we did, Mom walked in. Mom thought it was cute and got her Brownie Kodak camera and took our picture smooching. I think she showed it to Terrie's mom, but she didn't think it was cute. Terrie wasn't allowed back to visit.

The winters were long and cold and the summers were short and hot. I remember one school morning it raining and freezing as soon as it hit the ground. I had to walk up a hill from our government house, past the "nice houses" and I had my rubber boots on over my shoes. As hard as I worked to get up that hill with every step I took, I would slide back. Finally, I made it halfway up, and I was exhausted and very late for school, but I was proud of myself for making it that far. So with the next step I took, my feet started sliding backward quickly, which threw my upper body forward. I caught myself with my hands and gloves and instead of sliding down on my belly. I remained in this position in the shape of a capital A, my butt in the air sliding all the way backward down the street.

Forts and Flaming Noses

It was an adventure living in Warden and as kids we were always making treasure maps and creating forts to play in. Some older kids had made "an underground" fort at the end of the street, where the fields stopped planting and the road ended. It was dug out and covered with plywood and dirt. I wasn't allowed in it because I was a little kid and not old enough to be a part of their club. These were the big kids. I think they were twelve, and I was only six at the time. But one of them was a Bureau of Reclamation kid like me. He told me what it was like. You had to crawl down this long "hallway" and then make a sharp right and slip down into the "room" which had candles in it on shelves that you had to light and then there were shelves carved out of the dirt where they planned on storing candy, games and maybe a book or two. It sounded wonderful! I couldn't help myself. I watched the fort and waited for everyone to go home and I sneaked into it. As I crawled in and realized I couldn't turn around in the "hallway" which was very narrow, the thought came to me that there might be a snake in the room. It was dark, very dark. I started to panic, but I couldn't turn around so I pushed on! The hall wasn't as long as I had envisioned. In fact, when I fell into the room and felt for the candles and matches, I lit them and realized the room wasn't all that big or neat, either. But still, I was in! That's when I noticed on the floor little things crawling around! When I saw what they were I froze! They were scorpions. These were pale white ones not black like ones I had seen in the movies or books, but they had their tails curled back ready to strike. My older friend told me they were not poison like the black ones, but I wasn't going to stick around to find out. I blew the candle out and hoped they couldn't see me as I couldn't see them. I scampered out of there not interested in going back.

High Flying Low Feeling

The wind blew a lot, but this was good for flying kites. I got pretty good at it. I'd go down to the variety store and buy a kite and then get some string. I'd wrap it around a stick and let the kite go up as high as the string would allow. One time I got two spools of string (about 500 ft. of string). It took all day to tie them and wrap the string in one spool. The next day I added more tail to the kite to steady it as it went up and up! Higher and higher, it got so high I couldn't see it, just a dot in the sky.

And then came the time to reel it in, before Dad came home and we had to eat. First, my Mom yelled for me to hurry home before my Dad got there because she would have to have food on the table when he got home. But the harder I tried the more tired I got. Finally I heard my Dad yell for me, and he was mad.

I started crying and said I was trying; he just yelled all the more and finally told me to cut the line and get home. I told him I couldn't; I didn't have a pocketknife. He said he would do it! I said, "No Dad I don't want to lose it," it was a great kite! I don't know if my Mom spoke to him or not, but two hours later he came home with the kite intact and his dinner in the oven, he was burning mad. He was always mad, I don't remember him ever talking to me at all when I was little. When I got older he would just yell at me, or make sarcastic remarks which I didn't understand. I just knew he didn't like me. He used to beat me with his belt when I needed discipline and scream at me and call me names. He never ever hugged or kissed me, and he would never think of telling me he loved me as a kid.[4]

He played Santa Clause on Christmas Eve when Mom would look out the window and say I think Santa is coming to our house. Dad would go outside and bang on the roof. Mom would then say we needed to pretend we were asleep[5]. And then Dad would come in Ho Ho-ing, with a slur in his voice from drinking. Now, don't get me wrong, I don't think my Dad was an alcoholic. Christmas was the only time when I was little that I remember he was drinking, but then I wasn't sure if it was him or Santa that had a few too many!

I don't think he knew how to relate to me, I was different. I remember he gave me a BB gun for Christmas. He was a hunter and a fisherman. The first time I took my BB gun out hunting, and I saw some birds that looked like pigeons on the roof of the house across the street with the big picture window. I shot at one of them and nothing happened. They seemed to be ignoring me. I shot at a sparrow in the tree over my head and it fell. I picked it up and it was limp, its little head tipped from side to side. I saw blood where the BB went in and I began to cry because I had killed this living thing. It had been alive and chirping; one minute later it was dead, because of me! I ran home and put my gun up in the closet. I never wanted to use it again. When my Mom told my Dad, he laughed at me. And then a knock came at the door. It was the neighbor across the street. He said he had a big hole in his window. I had shot out his window with my BB gun. Dad asked me if I had been shooting at this man's window, and I said I hadn't, but I was shooting at some birds from across the street on his roof. The BB gun was not powerful enough to reach the birds on the roof so the BB dropped at an angle and put a hole in the picture window. It was an accident.

My Dad took me fishing with him at the insistence of my mother. Dad said he didn't want to have to fool around having to bait my hook and get my line untangled etc., but Mom pleaded and he gave in. I caught the first fish, and it landed on the ground with its mouth opening and closing like it was having trouble breathing. I freaked. I knew what it was like to struggle for your breath because of my asthma. I felt bad for the fish, but I didn't let on because I didn't want my Dad to laugh at me again. I didn't go fishing with him for a long time after that.

It was in Warden that I went to my first Baptist Church – the first time was that backward day I told you about and the next time was friend day. I don't remember much about church, but that the benches we had to sit on were hard and the church was small and everybody seemed to dress the same and all the men wore horned-rimmed glasses.

I didn't have church clothes, so I didn't go there much, but I liked the walk because I had to cross a huge football field cut into the side of a hill, and I had to walk down the hill and when I did, these little animals would poke their heads out of all their holes and then run around and jump in another hole. They were cute and looked like Chip and Dale. Mom asked my Father what they might be. And he said they were probably ground-squirrels. At five or six years old, I walked all over this town, both to church by myself and to the store or friends homes. I guess today they would call me free range.

Another church I remembered was called The Community Church. It was a Congregationalist Church. My whole family went one Easter. Dad thought that it might be like a Presbyterian Church, but it wasn't. It had its roots in Puritanism. I don't think they liked it because we never went back, and the benches were hard there, too. Then I went to the Mennonite Church. They were really nice and always ate a lot of food after church. They seemed like the Baptists, but more friendly and the ladies wore little lace caps, and long dresses and many of the men had beards. They didn't call themselves a church, one lady corrected me, they were a community.

Finally, there were the Mormons – the only thing I remember about that visit was that the kids went out during church to a kid's class not called a Sunday school. When I got home I told my mother what I had learned, that we all got our color and language from this large parrot that spoke different languages and taught it to the people and sent them to different parts of the world. Mom said she had never heard that one before. They had a lot of strange beliefs that were different from anywhere else I had been.

The Bureau camp in Warden began to get cut backs, I noticed families began moving and then their houses were moved, I don't know how the houses were moved. I guess I wasn't paying too much attention, but Terrie moved, and Jerri moved. The next thing I knew, their houses were gone too. Only a handful remained.

We did our part to try to repopulate what the government was moving, that's when my little sister was born. Her name was Shelly. Dad had named her after one of his favorite movie stars. She was much different than Pam or me. She was feisty, had long Shirley Temple curls, and loved to run around naked. Whereas Pam was sweet and awkward, Shelly was not afraid of anything. I remember we were having a family barbeque and my grandparents and my mom's sister and her kids were there and maybe a neighbor or two. When we were done with the hamburgers and hot dogs, the adults were sitting around smoking cigarettes and drinking beer while we kids were roasting marshmallows with limber willow sticks Dad had cut from our trees. The trick was to keep them on the stick and toasted over the coals, which were dying, without letting them slip off into the charcoal grill or catch fire. Mine was just about right. That's when Shelly burst into the yard not wearing a stitch of clothes! Mom got up to get her at my father's command, "Get that kid, Betty Mae." That's when she took off running around the yard, and in all the excitement Pam turned to see what Mom was doing chasing Shelly. But when she turned, she faced my cousin whose marshmallow had just caught fire and overcompensating, he flipped his willow stick upward causing the marshmallow to be hurled into the air and come down like a fire bomb right on the tip of Pam's nose. Pam began to scream as if she was on fire, which of course she was, and run around the yard in one direction as Shelly ran the other. Mom stopped chasing Shelly who was having fun in the pursuit, and ran after Pam who, by this time, was like a fire breathing dragon who had sneezed and the fire came out his nose. Mom grabbed bravely (with her bare hands) the flaming fire bomb taking the first layer of skin off Pam's nose and flung it into the yard where one of the kids trying to be helpful stomped on it with his flip flop causing the flames to go out, but several layers of leaves to accumulate on his sole, the sidewalk, and everything else for the rest of the afternoon. Shelly, whose attention had been stolen by Pam's flaming nose, went back into the house and returned dressed. I don't think that had anything to do with our move to Othello, but maybe the show we put on for the neighbors was the icing on the nose so to speak.

4
Where the Bough Breaks

OTHELLO WAS LIKE MOVING TO THE BIG CITY! After all, it was at least twice the size of Warden. I was excited! The Bureau had a house for us with a screened-in porch which would become my bedroom. I would no longer have to share a room with my two sisters, that is after they, my dad and my grandfather (my Mom's stepdad) finished it. My grandfather, who was a carpenter, said we could do it very economically. We wouldn't even have to insulate it because the wallboard he would use would have an insulation factor built right into it! He was so wrong about that, winters there would sometimes drop down into the teens, and I would wake up seeing my breath and run into the house and stand by the oil stove to thaw my frozen buns. But at least it was my own room.

While things were freezing in my part of the house, what I didn't know at the time was that my mother felt the only way she could save her marriage was to get pregnant again. Dad was always disappearing, going to friend's houses, going hunting and fishing. I remember going around knocking on doors trying to find him but I never did. When he was home, he was either sullen or yelling, or beating me with his belt. I remember the house being small and the kitchen table being up against the refrigerator on one side and up against the window on the other side. I had to squeeze in first next to the frig and the window and then Pam slid in. Dad sat at the end and Mom opposite Pam next to Dad. Shelly's highchair was opposite me. Once you sat down that was it, you had to stay until you finished "everything" on your plate even if it was liver. Dinner was never very pleasant. Dad never had a kind word to say. He complained the whole time he was at the table, but we were not allowed to say word, good or bad. Dad would scream at you the whole time if you "looked" like you didn't like the food. He went on and on about if your tongue was hanging out then you would eat it. I never knew what that meant, but it didn't make for a pleasant dinner time like "The Beaver" had, or "The Nelsons". I remember one time I was trying to force it all down, but it kept wanting to come back up. Finally, I *knew* it was coming back up and I better get to the bathroom so I asked Mom if I could be excused, which she then told me to ask my Dad, who then started the "tongue hanging out" thing, time was wasting! So when we finally got to, "Okay, go if you think you have to", I gave Pam a push because she obviously didn't get the urgency. Pam was not very coordinated at this time. She was what my Mom called "Pigeon Toed". She could walk across the room, and with nothing in the way, trip and fall. This time with my little push she got her foot caught between the chair leg and the table leg and began to fall face up screaming with her mouth wide open as I proceeded to climb over her pinned down body and empty that which finally would no longer stay down into the open hole in her face where the screams were coming from! Help, help she cried to no avail.

That only provoked my father further into a tirade about not being able to have a peaceful dinner. After all, he had earned it after a long day at work! Clean up this mess Betty Mae, I'm leaving!

Dad was cruel to me and Mom as well. I remember one time when I was told to take a shower, but I reminded Dad the hot water wasn't working. He said he had fixed it, just let it run a minute and get in it. I let it run and by the time I went to get in it was scalding hot with steam rolling out. He told me to get in it anyway. I tried twice and couldn't, it was burning hot. That made him really angry, and he jumped up and grabbed me and proceeded to force me under the scalding water as I screamed. Mom began to fight him off me; he shoved her into the wall. It was when my baby sister Shelly began to cry and pull on my father that he finally gave up, I was burnt red and in pain. He later admitted he had adjusted the thermostat on the hot water heater when it needed replacing.

One morning as I was running from my freezing room taking off my pajamas to jumping in the shower I found this white sticky glob of stuff sliding down my leg. When I told my Mom about it she got confused as she was trying to tell about the birds and the bees and boys bodies. When I corrected her, I told her it looked like the same kind of stuff, but how did it get in my bottom? She told me to talk to my father, which I did while he was reloading shotgun shells. He just stared straight ahead and didn't speak or look at me. It was as if I wasn't there, so I changed the subject to shotgun shells and thought we could go from there – still nothing. I wasn't even there, or my question heard, so I finally walked away. I never did get an answer, strange.

He Ain't Heavy

It was also at this time my parents met and befriended Marty and Maxine Hendricks, they would become my Godparents at the "Pilgrim Lutheran" church where we all would be baptized including my new little brother, Timmy. Mom said his name would be Timmy, not Timothy or Tim, but Timmy because she didn't like the formality, it was too uppity. I liked the Lutheran Church and the beer drinking pastor (I never saw him drink a beer except with my Dad when he came to visit) who had asked me to be an acolyte. I got to go to the altar and light the candles at the beginning of the service and then after the last song was over, I got to put them out and no one got to move until I did!

When we moved to Othello I was in the fifth grade, and my best friend both at school and after was Greg Esparza. His family was Mexican-American from Texas. He, like me, was quiet in school. He invited me to come to his house to ice skate on the frozen seepage from the big canal that ran just south of town. I remember getting too far from the shore, and I began to hear a loud crack. Greg had warned me about going out so far and just as I heard the crack, I saw it coming at me quickly. I got ahead of it and back to the shore just in time.

Then there was David Ipson. He was a bureau kid who had moved with us to Othello from Royal Camp. His brother, Artie, liked to hunt rattlesnakes, skin them and cut their rattlers off. I remember walking through our house with the TV on (the TV was always the first thing on and the last thing off even when no one was watching it), while the "Huntley – Brinkley Report" was broadcasting and heard something about Othello, Washington. I turned dead in my tracks to hear them talking about how the trash man in Othello had gotten the surprise of his life when he opened the trash can to empty it on Elm Street and found it crawling with live rattlesnakes. Apparently, Artie who was in a hurry had just stunned the snakes and pulled their rattle off and threw them away, unknown to him they were still alive! That was the first time I remember Othello making the national news.

David was my best friend after Greg. He liked to fish, drink beer and work on his Chevy Corvair. We used to "borrow" his brother's Suzuki 80 motorcycle and ride it out to "The Lakes" to go fishing or to swim in the summer. These were the Pot Hole Lakes, basically seepage lakes from the Potholes Lake reservoir. When they decided to irrigate the desert, the water seeped into the sand and started coming up in the lava beds left over from the last time the Cascade Mountains had erupted eons before[6]. One such lake was called Wind Mill Lake because it had once been a farm with a windmill in the middle. Now all you could see was the top of the windmill in the middle of the lake. In my imagination, I could see diving down to the bottom and swimming through the barn and the old farm house with skeletons still sitting at the table in the kitchen not knowing what had hit them! But of course it couldn't have happened like that, the water must have rose slow enough for them to get out of there, but not fast enough for them to take their windmill with them tied on the back of an old wagon!

Our favorite lake to swim in was Black Lake because it had cliffs where we could cliff dive (actually jump not dive). Nobody knew how high they really were, but they were high for us, and we liked to exaggerate their height just to psyche us up. The first one was "12" feet high, the second "26" feet high but the highest was "68" feet high. Black Lake was also where Artie said were the most dens of rattlesnakes. So we were always careful about where we walked and sat. "Diving" off the highest cliff wasn't something you could do right away. You had to work your way up to it! We would spend most of the time jumping off the "12" foot cliff. Then we might jump off the "26" foot one and by that time it was time to head back into town before it got dark. One day there were three of us at the lake and we start egging each other on to see who would go off the "big" cliff first. You know saying things like, "I bet you're chicken to go off it!" "I will if you will', and so on. Well we, all three, went to the top of the "68" foot cliff. Up there the path was narrow because not many people climbed it. While we were debating "you go first, no you go and I'll follow, etc." It was then that we all heard it together, the distinct sound of a rattler right behind us. We all jumped simultaneously not a moment to hesitate. All I can remember is it was a long way down and it felt like we would never get to the water, but when we did, we hit it so hard it stung my feet. I looked up as I entered the water and saw a tunnel of light over my head and then watched it close as my feet began to feel colder and colder as I went deeper into the dark. Fear gripped me. That's when I suddenly realized as I went down, I could put my hands straight out and slow my decent, after all I didn't know what was down there! Skeletons, frozen dinosaurs or the creature from the Black Lagoon! I swam to the surface as fast as I could and when I got to the surface I had to play it cool like nothing bothered me!

The rocks around the lake played tricks with your mind. You'd swear you could see Indian heads profiled in them, cowboys and faces looking over the terrain. The darker it got the more you thought you could see. Later on, when we "partied" at the lakes the beer, grass and LSD would only magnify the images in your mind.

Greg and I grew apart. It was the same with David. He kept drinking and fishing while I went on to other things. One day David sat his pole on the shore propped up with a rock. He had a few too many. Then suddenly he got a strike. His pole began to follow the fish. Seeing he was about to lose his gear, he dived in to get it and broke his neck in the shallow water. He then spent the rest of his life as a quadriplegic.

From fifth grade to the eighth I began to get "popular". I was invited to a lot of parties and my list of friends grew, but my shyness and insecurities continued to impede me. Girls suddenly started noticing me and flirting. It seemed everyone was pairing off. I would go to teen dances every week and my interest in music grew. I was too shy to talk to the "popular" girls even when they made eyes at me. My girlfriends were few, but I was faithful until they broke up with me. Rarely did I break up with them and when I did, it was more because I didn't want to be the one left standing.

My parent teacher conferences were always the same: "C's". The teachers would say that I was very helpful (something my mother had always told me), but not to expect too much. And there was that asthma thing. Mom told me C's were okay not everyone could expect to be an "A" student. After all, it was okay to be "average". But I didn't want to be average, I didn't want to be shy, I knew there had to be more for me than I was experiencing. I had to be worth more than my father's estimation of me, "not worth the powder to blow your ass away" as he would yell at me.

I began to slip into a darkness that only a teen could. I remember when I was thirteen my grandmother, my mom's mom set me up with a friend of hers granddaughter in Moses Lake. She was fifteen and had spent the summer before with an Air Force man who showed her a few things she had never experienced before. When I spent the weekend at her house, she expected me to do the same. I had an idea what to do, I had never done it before. And I was a "good boy". Mom had told me that I should never "use" a girl for my pleasure. I should show respect and save myself for marriage. The thought never occurred to me maybe the girl might want me for her pleasure. After all, Mom had told me she didn't like "love making" that much. I didn't want to think about my parents "making love". It was a disaster; first at her house and then a night at mine where we played childish games of chase.

"So you think you're a man now," my father quipped with a smirk. "You got yourself a tickle," he said. "Well you're no man." Then he made a muscle and showed it to me and said, "Anytime you think you can take me on you've got another thing coming!" I couldn't figure out what he was talking about! I thought I had been, 'good' and 'showed respect', etc. I got angrier and angrier, and more and more confused.

He's Leaving Home

By this time most of the Bureau houses had disappeared again except ours and those on Main Street. We had outgrown our Bureau house, and they wanted us to move. We found a three bedroom house with asbestos siding and an oil furnace. It was a corner lot with a small greenhouse in the back, three peach trees, one apple and the tallest Poplar trees that lined the fence between our yard and the Cunningham's. The Cunningham's were Mormons and some of the best neighbors you could ask for. The furnace had a thermometer and actually blew air into the house to heat it. No more oil stove, we never had such luxury! It didn't have an air conditioner, but because this was the desert you didn't need one. We had a swamp cooler[7].

Ever since living in Royal Camp, when we needed grocery's we would travel to Moses Lake where there were more stores to pick from. Mom would load all us kids into the car and drive us to Moses Lake to shop at the Pay and Pack or some store like that and then for lunch we would go to her favorite Chinese Restaurant. I liked shopping with Mom because she always said I was helpful. After all, I was oldest and could help with the kids and run for things she missed on the other aisles. We were on Highway 26. Mom pulled over crying. When I asked her what was wrong she said she would be okay, but she wasn't and it kept happening. Then Dad took off work and went with her to Moses Lake and a babysitter came over. When they got back and Dad paid the babysitter, Mom must have gone in the bedroom while Dad sat us down. He told us, as he was choking up, that we had to make some changes or we were going to lose Mom. The doctor had him pretty shook up. Things changed for a little while and then slowly went back to the same.

Mom and Dad decided that they didn't need the Lutherans anymore, and so they found another way to socialize. It was called the Moose Lodge, then the Elks and then the Eagles, and then back to the Moose. Every Saturday and sometimes on Wednesday and Monday night bingo, they would get dressed up and go there happy and come home fighting. I think the booze made Mom bolder to stand up to Dad. It just made him louder and meaner. He would get mad at me for something, when the belt beating no longer seemed to work, and he chased me around the house with a baseball bat. Mom wasn't far behind and stopped him. It wasn't long after this that Mom began having talks with me about Dad and how mean he was to her. He would hurt her on purpose when they were supposed to be "making love." Although she never said it, she implied that she and I were in the same boat as far as how we felt about Dad. She said she liked our "little" talks, but they got more and more frequent, and my loyalty and protective sense began to grow out of proportion at the same time. I was angry with Dad or confused, now I hated him.

I found myself getting out of bed after their night out and coming between them to stop the fighting, quite frequently. Then one night it happened I stepped in and got pushed out, I would have to take it a step further, as I heard my Mom screaming. I took my shotgun down just to scare my Dad to stop fighting and to stop hurting Mom, it wasn't loaded and I never intended on loading it. Dad came around the corner just as I started taking it down. He demanded "what was I going to do with that", I had to think of something and look convincing, so I started to load it, and I said, "I am going to kill me an old man". With that, he grabbed the gun out of my hand and hit me up alongside the head. The fighting stopped for that night.

Mom's talks kept happening and getting more detailed of things he would do to her, not real bad things, but things that should only be talked about between husbands and wives. I was becoming her emotional husband. I knew Dad didn't love me, I now suspected my mother didn't either. She only wanted to use me. And it didn't feel right. Things started falling apart everywhere for me. I stopped believing in the existence of God. My world at thirteen was small and growing smaller. I remember like it was yesterday walking down Main Street praying out loud swinging my fists at the air:

"God if you are up there answer me. What is going on in my life?"

"Do you even care what is happening to me?"

"Do you even exist?"

"Answer me!" I demanded.

Then I listened – no answer, no booming voice, no quiet voice, nothing. I smugly assured myself there was no god. Until one night I was awakened by a bright shining being standing at the foot of my bed. He beckoned, no compelled, me to follow him. We walked through the living room to the backdoor which opened by itself. Fear gripped me, everything in me wanted to run and hide but I couldn't! He then pointed out the door and up into the sky. I didn't want to move, but a force moved me. I didn't want to look up where he pointed, but something forced my head to move and my eyes to focus on the sky. Music began vibrating in the air and singing, beautiful singing, growing in volume! And then I saw the stars moving to form letters in the dark sky. The letters became words and the words began: "Our Father..." The Lord's Prayer was printed in the sky with Angelic beings. What did it mean? Finally released, I ran back into the house and fell on the floor hiding my face and when I thought it was safe I ran back to bed and hid under the covers shaking the whole time. I didn't know what it meant, but I would never doubt there was a God again.

I wish I could say I gave my life to the Lord and everything changed for the better right then. It didn't. In fact things began to fall apart at a more rapid rate. My parents took me to a psychiatrist because of the gun thing. He evaluated me and declared me sane, but angry. My grades got worse. Then the school counselor brought in a psychologist to do testing, two weeks' worth.

He looked at me straight in the eyes and said, "Rob what is wrong?"

"I must have done really badly on the tests, huh?"

"No you can't do badly on them they were IQ tests. You scored in the top 10%, but your grades are in the bottom 10%.

I said, "Then I have a good IQ? I always thought I was average or below."

"Below," he questioned. "I wish I had your IQ."

"What is it," I prodded

"It is 145, average is 100," he told me. "What is going on?" he asked again.

"Maybe it has something to do with what is going on with my Mom and Dad. I hate my Dad."

Now I not only felt angry, I felt empowered, I wasn't average so I started to apply myself more to my school work, and I began to speak up about things I thought were important, like the school dress code! At that time on the radio and everywhere, rebellion was in the air, literally. "Times they are a changing," sang Dylan.

We had a new vice principal, who had a crew cut and wore a suit. He announced to us that he was going to crack down on us and "things were going to be different". No more would he allow us to talk in the hall between classes, or to come to school with our hair on our ears, and boys were not allowed to have our shirt tails out. He walked the halls and if he spotted someone in violation of his rules he would write them up. After the warning came a suspension for two weeks and expulsion. I got written up, and suspended for the shirt tail hanging out just when I was trying to apply myself to my academics. Then I got expelled for my hair touching my ears. That was it! I started speaking up for what I believed. That this was wrong, very wrong for him to treat us this way. I told everyone who would listen that I felt the school was being run as if it was under a communist dictatorship. It got back to him and I was called into his office for several meetings, where I explained my Constitutional Right to free speech, and he proceeded to tell me I had no rights on the school grounds! After about three meetings where I refused to "give in" and as my views began to grow in popularity, I got kicked out of school once and for all.

By the beginning of the next school year I applied to come back, things had changed. The dress code had changed and a new vice principal was in place. But I had lost momentum in that year. Besides, losing interest in school I had been shifted around to live with various families, all good people who just wanted to help. I would always end up back at home. Nothing had changed at home.

5
American Graffiti and a Gun

THAT LAST YEAR AT HIGH SCHOOL, I BEGAN TO look for things to do, at night and on the weekends. We hung out at the bowling alley and played pool, pinball and drank what David would steal from his father. We smoked cigarettes, and acted tough. Once when my sister Pam had rejected the advances of a former friend of mine, he began to call her a whore. When I got wind of it, we cornered him in the bowling alley men's room and threatened him that we would beat him within an inch of his life. But when he refused to "take it back", I had no desire to follow through. I chalked it up to sour grapes. I wasn't a thug and that was as far as I could act like one, and I didn't like the act.

We once broke into the Tasty Freeze climbing in through the drive-up window. We jimmied it open and helped ourselves. I had an ice cream cone; David started to make himself a hamburger. This was really stupid because the Tasty Freeze was right on Main Street! We were just looking for something to do. I remember going into Potters Drug Store and they had a section for records. I started thumbing through them, when off to my side I saw some guy stuff some 45s into his pants and pull his shirt over them and walk out. I thought I'd try that too.

The guy who lived across the street and I went into Spouse Rites a five and dime store, and I tried shoplifting merchandise. I got caught and pleaded with the manager not to call my parents because my father would beat me. Mike backed me up, while I turned on the tears. I promised I wouldn't do it again and he gave into me. I guess he could see the fear on my face. It started out as an act, but by the time I was done, I wasn't sure I was acting.

Driving our cars up and down Main Street was the thing to do when you had nothing else to do, always looking for girls who would party with us. The rest of the time we would just honk at people we knew as they too drove up and down Main Street from one end to the other.

I worked in the potato sheds in the summer, sometimes in the fields changing sprinkler pipes or siphon tubes hoping all the while not to step on blind rattlesnakes during their shedding season. The migrant laborers from Mexico and from Texas would come up in the summer, and I would work with them in the sheds, fields and frozen food factories. I made many friends and learned some Spanish I didn't learn in school.

My old school friends started getting scarce. There was Thomas Morrison whose parents had adopted him. He was an only child who owned a stereo and free-weights. I envied him because he was adopted and because of the stuff he had. I remember walking in the halls in high school and Thomas pushing me into this new kid who was a Mexican, built like an upside down pyramid. He and several other of my "friends" told me I should fight him. Why? I don't know. I hadn't ever fought anyone before in my life. Pushing me into him they called me "chicken." He turned to me and said I don't want to fight you. The only thing I could think of was, "why are you chicken" (yeah right, I was 128 lbs. and stood 5'10" or so, he was shorter but about 190 lbs. of solid muscle). In those days there was a lot of tension between the migrant laborers and the locals. With me having called him chicken, that was it, we would meet after school, and I would fight him behind the gym with my "friends" cheering me on is the last thing I remembered.

They said I never got a punch in. He hit me, and I went down on my knees while he bent over me hitting me again and again and again. My head was like a punching bag on a spring. I was bloody and out cold when they dragged me into the locker room and left me there. When I came to, I somehow found my way home and it was at least two weeks before I could see out of my eyes again. Thomas and these guys who pushed me into the fight wouldn't be my friends after that. I would avoid them more from the shame of being a loser than anything else. I already felt that way without their help. Later, the object of my provocation told me he would be willing to teach me how to fight since he had had two years in the ring. I never took him up on it, but it was a nice offer.

I decided I needed to do something different, not just for the day, but for my life. So I started going one summer to the local radio station. I got to know the manager pretty well, and he told me I needed to get a license to be a broadcaster. Once I got that he would train me to be a broadcaster. I began to hang out with one of the DJs in particular who had the afternoon program, which was a top forty program. My love for music had grown from an early age.

Mom and Dad bought me a used stereo from the Hendricks for Christmas when I was thirteen. I had ooed and aahed over it when I first saw it at their house when it was new the year before. I appreciated it less when it was given to me a year older and second hand and no longer the latest. I also worked mowing lawns and bought a Silvertone guitar. I was determined I would become a rock star. I even took lessons from Carl Freedman (the same who had built the chicken coop with my Dad at Royal Camp) who taught me three chords and said that's all I needed to know; that all songs were essentially made up of only three chords. He was a country and western guitar player. I never liked country and western, it was always a rehash of radio pop songs sung with a twang by a rhinestone cowboy. I thought why can't they sing their own songs. I liked Hank Williams. He was original but I didn't like Merle Haggert. He was original but seemed to be mad at everything, especially young people looking to make the world better than they received it. David Ipson liked him, which only widened the gap between us.

I got my love for music and the radio from my mother who could play piano by ear and had a good voice. She told us she had turned down the chance to join several bands and go on tour because her kids always came first, even before my father. She said that with great pride not understanding the best thing you can do for your children is to love their father and/or mother not in exclusion of the children or more than but rather with them. She liked country music and could yodel.

Jim let me sit in on his sessions and told me he had come from a much bigger station and had used many "stage" names. When I asked him what his real name was, he said something unintelligible, I never did get a straight answer out of him, which didn't really bother me. I would make suggestions to him of who he should play that were my favorites, which at the time was mostly the *Beatles*, the *Byrds*, and or the *Sonics*, (a Seattle band that was popular in the NW). He would most often go by the Billboard Magazine's top.

I was good at making frog croaking sounds. Because I didn't have a license, I couldn't speak on the air, but I could make frog responses when he queued me in. I was George the frog, *riggit, riggit*, it was fun. I got to know him really well and his wife and their new baby.

One afternoon when I got home from the station, I got busted. My mother said she was listening to the radio and heard someone making frog sounds that sounded a lot like me. I never was a good liar, so I told her it was me. She told me that I should be careful hanging around Jim, after all she had heard that Child Protective Services (or whatever they called it back then) were watching him and they might take the baby from them for being unfit parents. I had always sensed there was something not quite right about him and his wife. It was like they were hiding something. Besides that I seemed to be the only friend he had, a fourteen year old kid.

I felt a certain loyalty to him as a friend and thought I ought to warn him. When I did with as much concern and grace as I thought possible, I thought he would thank me and be careful not to do whatever it was "they" might be watching him for. As soon as I told him that, in a flash he had a gun out pointed at my head demanding that I tell him who had given me that information. I couldn't tell him my mother had told me and then have him shoot me and go after her. Besides I had promised her I wouldn't tell him, and I always kept my word.

"Jim," I said, "what are you doing? I'm your friend; I can't tell you who told me that!"

He proceeded to cock the rife (I think it was a .22). "You either tell me or I am going to kill you on the spot."

"Go head and kill me then, I can't tell you and I won't." Tears welling up in my eyes.

"Then I'll find someone who will get the truth out of you, go out that door," he said swinging the gun in the direction of the door. I thought he might take me outside so as not to get blood on the carpet, his eyes looked crazed and his nose was running – but his nose was always running and so was his wife's. We left his apartment with him walking behind me with the gun pointed at me. We walked across the high school yard and over an empty lot, to the city hall with the Police station in it. He demanded to see Lou Johnson, the Chief of Police, who I was well acquainted with. I thought to myself — he is going to open fire in the police station. But the Chief who was a great guy sat down and talked to us, and told him nobody could make me talk if I didn't want to and not to worry about what I had told him. If the child protective services were going to charge him for something there was nothing he could do to stop it and if it wasn't then nothing would happen. I never let on that the rifle he came in with was pointed at me all the way there. But after our visit Jim and I parted ways and he soon left town.

Moose to a Gotten Goose

When Mom and Dad were at the Moose, us kids would have parties at our house. Early on I would put on "concerts" by hooking my guitar and an old microphone up to the second hand stereo, and we would turn off the lights except for the pole lamp pointed at me and I would be the star as I made up songs. That was fun at first, but after a while grew old and because it seemed like they were at the Moose most of the time we found other things to do. We kids, me mostly because I was the oldest, complained about them being gone every night and coming home with at least a buzz on and getting in fights, which I hated because I felt responsible and would then have to get out of bed and stand in-between them. When we did complain, Mom would go off on a diatribe about how the Moose helped orphan children back in Illinois or somewhere. I guess they thought they were helping other people's children while leaving theirs at home alone.

That's when I met Ron, who I barely knew, and we started scheming one night about running away. I had run away by not coming home, but not really going anywhere. He was adopted and lived and worked on a farm with his adopted parents. I had a reputation in town of being "wild", and he sort of looked up to me. It was a "Moose night" and he was at our house. That's when I came up with the idea of running away. He surprised me when he said, "let's go". So, we hopped into his father's truck and drove to Boise, Idaho where some elderly relative of his lived. It was as far as the gas in the truck would take us. He thought his father would have had reported it missing by then, and have the police out looking for us so we were always looking behind us.

His relative was old, in his eighties and had a '58 Chevy in his garage. We talked a while, but he didn't seem quite right. He told us we could sleep on the bed that was set up in the living room. When we asked him what the bed was doing in the living room he proceeded to tell us that was where his wife slept. We said, "oh" and looked around but we didn't see anyone else! Then he said with glazed over eyes and tears filling them, "That is where she died," he said. "When did she ..." I stopped trying to think how to put it delicately, "pass away". He said two weeks ago. Suddenly, I wanted to get off the bed I was sitting on; it didn't look like it had been made in two weeks. I felt creepy about the idea of sleeping in a bed where someone had just died, plus the place smelled like a convalescent home. He suddenly jumped up, startling us as he did and said, "Do you want some ice cream?" We were both starved, "yeah," we said. He came back from the kitchen and said I have to go get some. "We'll wait here," we said a little afraid to get in a car with him driving.

The garage was set away from the house like it was an afterthought. He went out to the garage as we watched from the front door. Suddenly! He came crashing out the back of the garage in reverse, boards flying everywhere. The car made a complete backward u-turn crossing the street behind it. It was a good thing no cars were coming. We got a glance of his face as he went flying by and could see him looking forward as if his brain had just shut off while his foot floored the gas in reverse. He stopped in the parking area beside the garage. The garage that now looked like a covered bridge open on both ends. He shut it off and got out and came back in the house and said he was tired and was going to bed. Not a word was spoken about what had just happen, I'm not sure he knew. I know we didn't. My guess was that he had forgotten where he was going and we were not going to get any ice cream, my stomach growled in protest.

By then it was getting dark and neither of us were going

to sleep in the haunted bed. Ron said that we needed to ditch the pick-up and take the '58 Chevy. As we drove off in the car he said he had an uncle who lived in Vegas. Off we went in a stolen car – neither one of us were old enough to have a drivers license, I was fifteen going on sixteen he was fourteen going on fifteen. In Othello, farmers kids were allowed to drive without a license as long as they stayed off the highways, he knew how to drive, me not so well.

A good example was when my parent's had gone away for the weekend a couple months before and let me stay home by myself. Dad always kept a spare set of keys in the dining area cupboard, and when the friend who lived across the street suggested we take it out for a spin. I said, "I don't know" and then said, "okay, but we'll just go around the block." Away we went in my parents' '56 Ford red with white wide-striped station wagon and headed down the road. That's when I saw some older friends on the corner that looked surprised and pleased to see me driving. Well, I had to make a good impression, and I had heard about "power braking" to make the wheels squeal, so I tried it – as I turned the corner in their direction, big mistake. The tires squealed all right and slid sideways slamming right into the curb. My friends looked wide eyed, pointed and laughed at me. I drove the car back around the block pretending I didn't notice the wobbling and shaking I had caused by bending the tie-rods and knocking it out of alignment. I put it back where it was, hoping my father wouldn't notice. Hum, he noticed as soon as he got home and got in the car, so I was told, because I had made myself scarce. I made sure I wasn't there. But had somewhere else to be for the rest of the week, until the heat died down and the car was fixed.

It wasn't that long after leaving Boise, when we crossed the border into Nevada and our eyes were getting heavy. The problem was that there were no rest stops so pulling over meant just pulling off to the side of the road. When we did, I noticed shadows of what looked like men with their arms upward of various sizes all around us. Then I started seeing pairs of shiny lights approaching us and surrounding us, but keeping a distance of about forty feet. We locked the doors and closed the window, and I fell asleep. When we awoke I saw what the "men" really were, tall cactus, but the shiny lights were gone. I suspect they were just some curious, hungry, desert animals. We hit the road again. It was long and straight and there was always a pond of water just in the distance that we could never quite reach. The road was hypnotic and just as you felt like it was taking you under its spell, it would change colors from black to red and then red to black. It was hot, very hot and I don't remember the car having air conditioning. At one point, it overheated, and we just happened upon a gas station / bar. Ron must have had some cash. Where he got it, I really didn't know and wasn't going to ask because he was able to buy some gas and some Ho-ho's and a bag of shoestring potato sticks with a couple of pops, enough he said to get us to Vegas. I hoped he was right because there was nothing, nobody out there, and I knew if we didn't make it down there we would die here.

As we traveled down Rt. 95 I remember seeing signs for Death Valley. In my mind's eye I could see us breaking down right about there and crawling past an old steer's skull as we did with the sun only inches away and our tongue hanging out (maybe that's what my father had in mind when he chastised us for not wanting to eat something at the table). The gauge on the radiator kept going up, we just ignored it. What else could we do? We decided we would take turns driving while the other slept. The worse that could happen with my driving skills would be I would drive off the road and hit a cactus. How bad could that be? I certainly had no desire to squeal tires in the desert.

6
Viva Lost Vegas

WE FINALLY REACHED VEGAS. IT WASN'T WHAT I expected it to be. I thought it would be like, LA or New York, even though I had been to neither. It wasn't much larger than Moses Lake at the time, two main streets with roadside hotels and casinos. There were slot machines, and more slot machines everywhere, on the street, sidewalks and even the gas station bathrooms, ringing, blinking, and spinning – making all sorts of noise!

Ron found his uncle's place with ease. He had, like everyone else, a stucco house with a tile roof and a pool in the back and a palm tree in the front. I had never seen a house with a pool before, except at David Muscot's where he lived in the back of a funeral home. His Dad, the mayor, was also the funeral director. I could never figure out what would motivate a man in his profession to want to be mayor, judge maybe, he could then hang 'em and bury them. In Othello we had a public pool at the Lions Park where the huge water tower was. It was painted red and white striped (high school colors), but very few had a pool of their own. We used to sneak in the pool and skinny dip with girlfriends after dark. Then take them into the tunnels under the pool where it was dark and spooky and they clung to us – well some did. The Police took all that fun away by shining their spotlights over the pool as they patrolled.

Ron's Uncle was an ex-movie star of sorts. He played as an extra in enough movies to buy this house and live in Vegas. He told us about playing in a bar scene with John Wayne, where a fight was supposed to break out, and he was to pick up a "special" chair and break it over John Wayne's head. But he grabbed the wrong chair and you guessed it, he knocked John Wayne out cold. He laughed and said he never got another part in a John Wayne movie after that. He asked us whose car we had; Ron told him it was mine. I don't think he believed us.

We went out as it got dark and started driving up and down the strip to Freemont Ave. There were so many lights on the buildings flashing and shinning; it was brighter there at night than it was during the day, my eyes were as big as saucers. We were just cruising up and down the strip taking it all in when a police car came out of nowhere flashing his lights. Ron was driving. The policeman came up to the window and shined his flashlight in the driver's side (you know the kind of flashlight you could use as a light or a club) and said "do you know you have a brake light out?" I thought the incident with the garage must have had something to do with that, when the old guy backed through it. We hadn't even thought to check it. "Where are you guys from?" We told him California or something which raised his eyebrows; we forgot the car had Idaho plates on it. "Where'd you get the car then?" "We borrowed it from his uncle," we told him, which was sort of true. "May I see your license and registration?" Quick thinking we said, "Our wallets were stolen when we stopped at this gas station/ bar with the slot machines in the bathroom." He didn't buy it. Next thing I knew we were in back of the cruiser with handcuffs on and headed for jail.

It was my first time in handcuffs – connected behind my back and I didn't know you shouldn't lean on them as you sat because they just got tighter and tighter with every bump in the road. While my wrists were killing me, my hands were turning blue, my bladder was ready to burst, and they seemed to be taking their time getting us there and processing us into the juvenile delinquency center.

Ringo Rob

It was 110 degrees at nine o'clock in the morning. There were bugs crawling out of the torn mattresses that lay on the floor, without bedding. There were casement windows in the unpainted cinderblock walls with panes broken out of several. This was a good thing or there wouldn't have been any air in there and it let some flying bugs out and some flies in. The cell was about 20'x 15' with nothing but bars on the opposite wall from the broken windowpane wall. There were about twenty kids in there. I was taller than most of them, and must have looked meaner. When I got there the night before I looked around and all the mattresses were taken. Some kid said "here you can have this one." They put Ron in another cell.

There was this ADHD black kid in there with us. He was a scrawny little, squirrely guy who couldn't stop talking. I was tired and not too happy and didn't want to play twenty questions. The first thing he asked was what are you in for – I smiled and said, "Murder."

I guess I didn't look like a murderer, cause he said, "Na-ah".

Then I said, "Interstate transport".

"What's that?" he said.

Someone from the back said, "Stealing a car and taking it from one state to another."

"That's right," I confirmed.

"Cool", the black kid said.

"What kind of car was it." I heard someone else ask.

"'58 Chevy", I replied.

"Nice" came the reply.

Then the black kid asked, "Hey where are you from? You talk funny!"

Before I had a chance to answer he answered for me, "You're one of those guys from that group the *Beatles* aren't you?" At the time I had an early Beatles hair cut and wore a lot of rings."

"You're, you're that guy that plays the drums, what's his name?"

From the back of the room again came a voice, "Ringo, is his name, that's not Ringo."

That black kid said, "Are you Ringo is that your name?"

"Yeah, I am Ringo," I said sarcastically, with a little intrigue at the idea. There after my Pacific Northwest accent changed into a Liverpool one for the rest of the duration!

As I lay down and started to doze off, I felt something at my feet, and heard "flick, flick". I looked down and the black kid was placing matches between my toes trying to light them with a lighter he couldn't get started. I came off the mattress with my fist balled ready to strike; he backed away and started apologizing profusely! He and everyone else left me alone after that. Next thing I heard was, "Hey Tracy, come 'ere, baby".

I looked up and there was a pretty young girl about my age coming toward us from down the hall with raccoon make-up eyes, wearing nothing but a cut-away T-shirt and panties.

"Hi guys," she said, "waving as she walked up to the bars."

"Tracy, get away from there," came a voice from what I thought might be the night guards. "You get out of your cell again? Come on get back in there."

I wondered how she had gotten out, I could only surmise either her cell was more dilapidated than ours or she was "let out" for obvious reasons.

Five days later, the guard came to the cell with the keys in his hand. "Carl?" he said.

"Yeah?" I said.

"Come with me."

"Where are we going?"

"Your father is here," he said.

"Here, in Vegas? This is going to be good," I said to myself expecting the worst. When I got to the front desk, there was Ron with a wrinkled sun beaten farmer that had to be his adopted father. He didn't look none too happy. And there was my dad, signing papers. I followed the three of them out of there, and we got in the back of the car. Ron's dad was driving. My dad sat in the front seat.

Nobody was talking in the car except my dad. Ron just stared as his father drove all the way back to Othello. I don't think Ron's father said a word as my dad who would normally be the quiet one, but now he was talking and laughing with a little nervous laugh like people do when they realize the conversation is one sided. Ron's father just kind of grunted. What I thought was strange was not that Dad didn't have much to say to me, but that he seemed to be having a good time! Maybe he liked getting off from work and taking a little trip to Vegas, I didn't know. Or maybe he too saw the signs off Route 95 for "Death Valley" and he was planning on throwing me out of the car there and leave me with my "tongue hanging out!"

It wasn't long after I got home that Dad came to me and told me that Johnny Jones and his wife were offering to "take me in". I didn't even know that Dad knew Johnny Jones or he knew Dad. Johnny was one of the town policemen. When I spoke with Johnny, I asked him if I was going to be his foster child or something. He said, "We'll see, let's just give it a try." They were a great family and had two younger boys. They treated me with respect and I them. But, when the oldest boy, about ten, started asking me questions about, "What it was like, going to jail, being with girls and how did you do it?" The Joneses decided it wasn't working out and I had to go. I was disappointed, I liked them a lot, and I was just trying to be helpful. I always told their son not to take my word for it, but to check it out with his parents.

I then spent a couple of weeks with my cousin in Moxee, they didn't live far from my grandparents. Gaylord and I were about the same age and had always gotten along well. His mom, my Aunt Ginny, was my dad's younger sister and was a single mom. She was left high and dry with two young boys and gone through difficult times. Aunt Ginny was tough, but good to me. She was a strong woman whom I loved and respected. After a couple of weeks I was back home again, but not really.

I came and went as I wanted – I was out of control. The drinking increased. And my group got larger. We would get a case of beer and drive out into some farmer's field and drink and act stupid like making cow sounds, trying to copy them. I got pretty good at it and would have won a prize if there was one to be won! Some of these guys got a bad rap from my parents. They figured that if I was with them they had to be bad. One was George Grover, he lived just outside of town. He was slightly older than me, but a lot bigger and became an unofficial bodyguard. When we went to see bands, like the *Bards*, the *Kingsmen*, and the *Wailers* when they came to town, George would look out for me. Fights often broke out at the Odd Fellows Hall.

Christmas in the Clink

In Othello, the winters are long and cold and the summers short and hot. It was Christmas, one of the few where I remember everyone being there, both grandparents and all us kids. Mom wasn't wearing a patch on her eye or a cast on her foot and Dad even seemed to be sober. One year Mom had a fight with the Christmas tree. She wanted to put tinsel around the back of the tree which was bigger than her and on the side where the branches faced the windows toward the front of the house. As she persistently forced her reach to toss the tinsel to just the right spot, she inadvertently bent several fir tree branches to the point where it just couldn't take it anymore and it swung back at her as she was making her reach for more tinsel in the other hand. When it did, it got her right in the eye, so that is why the white gauze covered her eye that Christmas and there were no family pictures allowed. The other memorable Christmas was when I was giving grief to Mom most likely just to be smart because I knew I was agitating her. She warned me to cut it out and I kept at it. That was when she kicked me in the shin as hard as she could and though I didn't feel a thing, she did. I began to laugh but she didn't, she had broken her toe.

This Christmas wasn't like either of those. Since the trip to Vegas, both my parents seemed to have been taking a new tack that was to leave me alone, except to make suggestions. I guess they thought I would finally learn my lesson albeit the "hard – way." Since Vegas I had turned sixteen, got a job at the potato sheds, and bought my first car. '57 Ford Fairlane convertible with a 350 engine and a Lincoln transmission that was too large for the car so the firewall had to be cut out for it to fit, then the space was screwed in with sheet metal. Sheet metal is thin and not much of a barrier for the engine heat which came into the un-air/conditioned cab. Not only did it create an unbearable condition while driving, but the convertible top wouldn't stay latched while doing sixty miles per hour going down the highway. So you can imagine how difficult it was to drive with one hand on the steering wheel and one hand on the top to keep it from flying back when it came loose, the whole time sweating like a pig. I think I got rid of it as fast as I had purchased it.

It was cold this Christmas Eve with all the family gathering around all laughing and making merry. It felt like the most normal Christmas we had had in a long time. That is until a knock came at the door, it was "Barney Fife." That wasn't really his name but that is what we called him. He was a deputy who didn't seem too smart and always acted too hard to look the part of a tough cop. His voice would drop a notch in pitch and he pulled his stomach in as he puffed his chest out to say something police-like. Of course it had to be my dad who went to the door. Dad never answered the door, one of us kids did, or Mom. "Red," he said, "is Robert, here?" I was standing right behind him, and he could see I was there unless he had forgotten what I looked like. His eyes looked like they were going to pop out as they got wider and as his voice dropped in pitch, in went his stomach, and out came his chest. "I am afraid I have to take him down to the station for some questioning." The handcuffs came out of the belt loop as he pulled my arms around behind me, right in the doorway in front of everyone. I could hear Mom gasp and begin to cry as I got escorted to the police car out front where he had parked it with the lights still flashing and the neighbors peeking out from behind their curtains. My dad asked Barney, "What did he do this time?" And Barney whispered something to him as we walked away.

The Great Grain Store Robbery

A couple of months before, a bunch of us guys got together, about thirteen in all and decided after the beer ran out that we would take a trip out to "Bruce". Why? I don't know, we just longed for something to do I guess. This wasn't my usual crowd. Three of them were older, 'hardcore' and rough around the edges. They liked to drink and bust things up and get in fights, etc. I wasn't like that, but I was flattered they wanted me along. I guess they were impressed because I had stolen a car and done time in juvey, even if it was only a week.

When, in the past I had gone out to Bruce, it was to ride the grain elevator up and down. They had a rope drawn elevator that worked with pulleys so that the elevator moved smoothly and easily up and down carrying one person at a time about a hundred feet off the ground. Bruce had a granary storage silo and a farm supply store with a couple of potato sheds and that was it. What kind of trouble could we get in anyway? Well, we all piled out of our vehicles, and I headed for the elevator thinking that was what we were there for, a couple started following me, others just started milling around, some finishing off the beer left in their bottles or smoking cigarettes. Next thing I knew, someone said "hey they're in the store, come-on let's take a look." So we all filed in the store – "It was a farm store, what could be of interest to us?" I wondered out loud. We looked at nuts and bolts, some farm tools, shovels, post-hole diggers and so on. But, suddenly from the back hall one of the older guys said, "Look what I found." We all turned to look and here he came rolling a safe down the hall, back to the door where we all came in. "Grab a cutting torch and let's open it," he said not looking back. I had only seen one of those in metal shop in high school. Someone looked for it and announced they didn't have any but they did have some chisels and hammers. They took them while others helped lift the safe into the open trunk of one of the cars. The back tires looked flat. We all piled in.

"What are we going to do with that?" I protested.

Someone said with glee, "We are going to crack it".

"Crack it," I thought, "it is not an egg" and I am sure no one in our group knew how to listen to the tumblers fall as they spun the combination, the way they did in the movies. Next thing I knew, we were in the middle of a field somewhere, and we were all in a line while three of them took turns hammering away at the safe. This went on for hours, and I do mean hours. It was shortly after dark when we headed to Bruce. Now I could see the sun starting to come up over the fields while we stood in the middle of some potato plants. I was tired; I just wanted to go home. I had been saying this for hours trying to build a consensus. A couple of the other guys at my end of the line agreed with me, this was stupid and fruitless. We'll never get that open, besides we don't even know what is in it, if anything. The guys working on the door warned us, "You're not going anywhere. We are in this together." I didn't feel like getting beat up in a potato field, and I wasn't sure which way was home anyway so I waited. Just then a burst of light came streaming across the field exposing the tiredness in our eyes, and weariness in our faces. It was about that time that I heard shouts from the front of the line, "We got it open and there is money in it!" Next thing I knew fists full of cash was being handed down the line, while stuffing their pockets. By the time it got to me, it was very small. So much so that it was a dollar here and a dollar there, till I counted what my take was, $19.39. I didn't even want that, I didn't want any part of it.

Barney undid my handcuffs as he unlocked the cell door and down the jail corridor, I heard someone say, "Who's there? You keep your mouth shut. You know what happens to someone who rats!" I thought to myself, "well it looks like someone already has. How else would the police have known to pick me up with this group?" The next day the *Othello Outlook* our prestigious newspaper reported that a gang of bandits stole the safe at the Bruce Farm Coop and took it to an undisclosed location where they "pealed" back the door. It sounded so dramatic, if they only knew how boring it was. $13,000 was taken from the safe, it concluded. When I read that I thought about the guys stuffing money in their pockets, and I thought about me and my $19.39 and I am in the same boat with them?

Barney brought me into the Chief's office the next morning, Christmas morning. Barney lowered his voice, pulled in his stomach, and puffed out his chest, "We know all about your part in this, the other guys have already told on you."

"So why don't you make it easy on yourself and tell us what you know," he said, eyes bulging.

The Chief said, "Look Barney get on out of here, and leave us alone." Barney looked offended, huffed and then walked out.

I looked at the Chief and said, "Look, I don't know what anyone else said about all this, and I have nothing to say about them. What we did was stupid and I told them so at the time. They threatened me, and I had no way of backing out once it all started taking place. I can't say who or what anyone else did in this, but I can say what my part was and quite honestly it wasn't much."

I was told that they were releasing me and that I should wait to hear from the courts. I never did. I had very little to do with those guys after that. My guess is they either 'fessed up or gave back what they had taken or something because nothing was ever spoken about it again.

Box Car Boss

I lied about my age and got a job at "Chef Reddy" working on loading the box cars. Mom gave me a "modified" copy of my birth certificate, which indicated I was eighteen, you had to be to work there driving a fork lift. I was only sixteen at the time, and I was made supervisor on the midnight shift. That's where I met Sylvester Deleon; he was Hispanic and a Christian. He wanted to talk to me about a personal relationship with

Jesus Christ and the power of the Holy Spirit. He was what he said was called, Los Hallelujah's or "Pentecostal." What I knew about the Pentecostal church came from my mother who visited one as a child when they were called "Holy Rollers". She said while she was there some lady had fallen in the aisle and started shaking. And then someone else jumped over a pew and one lady threw herself on the floor and threw up her skirt. She wasn't wearing underpants. When they tried to cover her up for modesty, she shouted as she threw off the covering, "Let all glory show." I laughed uncomfortably when she told me that. She said that they scared her to death as a little child, and she never went back.

I gave Sylvester a hard time, but he never seemed to mind. It was his demeanor that spoke to me the most; he had a gentle spirit and a kind and glowing face. There was nothing but humility and love for his Lord about him. Sometimes, I would ask him hard questions just to try and trap him, other times just because I wanted to know what he thought. I don't think he ever knew it, but he had an impact on me that I could never quite shake.

I was a terrible supervisor. These guys were trying hard to support their families, and if work got done early, or it was a slow night I would give them a choice of whether they wanted the rest of the night off or not. Of course you can guess what I wanted. I liked the money, but I liked getting off and going out with my friends and partying. Most of the time they wanted to stay at work which meant I had to stay and supervise. As a result I would give them menial tasks like sweeping the freezers out, over and over – till they caved in and we got off. Now the freezers were huge, about the size of a city block and below freezing for the frozen French fries and tater-tots. This was no small job or an easy one. Often the guys would cave in and we would all punch out. But, no one ever complained to my supervisor or to me for that matter. I was good to them in other ways that made up for my immaturity. I let them go early if they had something important to do and not dock their time. Or if they got sick or needed a day off, I would cover for them. But we still got the work done and were often praised for our completion when the other shifts were seldom done.

California Scheming

When the orders slowed down and nothing had to be loaded into boxcars, Chef Ready laid off the night crew. I was out looking for another job when I heard this new guy and his wife had just moved into town, and he was a plumber looking for a helper. He had moved in from California, and he was different in many ways. He spoke differently, he acted differently and he seemed to be full of ideas. He was living in a hotel and managing it while his home was being built for his wife and son. She was also different in a good way, very carefree. They welcomed me and he gave me work when he needed me to help him lay pipe. One of his projects was going to be a club called The Fun Factory. It would serve as a place to hang out and play pool and serve sandwiches, pizza and sodas during the weekday. It would be a dance club on the weekends for young people. I thought it was a great idea especially when he wanted me to run it. He intended on keeping a plumbing shop in the back, but his plumbing business grew too quickly, and he needed more space. So I moved in the back and put a cot in there to sleep on. This was perfect for me, ever since Vegas, I had lived anywhere but home.

At the same time, I met a friend of mine whom I hadn't seen in a long time – maybe a year and a half. He had just gotten back from San Francisco. And he looked different! He had odd combinations of colors on for clothes; they were bright reds, orange, yellow and striped pants with a bandana around his neck. The weirdest thing of all he wore make-up, like eye shadow, lip stick and rouge, nothing I had ever seen before. I asked him what was all this about and he told me that in San Francisco there were a lot of people who dressed like him. A lot of people thought he was gay, but he still liked girls. Even though some of the people who dressed like he did were gay, but you didn't have to be to look like that. "There were two main groups there in Frisco," he said, "One was the "Heads" and the other the "Mods". He identified with the Mods. I asked him if he did drugs like LSD and he said yeah everyone did. I told him I wanted to try it, and he said if I did, he would get me some. It would cost me $20. That was a lot of money for me to get high on when I could buy a case of beer for less. He said to give him some time and he would get it for me. This was 1967 and there was a lot of talk about what was going on in San Francisco and the Summer of Peace and Love. I was listening to *Country Joe and the Fish, the Doors, the Who's Tommy* and *Jefferson Airplane*. Things were changing even the *Rolling Stones* followed the *Beatles* June release of "Sergeant Pepper's Lonely Hearts Club Band" by putting out a Psychedelic Album: "Their Satanic Majestic Request" in December. I guess this was to solidify their bad boy image, oppose to the *Beatles*. The world would never be the same. He handed me the little pill he called

"White Owsley" and I gave him the money. I carried it around for a while, not knowing if I wanted to try it or not, I had heard the horror stories of people trying to fly off buildings, *et cetera.* But "everybody" was doing it so why not? I got David Ipson to try it with me, we made ponchos out of beach towels to look more "hip" and cut this tiny pill in half. Then we took it and went to the Fun Factory where there was a dance that night with strobe lights and black lights and loud psychedelic music. It was my first "Trip" and would not be my last. Soon I was trying whatever came my way, which wasn't a lot in Othello. You had to go to the Tri-Cities, sometimes Moses Lake at the old Larson air force base which was now a Job Corp Center or Seattle to buy more. This first trip was not that impressive, the worst was yet to come.

7
...Not Behind the Plow

I WAS READY TO LEAVE OTHELLO FOR GOOD BUT how would I do it? 1967 seemed to fly. Next thing I knew it was 1968, and I had joined the Army at seventeen. Nobody joined the Army. People were burning their draft cards, not joining the Army; I was RA instead of US. The Viet Nam War was going on hot and heavy at the time. I had no idea what was ahead of me. I had gotten my GED that past summer and gotten my mother to sign for me to join. I was sent to Ft. Lewis near Tacoma, which was south of Seattle.

As we filed in from the bus into the base there were two lines, one going in and one coming out. The one going out were those being discharged and the contrast was stark! These guys had sun beaten tans, muscles bulging and they wore the expressions on their faces of war weariness even as some laughed and cut up, others not so much. We going in on the other hand, were pale, puny, and know-it-all. But our line grew quiet as we watched them; they didn't even seem to see us.

The recruiter asked me what I wanted to do in the Army, and I had selected Helicopter Mechanic because I thought I couldn't screw that up. I liked working on my car which by this time was a Corvair, one that I would take apart for the fun of it and put it back together, jacking it up and dropping the engine out the bottom.

The Army ran me through a battery of tests to see what I would be best suited for and if I was suited for them. I qualified for Helicopter Mechanic, but was brought one last time into the office to discuss my MOS (Military Occupation Specialty), before being assigned. This was unusual.

The officer told me to sit down and then said, "Are you sure you want to be a helicopter mechanic?"

"Why," I asked, "do I not qualify?"

"Oh, you qualify alright, but our testing says you could qualify for a whole lot more."

"What do you mean? What kind of tests were these?"

He said, "Well, there were several and one of them was an IQ test."

I said, "What did I score on it?" They said we are not supposed to tell you, but it was above average. I told him then about the one I had in high school which had lasted a week and I scored 145.

"Well it wasn't that high but this test is not that detailed." He sighed and said, "It was, 135."

I said, "I'll stay as a helicopter mechanic."

"OK." He sighed again and then stamped my papers and said, "You can go now."

The Sergeant First Class, with the patch of the horse looking back on his shoulder meant here was a 1st Cavalry division coming out of combat, the first to go into Viet Nam. "You had better give your heart to Jesus", he said for the next few weeks, "your ass belongs to me!" As the spittle shot in all directions.

Basic training was hell, but it was meant to be. Most of the Drill Instructors (DIs) had done too many tours in Nam and some were no longer wrapped to tight, so they were no longer fit for combat but would do quite well as instructors for the trainees. What I found out right away was you were not allowed to eat, sleep or leave your locker unlocked, and never ever call your weapon a "gun". If you did call your weapon a gun and it was overheard by one of the DIs you would then be told to proceed fully exposed to everyone in the barracks, with one hand on your rifle and the other holding on to your "gun" to explain which was your weapon and which was your gun, which was for shooting and which was for fun.

The routine was the same every day. We would polish the middle isle of the barracks, which was taped off so no one would walk on it. We would change the butt can water for cigarette butts, which no one was allowed to use. We cleaned the latrine, sometimes with a toothbrush, and about an hour before revelry, we bunked. Then within the hour came the screams of the DIs to wake us up so we would S.S.S. (sh-t, shower, and shave) while they screamed at us about being slow or lazy, then dress and make our bunk so tight a quarter had to bounce on it. Lockers, had to be locked, foot lockers pad locked, our boots shined and our weapons cleaned, ready for inspection. Or, they would come in and tell us within fifteen minutes of hitting the bunk that we did a lousy job of polishing the isle. They then started turning over the butt cans into the "no walk zone" and then dump the trash can (which had been polished with Brasso) on top of the water, while they ripped the bedding off the bunk and threw it on the floor and then tell us to start over again, those nights no sleep was allowed.

Then came the chow line, all the while the screaming continued. "Pick up that tray, eat, stupid! What do you think you are doing here? Sit down and eat! Why are you sitting down? What is wrong with you, can't you hear?

"Who told you to sit down?"

"You did sir!"

"What did you call me!"

"Sir. Sorry, Drill Sergeant."

"Sorry? You are a sorry excuse for a human being. Do you see these stripes on my shoulder? I work for a living, you will not call me sir, now get your dumb ass out of here, before I make you drop and give me fifty." And on and on it went. The blood vessels in their faces would bulge so bad you thought they would burst!

Blood and Noses

We were standing at attention in a circle. We had just run with full pack on and then crawled through the snow and the mud, and now we were in a parade field somewhere in the heart of Ft. Lewis. Those fifteen minute night sleeps were getting more and more frequent. And it was cold, very cold, not only could I see my breath, what there was of it, the cold air was always the hardest for me to breathe with my asthma, something I failed to write down when I signed up, but shivers were running through me as the wet fatigues stuck to me. You had to keep your eyes straight ahead as the DI droned on about how we were all a bunch of pukes. Out of the corner of my eye, I saw one guy teeter as he struggled to stay awake, the DI didn't catch it. Someone chuckled, he caught that. "What's so damn funny," he screamed about a half an inch from the face of the offender. "Drop down and give me 100 push-ups."

Then it started happening to me, oh no, don't let it happen to me! My eyes wouldn't listen to my demanding thoughts, they were fighting me as my vision began to blur and I began to drift away to somewhere else – anywhere but herererere. "What the hell do you think you are doing you afterbirth of a bastard rabbit," he said just as I caught myself stumbling out of formation. Then he ripped the M-14 out of my frozen fingers and slammed it against my helmet-covered head. The tirade would have continued, but just as he handed me my weapon, someone else fell face first into the snow, barely missing the troop now on his fifty-seventh push-up. Sometime after stumbling, it dawned on me we were running in cadence back to the barracks.

"What's that all about?" someone commented as soon as I got back.

"What do you mean," I responded.

"That blood running down your face," he pointed. I hadn't noticed, but I knew right away what it was – a bloody nose. I used to get them a lot when I was younger. I ran into the latrine glancing into the mirror as I headed into the stall to grab some tissue. I got out of my fatigues and lay on my bunk with my head back.

"You're going to miss mess," someone reminded me.

"Big loss," I replied, as the tissue reddened.

Discharging Honorably

No eating, sleeping and do nothing but meaningless work — it was meant to take the individual out of you and to put the conformity in you. This was a hard thing to do to someone in the '60s, especially someone as proficient at rebellion as I had become and others like me. Many in our company were "opting out" of the Army. By that I meant there was a lot of scheming going on, I saw one guy asking another to slam his trigger finger in the window, hoping to get out that way. Some suddenly had maladies such as 'bad backs' and were sent to the infirmary to check it out, David Ipson was one of them after asking someone to break his crutch across the small of his back. Some came back right away and were given extra duty; others like David never came back.

Like jail house lawyers, there were also the 'army experts,' these took pride in knowing the answer to any question you might have because they had a brother or a father who had been in the Army. And everyone discussed their MOS, most were going into the infantry. I remember talking to one of these "experts" who informed me that, "All helicopter mechanics have double-duty," he said with a, "don't you know that, dummy," look on his face. "Not only do they work on them, they were expected to ride along and serve as door gunners," his instruction concluded. Door gunners were the ones hanging out in the open with a machine gun, firing at the enemy as the 'copter' flew over. I was told they had a life expectancy of three days. I didn't know if that was true, but I didn't want to get to Viet Nam and then find out it was. But, you couldn't "unjoin" once you had joined that was called "desertion" and all deserters were sent to prison or shot. I could see myself standing up next to a wall with my fellow troops standing in a line in front me while the DI asked if I wanted a cigarette and a blindfold. No, I wouldn't even consider desertion, besides Canada was too cold for my liking.

The bleeding didn't stop; in fact it got worse as I bled into the night and got blood all over my pillowcase and sheets. In the morning about 3:00 a.m., the DI sent me to the hospital. You would have thought I had a bullet wound or something the way people were running around me.

The hospital was nothing like the barracks. Manigan was designed in 1944 during WWII. It was spread out with fourteen miles of halls and corridors. The idea behind it was that if we were ever under attack, the bombed out units that were damaged could be closed off and the rest of the hospital could continue to function. As soon as I got there I was put in a wheelchair, just as a 'train' went by down the halls. These electric cars were used to travel the fourteen miles of halls and to get there and back in a hurry. Just as the train passed someone asked if they could get a hand moving me to the 'so and so' unit. I heard a voice I thought I recognized, "I will," but somehow the face had changed. Then it hit me – it was Wally Neuckirt. "Wally," I said it's me Rob Carl. He too studied my face and said slowly, "Robert Carl from Warden?" Wally was a bureau kid, he was a preteen when I was pre-school, but we knew each other – all the bureau kids knew each other. I used to play on his mom's piano, that's where I learned a mean rendition of "Chop-Sticks", using *both* index fingers on each hand!

"What are you doing here, and when did you get here?" He had question after question.

"I said well Wally…" he stopped me, as he looked around at his fellow workers and said, "It is Specialist First Class Neuckirt in here, private."

"Oh, sorry," I said. They told him where to take me and we went down several halls and corridors talking all along.

"How'd you get in the Army, didn't you have asthma?" he asked.

"Yeah, I didn't tell them." Blood dripped down my chin, my tissue was uselessly soggy by now.

"You can't do that," he said, "what if you get in combat and have an attack and they're depending on you? What is your MOS anyway?"

"Helicopter Mechanic," I said.

"Ohhh", he responded with a knowing in his voice and a concerned look on his face. "Look he said, with your permission, I'm going to include the Asthma on your chart."

Before I knew it, I was in what looked like a dental chair, with about half a dozen people gathered around. Wally disappeared. The Doctor / Captain started explaining to his interns or whatever they call them in the Army, what he was about to do with this long needle, that looked to me to be about two inches long.

"I am going to go up through the roof of his mouth into the sinus cavity, if I go too far the needle will pierce his eye and blind him, if not far enough, a pocket will be formed in the roof of his mouth and create an abscess," he instructed.

"Great," I thought. I could see myself with a patch on my eye.

"How'd you lose your eye?" I'd be asked.

"I lost it in the Army," I'd say.

"Oh, you lost it in Nam?"

"No, I lost it in a dentist chair."

"Oh my god!" They might ask, "What happened did they pull too hard on a tooth and your eye came out with it?"

Backward I went, my mouth propped open, in went the needle, and up went the plunger. It felt good, very good, too good! The bleeding stopped, and the group filed out. The doctor told me I would be on light duty for two weeks. Two weeks, I thought, and basic training would be done! What I didn't know at the time is that by that following March, I would be out of the Army with a medical discharge for none other than asthma.

A medical discharge was an "Honorable Discharge." When I was asked if I wanted to remain for the rest of my time in the Army and that I would be assigned as a clerk with a desk job and remain a low rank for the rest of my tour, it took me two seconds to decide. The trip back down the halls and corridors was more fun going back than it was coming to the unit with the dentist chair.

"How are you feeling," Specialist Neuckirt asked on the way back.

"Weee," I said, "I feel great," as the corners seemed to stretch out like a carnival ride. "What was that they had shot up there?" I said struggling to get my words straight.

"Cocaine" he said, "pure cocaine".

8

Not So Magic Bus

"*I* SMELL A DIRTY HIPPY," DAVID MUSCOT SAID AS he came crouching around the bus at the station, on the corner of 12th and Pennsylvania Ave – Washington, DC.

"What you smell is five days and twelve hours of Greyhound bus ride, from Moses Lake to DC," I replied with a grin. I could still feel the bus moving under me even though I was standing still. I couldn't believe it. I was in Washington, DC! The farthest east I had been to was Coeur d'Alene, Idaho (or maybe that trip to Vegas). David had contacted me after I got out of the Army and told me to come out to DC with him and we would hang out there for a while and then go out to California. David said, "follow me." I picked up my military bag with all my worldly possessions in it including my fatigues issued by the Army. I tried to give them back when I was discharged, but they didn't want them. I wore a white beaded leather jacket with long fringes on the sleeves, a girl had given it to me to remind me of her. I loved that jacket it was perfect for a hippy-wanna-be. We got on a city bus, with a lot of angry looking black faces which didn't smile back at me as I walked by. We sat in the back of the bus.

"Where is the Whitehouse," I asked, making the same mistake a lot of tourists make, thinking the Capitol was the Whitehouse not realizing they were two different buildings with two different purposes. I never watched the news, except when Kennedy got shot and I couldn't vote. I knew nothing, absolutely nothing about Washington, DC except it was the nation's Capitol and it was where the president lived.

"Its two or three blocks that way," he pointed south.

"Hey, what's with all those burnt out buildings I saw on the way into town?"

"That's from the riots, last year,"[8] he said while his eyes shifted back and forth across my face.

I didn't ask. I figured I'd find out eventually. Besides I already felt stupid enough. My eyes searched down the street for the Whitehouse as we headed for Arlington, Virginia where David worked as a maintenance man for the Quality Inn across the street from Ft. Myers.

"Why are we going all the way to Virginia," I asked not knowing it was minutes from downtown DC. In Washington state (I learned quickly to identify where I was from with the postscript "state", otherwise I was thought to be saying I was a local, and it was obvious I wasn't). The boarders of the state were hours from Othello, not minutes, so I was wide eyed as we crossed the Potomac with the sun going down in front of us blinding my tired eyes and the Washington Monument and the Lincoln Memorial behind us. As we passed the Iwo Jima Memorial on the left, I couldn't believe I was there. I slept till noon in a room at the motel that David had arranged with the manager since it wasn't booked, I was exhausted.

There were three main places in DC where we "hung out,"

Georgetown, DuPont Circle, and P Street Beach. In fact, P Street was the main through-fare from one to the other. The motel manager ended our stay, David lost his job and I never got one there. We had hoped I would. But this was the sixties you didn't need a job, you were a part of something special, "The Movement". It was a movement of "peace, and love" and it was a time of "flower power" and as a "head" you were a part of a brotherhood. The brothers and sisters took care of each other. We were going to change the world, first we had to change our names and the way we looked. Our names were Turkey, Weasel, Rabbit, Dog, Doc and I was Mother, according to David who said he was Dog. Normally, the names were given to you because of your personality or something you did. We would stay wherever it was convenient to crash, which normally meant to come down off of a high. At first, I had trouble fitting in because everyone thought that I was a NARC because of my short military haircut. David convinced them I was cool, and I was no Narcotics Agent, so they didn't have to be afraid of me.

One day David and I were hanging out at this apartment with a bunch of other heads. Rabbit was sitting on the couch with his pet rabbit running up and down the back of it. He had a gun in his hand, a small pistol. He had dumped all the bullets out (so he thought). He played with it pointing it toward the floor and in front of the entrance. About that time in walked Weasel who sounded like a weasel when he whined about wanting to find the "Flower Children." He had the longest, waviest brown hair I had seen up to that time. I thought that this guy couldn't be for real. He looked like he had lived in a commune for ten years. Truth is he was probably some rich kid from Fairfax. But just as he stepped in whining, David signaled to me he wanted to go. So as I made two steps toward the door, David took one step, and as Weasel stepped past us into the room, the gun went off just missing me first and David second – hitting Weasel in the inner thigh. Everyone ran out as fast as we could, leaving Weasel on the floor clutching his leg and crying. I never saw Weasel again.

David had crashed at this guy's house that was gay. David asked him if it was okay for me to spend the next night on the couch. He said yes and fed us and let us clean up before leaving. I was amazed at some of the kindness I ran into during this time. Perfect strangers would take me in sometimes to feed me, other times to give me a place to sleep. I noticed this guy had a wig of long brown hair sitting on a Styrofoam head, he was bald. After some talk about it and as we were leaving, he gave it to me when I gave him a key I had found it in the street. It looked like an old key for winding a clock. He looked at me, tearing up as if I had done something profound. We said our good-bye, thanks for the wig and a place to spend the night as we left. The wig gave me "long hair" over my ears not quite down to my shoulders, sort of like I wore it before the Army. I took my dress fatigues and split the seam and sewed in a wedge so I had bell bottoms. With my white leather beaded jacket, and a tie-died shirt or no shirt at all, I fit right in. Later, we would shop for clothes at Good Will or Sonny's Surplus where they had Navy bell-bottom jeans, the real deal. Soon I was posing for pictures with tourists in Georgetown who asked if they could have a picture with the local Hippies! I lost David in the fray, but was very comfortable living on the streets on my own.

Many of us made money by selling the "Freepress" newspaper. They would give us twenty-five or so and we would sell it for a quarter. Then we would go back to the paper with the money and pay them for the ones they had fronted us for about ten cents each. With that little amount of money, we would buy lunch or drugs depending on what we were in the mood for. If we knew someone who needed help "unloading" some drugs, they would give us some to sell and some to do. We in turn would give them the money so we could keep the channels flowing. But, my most lucrative means of making money was "pan handling." My favorite pan handling turf was downtown on Connecticut Ave., NW. This was the business district, and many "a suit" from noon till three would be very generous with their, "spare change to help feed my people." I made at least $30 an hour in the very same area where I too would become "a suit" many years later as I climbed the ladder of property management. The irony of it always took me back as I thought about it years later. Truly my life had changed 180 degrees.

Pagans and Parks

At this time, DC had the dubious reputation of being the murder capital of the country. But, I was oblivious of this fact until I began to be confronted with it. That's when I ran into David again. I asked where he had been and he said he partying with "The Pagans".

"What do you mean partying with pagans?"

"They are a local biker group, they are out at this chick's house in Potomac, do you want go?"

"Sure, why not."

We hitched a ride out to a very posh Washington Suburb and this big beautiful home with all these bikes out front. The owners of the home were away in Europe, I was told. David walked up to this big biker and told me to stay in the doorway. When he came back, he told me with a worried look on his face, "they say you can stay."

I said, "Great".

"There is one thing though, you can no longer call yourself Mother, this guy tells me he is 'MOTHER' and there is no other!"

"I'm okay with that." I wasn't that partial to the name anyway.

David disappeared again. I just kind of moseyed around trying not to show the discomfort I felt being there. I picked up a beer and started drinking it – it was warm. Most of the "partying" must have taken place in the days before because the place was empty except for about a half a dozen bikers and a couple of girls with raccoon eyes.

I noticed things like holes in the walls where fists must have landed, chairs turned over, and patio furniture in the pool. With my warm beer in hand I thought I would head upstairs to see what was happening there. I poked my head in a couple rooms that were just as trashed. All that kept going through my mind was, "what are this girl's parents going to think when they get home." I would have loved to grow up in a mansion like this, it was a shame. Then I heard laughing and a gun going off with more laughing. In my mind, I could see some poor sucker like me dancing as the bullets hit the floor around his feet. I ducked into this empty room with nothing but a mattress on the floor and a projector showing porn films on the wall. This was no fun. I stealthily slipped down the stairs and out the door looking for the nearest bus stop and headed back downtown.

It was getting late and I started asking around for a place to crash, nobody had a place to stay. This was unusual, but it was late. One guy informed me a lot of people sleep in P Street Beach Park. The park was empty and dark, the bridge over the stream would provide shelter if it started to rain. I lay down exhausted, and just stared up at the starless sky, something I couldn't get over being from the country where on some nights the sky was so clear you felt as if you could reach out and touch the stars. Just as quickly as peace descended upon me, it was disrupted by, "Hey what's going on?" I looked up as this big African-American man plopped down beside me.

"Nothing," I answered, "just laying here."

He took a drink from a paper bag and started to sing, he couldn't get much closer to me. "Here, have some." He waved the bag-covered bottle at me.

"No thanks."

"No? You're not going to have a drink with me?"

"I had enough already today, (the one warm beer)."

He started singing again. Lord, I thought is this going to go on all night?

He said, "Sing, SING!"

"OK, I'll sing," I responded, but the first song that came to my mind slipped out of my mouth before I could think about the words, "Rocky Raccoon." I sensed him tense up as I sang.

He said, "I wish you hadn't said that," as he flipped back his sports jacket revealing a gun tucked into his pants. I thought quickly — he is thinking I am calling him a racial slur, if I try to explain it to him he'll think I am just trying to back down so as not to get shot. When he senses fear, he'll shoot me anyway. So I decided not to stop singing and act as if I wasn't afraid, even if he wasn't a *Beatles*' fan! "...checked into his room only to find Gideon's Bible..."

He said, "Oh" and threw back his jacket over the gun and stumbled off, while I finally fell asleep.

Sex, Drugs and Rockin' Roll

By this time, I was starting to feel a fear deep down inside. I had stepped off the curb too often and had been pulled back by a stranger, who saved my life from a car running a red light. And, I had never seen so many guns in a city that had outlawed them. I felt as if there was a murder taking place just beyond the next corner. The stories kept getting stranger, like one where there were a group of "heads" living together in an apartment when one of them OD'd. Rather than take him to the hospital they let him die and then chopped him up and flushed him down the toilet, to not spoil the good thing they had going. They didn't want to draw attention to themselves and their drug usage. And I noticed the people with the most drugs to share had the most friends, and those who didn't – didn't. Then there were the ones who suddenly had runny noses, shaking all over telling us they needed money for a fix. We would just look at them and say "Oh, no not you too"! Peace and love was a farce or so it felt. One thing I decided was I wanted to stop roaming around alone.

One night I ran into this guy and asked if he had a place I could crash. He said sure he was staying in this apartment with some friends.

"Are you sure they won't mind me staying there?"

He said, yeah he was sure; he didn't even know where they

were. Leon led me up to this apartment and put a record on by a group I hadn't heard yet called *Led Zeppelin* "Good times, bad times, you know I had my share..." it sang.

Leon was a lot like David, aloof, self-confident and independent. I started hanging out with him. One night in DuPont Circle he came back to a few of us that were there and said he was able to score some "new drugs," if we wanted to try them.

"What is it?" (Not that it mattered that much), I asked.

"It is called PCP."

"I had never heard of it."

"It is like some kind of elephant tranquilizer, I think," he said. I pictured him sneaking into the zoo and taking some elephants' prescription for their nerves, while they were not looking. The next day the *Washington Post* would have an article about an elephant that had gone berserk running all over the zoo.

We all took one out of the baggy. It didn't take long to take effect. I remember looking up at my friends talking to me, but I really didn't know what they were saying. I must have passed out on the bench around the fountain. The next thing I knew a man with a billy club and a uniform was poking me in the side asking if I was OK. I'm fine I tried to say but I couldn't get my eyes to focus and everything was strange. Where were my friends? Had they left me there because they didn't want to chop me up and feed me to the toilet? The policeman took me to a Lafayette Park booth station across the street from the Whitehouse and made me stay until I sobered up, then let me go.

Leon found us a place to crash in Chevy Chase. It was a

beautiful old home, white with a huge porch that went half way around it. While there, we got stoned as people came and went. On TV we watched the first astronauts land and walk on the moon. Watching it was very cool and surreal. There were always a lot of people coming and going and one guy there who'd take their money and give them little baggies of pills and white powder.

One day that guy said to some buyers, "Yeah I have a whole bag of uncapsulated LSD that I have stashed in the attic." The problem was there was also a raccoon that liked to climb the trees outside and get on the roof and into the attic. The dealer had just gotten it from the chemist and hidden it from the rest of us so he could sell it, but when he came down from the attic he was three shades of white. The raccoon had gotten into it and spread it across the attic. I pictured some stoned raccoon jumping from tree to tree screaming "I can fly, I can fly" as the colors raced past him.

The deal was a bust so he went up to the attic with a hand towel and wiped as much of it up as possible and put it in a huge bowl and added water to it and told everyone to help themselves. Now normally, one capsule would be enough to keep you high for several hours – but with this concoction you had no idea how much you were getting. I took a small shot glass and drank some, but another guy took two glasses. Not to be outdone, I did another one. By this time, I was on a full blown psychedelic trip with tracers and hallucinations. I had tripped before but not this intense. I went back in the living room and sat back down to watch more of the moon. Someone put the *Rolling Stones*' "Beggars' Banquet" on the stereo. Suddenly, the plastic flowers in the vase beside the TV began to melt and the colors started running up the wall, the ceiling and I could feel them. The moon was no longer interesting.

The music was loud and the record got stuck on the "woo woo" part and kept saying it all over again. "Sympathy for the Devil" was a song I didn't particularly like anyway. The house that had been full of people apparently emptied out, except for Leon and two girls who had gone up to a bedroom to "train him." I don't remember seeing the others go, now it was just me and colors running all over the place. At one point I kept hearing this little voice say, "Hey, let me in" then I saw a face in the window, I thought I was hallucinating, (but it really was someone wanting in, the door was locked). I wasn't going to let a hallucination tell me what to do, so I just smiled at it. But, I was going to fix that skipping record, "woo woo, woo woo."

As I went over to the stereo, I reached for the arm with the needle in it to move it over a track and it turned into a snake, which I dropped promptly. It screamed as it slid across the record. I kept telling myself this wasn't real it was just the LSD. But I knew I was losing control, so I decided I needed a different environment. I went to the bus stop and while I was there I started praying. "God if you get me out of this alive, I'll never do drugs again," I suddenly started getting my wits back, the prayer worked. I wish I had kept my end of the deal but that would come later.

The next time I found David he was walking across the bridge railing that was an overpass on the Rock Creek Parkway. When I told him he was crazy zigzagging like a person on a tight rope while cars just thirty feet below drove fifty miles per hour, he just laughed at me. The rail was concrete and about six inches wide, but it still made me nervous, and seemed to embolden him. So I ignored him and he finally got down. I asked where he was staying. He said he found this flop house near Georgetown, it was like a huge room with a lot of sleeping bags in it, and a loft with a girl in it who called herself "Flower". She warned everyone that she had "the clap." I didn't know at the time what that was, but I was pretty sure about two things: 1. You got it by having sex and 2. I didn't want it. We left her alone.

Buddhists and SDS

One afternoon some guys came up to us in the Circle and asked if we would help them. They informed us they were part of a group called Students for a Democratic Society: SDS for short. They had just taken over the administration building at American University. They had a list of demands and needed our help. So we said sure, why not? We weren't doing anything anyway, besides they were offering free food. When we got to the campus, there was a large crowd gathering around the admin building demanding the SDS guys to leave. The guy who picked us up knocked on the door and let those inside know who he was. They let us in.

As the night went on, the crowds outside got bigger and then there were the TV crews and reporters joining them. That's when someone knocked on the door and announced they were one of us. The SDS leader told me to let them in, but just as I cracked the door, something came flying out of the crowd and hit me right between the eyes. I wore wire frame glasses at the time and they broke as something cut into my face and blood began to run down my cheeks. Suddenly, there were TV cameras everywhere, and I was on the nightly news, up close and in color. We eventually negotiated settlement, for what? I have no idea. That was my first and last sixties protest I guess.

Then there were the Buddhists coming down to take us to the "meeting". The Buddhists evangelized us, taking us home and feeding us and then taking us to their meetings. This one meeting I went to was filled with about 60-100 people and the speaker sat up front dressed in normal casual wear while he talked to us about the benefits of chanting in this particular mantra. He had an aura about him that made everyone feel great, comfortable and a part of something bigger than themselves. And, when he talked there was very little I could find in my uneducated theological mind wrong with it, except one thing that kept coming to my mind – "Where is Jesus in all this, and what does He think about it?" Now I was not a practicing Christian and I knew it, but there was something in my heart speaking to me telling me this was wrong, and I should not get mixed up in it, but to wash my hands of it. I literally got up walked to the back of the hall near the entrance where the water fountain was and stuck my hands under the water and washed them. When the girl who had brought me here asked what I thought about the meeting the only thing I could say was "Where is Jesus in all this?" She told me to talk to the teacher and ask him. I did and was told that Jesus is everywhere and he knew a lot of people who chanted to get closer to him and that I should try it! For about five seconds I believed him but the further I got from him the clearer I knew that Jesus wouldn't have anything to do with this so called "chant for anything you want, and you'll get it".

The girl brought me to her house after the meeting, and

showed me her little box where she kept a "holy" scroll. She had to put something between her teeth when she opened it so as not to get bad karma on it or something. Then she took her prayer beads in her hand and began to recite the magic words, which would get you anything you wanted, over and over. When she was done, back went the stick in her teeth and the box locked and her beads put back on the box. She said I didn't need a box or a holy scroll or beads, I could just chant and get whatever I wanted! I tried it a couple times and got nothing but this eerie feeling that what I was doing was wrong. I felt like I needed a cleansing in my spirit. I didn't understand why, but I now believe it was the Lord protecting me and me having a sensitive spirit to hear Him, even before I had surrendered my life to him.

It was at the Georgetown flop house that I met "Doc". Doc was recently discharged from the army where he had been a medic in Viet Nam. So I called him Doc. I told him he was welcome to stay with us even though like most, I wasn't sure we should trust him, after all he had short hair. He could be a NARC! (How soon we forget.) One day when Doc and I were sitting on the floor, Flower suddenly spoke up from her loft and said she was over the clap, and we could come up and have sex if we wanted to. I told Doc to go ahead I would just stay down here. He wasn't up there too long when I heard them talking and suddenly Flower said, "Rob you can come up too." I had never even thought about a threesome with two people I didn't even know or care about that way. In fact, I hadn't even given the idea much thought and wasn't going to now. So I told them, "That's okay, you and Doc have a good time, I am leaving for a while. Then Doc spoke up asking me to come up; I said I don't think so and left. In my heart, I could still hear my mother telling me that sex was for marriage and for the one you loved – that wasn't always my thoughts but this time it was.

I ran into David again on the street, who was talking to some straight looking guy with a tie on. David told me that this guy had some new drug the government was working on that was supposed to increase your awareness and maybe your IQ. He told me what it was called, but it didn't ring a bell. The three of us shared a needle and tried it – I didn't notice anything different, as far as I could see he gave us water. Later back at the flop house, Doc was main lining some speed, he asked a couple us if we wanted some too. We shared another needle, something I would soon regret.

I ran into Leon and he had brought a friend with him from Bryans Road, his name was Paul. Paul had long, sometimes greasy looking hair and he was one of the nicest, smartest guys I had met up to this point. We hit it off and became great friends. Paul and I became inseparable. He had grown up in a home with an ex-marine for a father. He too was very hard on him, so we could relate to each other without talking about it. One day out of the blue and boredom I asked Paul if he would like to hitch-hike out to Othello with me, meet my family and friends and then hitch-hike to California with me. To my surprise and delight, he said "why not". The idea had originated with David Muscot and he could barely be found. It was a 3,000 mile trip or so, I really didn't want to do it alone.

9
Sick to Death

I DON'T REMEMBER MUCH ABOUT THE TRIP EXCEPT we seemed to get rides quickly until we got to North Platte, Nebraska. Then there were no more cars for miles and hours at a time. It was late in the evening and I started getting sick, no sleep, no food and stuck out in the middle of farm country just as they were starting to roll up the sidewalks. I felt weak, very weak, my skin was clammy and turning yellow. I couldn't hold my head up. I was paying the price for sharing needles. There was a pump house way off the road in the middle of this field. We walked out to it and it was open, no heat and a lot of space between the boards, and the temperature was dropping. I fell asleep, but I don't think Paul did.

The next morning we walked into town. We tried to get a job at a restaurant just for food to eat, but didn't find any takers. The rest is a bit of a blur for me. I think Paul got us a ride with a truck driver at the restaurant. I couldn't be sure. By the time we got to the Columbia Basin, I could see Othello on the horizon with its red striped water tower and its name written across the top. I walked into my parent's home and nearly collapsed. My mother took one look at me and took me to the doctor and he announced after looking at the blood work I had "infectious hepatitis". Either my country doctor didn't bother my parents with the type – A, type –B, or type – C thing or they didn't divide it up like that back then, I don't know. All I know is I was sick and would be for weeks to come.

My parents house became quarantined, no one was allowed in that hadn't already been exposed to me. In my mind I could see this huge sign posted in the yard with red letters saying "Quarantined, Stay at least 50 feet from house – Loser Son Rob has Infectious Hepatitis from being stupid by using dirty needles." And then there would be yellow tape across the door that my family would have to duck under every time they went in or out. But, there was no sign or treatment for it either. I was laid out on the couch and told to eat hard candy. Paul, because he had already been exposed was allowed to stay. He was welcomed because he was so polite and helpful, that is until my parents came home and found my sister sitting in his lap. That was the end of that – Pam found Paul a place to stay on a couch at "Grannies".

Grannies was a huge old Victorian home owned by a friend of mine's grandmother, Johnny Lowen. She had it divided into rooms to rent and every "hippy" who came through town knew Granny. She was sweet and never had a negative word to say to any of us, she loved us and we loved her. Even the loud music that came out of the rooms either from electric guitars or stereos was allowed. I think she took her hearing aids out. The only thing she objected to was the smoke that sometimes seeped out around the door – "What are you burning in there" she would ask. "Nothing," would be the answer when the face came to the door with a silly grin.

I slowly got better over the weeks to come. Years later after becoming a Christian, I got prayer for the hepatitis. It is supposed to stick around forever and can kill your liver (David Muscot who I had shared the needle with eventually died from liver disease). Over the years I have had blood work done to see if it was missed, and it can't be found. It is as if I never had it. Our God is a mighty God! I kept my promise to my parents to be out of their hair as soon as I was able.

California Here I Come

One minute we were standing in Johnny's living room the next we were on our way to California. I mentioned, that for Paul and I, Othello was supposed to be a temporary stop, that I had gone out to DC with the idea that from there I would go with Muscot to California. But I lost David and found Paul and that's where we were going next. Suddenly, Johnny chimed in I'd like to go, and then Tom Valdez said he had family in LA he'd like to see, we all turned and looked at Tom Dirk – he had a car. "OK," he gave in, "I'll drive." The biggest non-thought out problem with this scenario was that Paul and I were the only ones at least eighteen years old. We were legal to make such a trip without parental permission and none of us had any money. Oh well, it was the sixties who was going to let money or age get in the way?

I told everyone I wanted to drive down US highway 1, which ran right on the edge of the Pacific Ocean. So away we went. We drove through the Tri-Cities and then across the Columbia River and following along its banks going west till we passed Mt. Hood on the left and the majestic Mt. Rainier, Mt. Adams and Mt. Saint Helens on the right, the Washington side of the Cascades. Oregon seemed to go on forever because it looked a lot like Washington. When we turned and headed south before we got to Portland. We were more inland than I would like to have been and it was boring. Someone spotted the "Now Entering California" sign that's when we all woke up. We were on our way.

We skirted the Redwood Forest. I would like to have stopped, but what I soon found out, there would be little stopping. I wasn't driving and so I had no room to complain. It grew dark and we fell asleep. In the middle of the night I heard one of the guys say yeah this is the Golden Gate Bridge and that is San Francisco behind us, again I would like to have stopped. After all, Haight Asbury was the place to be, but these younger guys had no interest in it.

We finally did stop. The breeze off the ocean came across the rocky shore, sandy beach and hit the cliff and careened straight up where we stood stretching our legs and past us to the tall pines across the road up the hill. We were at Big Sur. We were, according to the sign at a scenic overlook and was it ever! On the large rocks partially lining the shore were seals and sea lions, it was breathtaking. But taking a breath was about all we could do we had to keep going. I wanted to go down to the beach and get closer, but our driver was on a mission.

Sometime in the early morning we saw a lone hitchhiker, I said let's stop and pick him up. He had blond curly longish hair, bellbottom jeans and a T-shirt. I said, "what's a hippy like you doing out here and where are you headed?" We used hippy as a derogatory remark not as a complement. His eyes got wide and wild with excitement, "Hippy, Hippy" he said. "Do you really think I look like a Hippy?" You would have thought I said he looked like Eric Clapton. He was so excited to be recognized as one of the "groovy" people.

"Where are you headed," I asked.

"Oh, I don't know where are you guys going?"

"We are just here for the ride I said, no place in particular."

"Oh, then I'll come too!"

We soon realized he was no more real head than a plastic flower. And he was younger too. When all of us were scraping our funds together to buy food or gas, he just shrugged his shoulders. He indicated he was completely broke. And we sacrificed what we had with him. When it looked like we were stuck and not eating or traveling any further on our funds. He said he needed to make a phone call. We all thought he is going to do what he could to help us. Then he made the fatal mistake of taking out his wallet looking for a phone number. That's when I saw the twenty folded under a flap.

"You are holding out on us. You had money the whole time and you let us provide for you until we ran out. And you never offered to help?"

We found out his father was a Senator and he was no more a street person than the man in the moon. He called his mom to send a car to pick him up.

Church is Middle Class

It must have been Sunday and we had pulled over to get some gas. Across the street was this fairly large Catholic church, people were filing in. I said I wanted to go to church. Everyone else said why not so we got in line. As we got to the door the usher at the door put out his hand and said, "Where do you guys think you're going?" We told him we were going to church! He said, "You're not coming in here like that. These are nice people here," he kind of stuttered over the word nice, "and you're not coming in here looking like that." We looked at ourselves: I had jeans and a T-shirt on with flip flops. Paul had jeans and a button down shirt with tennis shoes and greasy long hair. Johnny had a shirt with shorts and flip flops and none of us had had a bath in days or a change of our clothes – what was wrong with that? Johnny was turning three shades of red and about to exploded, I looked around and the people there were all dressed like dandies, we hung our head and got back in the car and headed south. Johnny would tell me later he would not go to church for another seventeen years after that because of that rejection. When he did, it would be a divine appointment. His thoughts were, "Jesus wouldn't have turned me away."

US 1 turned into 101 and headed to the LA Freeway. A car in front of us suddenly lost its drive shaft and as the sparks came off the road we decided to follow it onto the North Hollywood exit to see if we could help. We followed the car to the side of the road and suddenly there were two police cars there as well. They wanted to see our IDs and wanted to know what we thought we were doing there at this time of the night. One officer warned me the city was dangerous ever since the riots in Watts. I remembered the burned out buildings in DC and told Paul we needed to get out of there. They soon discovered that three of us were underage. When Tom Valdez told them he was here visiting family they let him call them. We went there and spent the night.

The next day Paul and Johnny and I headed south with

our thumbs out, the Toms stayed in LA. I told them I wanted to go to San Diego, I had an Uncle who lived there who I was sure would take us in. A car pulled over and a man in his fifties picked the three of us up. Normally, you could get a ride if you were by yourself hitchhiking or if you had a young lady with you. To get picked up by one "old" guy when there were three shady looking hippies was not likely and we were not feeling good about ourselves since we got thrown out of God's house. So the Lord sent this man to us. He asked where we were going. I was in the front seat with him and did most of the talking.

"To my uncles' in San Diego," I informed him.

He asked where we were from, and so on. Then the subject changed. He asked if we knew Jesus. Now I didn't want him to suddenly stop the car and throw us out, if we said we didn't. I heard Johnny mumble something in the back seat, Paul just sighed.

"Yes, I am a Christian." I really thought I was since I was born in a Christian nation. That is what I had been taught in my small town school.

"Do you have a personal relationship with Jesus?"

"Yeah, I pray," (remembered my prayer on my LSD overdose) I told him.

"Do you read the Bible?" Now he was digging in, I hadn't read the Bible since the time I got stoned and read Revelation. I got really freaked out over the wearied creatures with eyes all over. They had to be extraterrestrials.

"The Gospel of John is my favorite," he said with a pleasant smile of someone who was talking of a dear friend.

Thinking quickly I said, "My favorite Gospel is Matthew."

"I like John because he describes himself as the one whom

Jesus loved, he laid on Jesus' breast at the last supper – he loved the Lord so much," he concluded with a smile and a faraway look in his eyes. I needed to reciprocate and quickly my mind raced to what I knew about Matthew.

"Yeah that is true but in Matthew, Jesus tells us how we all need to live in the Sermon on the Mount and it is so beautiful."

He concurred.

I sighed a sigh of relief, hoping he hadn't noticed.

"You guys look like you haven't had anything to eat in a while." We agreed. Actually, we had stopped at this gas station that was closed. It had a soda pop machine, the kind that had the top of the bottle sticking out as it lay on its side and when you put in your quarter it would release the bottle and you got your soda. I found an old paper cup (who knows where it had been, but we were desperate). I told Johnny to hold it under the end of the bottle while I opened, it and it spilled into the cup. Then we would all share it to take the edge off. I got the top off with an opener I had in my pocket (they didn't twist off in those days) and the coke started flowing into the cup. When it finished pouring Johnny quickly drank all of it! Paul and I just stood and looked at him with unbelief written all over our faces. Johnny's eyes got big and said, "What?" He had forgotten in his thirst the share part, and we were not happy.

Our driver said, as he pulled into this Safeway parking lot, "I have to run into this grocery store I'll be right back." He must have trusted us because he left us in the car while he went in. If I was him I might have been concerned that these guys might run off with my car. He came back with a large bag of groceries with bread and fixings to make sandwiches, plus a six pack of sodas! He handed it to me, I was dumbfounded at his kindness and I never forgot him and our conversation. He not only used words to witness to us he used actions. We got a ride as far as Laguna Beach, and it was getting dark as we ate our sandwiches and drank our sodas.

Wipe Out and Wild Woman

"Are you guys here for the festival?"asked the first Head we ran into.

"What festival I asked?"

"The one in Monterey," he said with a spacey look.

"No but do you know a place where we could crash for the night?"

"Oh, yeah there is this place," he hesitated, "a couple of blocks from here but I am not sure you would want to stay there."

"Why not," I asked.

"Because they will keep you up talking about Jesus, it is called the House of Shiloh."

"Oh, maybe we'll look it up."

About that time one of the guys said anybody wants some Chocolate chip acid?

"Yeah" I said, "where did you get that?"

"That guy up there just gave them to me."

"Cool."

We took the acid and found our way down to the ocean. We couldn't stop laughing. We started playing tag with the waves. I had never seen such huge waves so close to the shore. They would draw back and rise up, way above our heads. We kept getting braver and braver, getting closer and closer to the rise of the wave, and then run like the dickens to get away from it before it crashed down on our heads. That is until I got the wild idea that we should stick our finger in the wall of water and then run back from it. That slight hesitation was all it took and then the wave hit us like a brick wall. It tossed me like a toy, twisting me every which way. I finally pulled myself up and out of the wave, surf and water. It was dragging me back as I moved toward the shore. I made it, frightened and beat up. I looked around and Johnny was nowhere to be found. I feared he had been pulled out to sea. I looked off to my right at the receding surf. There was Johnny on the sand doing the breast-stroke as fast as he as could. Wet grains of sand were being flung behind him. I yelled at him, "Johnny the waters gone you can get up now!" We all laughed so hard we could hardly catch our breath for a long time after that. Paul was safe. He hadn't gone in as far as we had. He was always the smart one of the group. We sat on a bench and Johnny dozed off a little but the night was nearly over and light was beginning to appear behind us as we watched its reflection reaching out for the darkened ocean that lay endless before us.

In a couple of hours, we were back on the road with our thumbs out. The morning sun and breeze off the ocean had dried us out. Our clothes were wrinkled yet a little cleaner, our eyes had deeper smile lines in the corners but darkened puffy shadows under them. Hunger was trying to take hold of our consciousness from within. That's when the '49 Ford pulled over to the side of the road. The young heavy-set driver leaned over and opened the passenger door and asked if we needed a ride.

"Yes," I informed her, "we do thank you."

"Get in."

Paul and Johnny climbed in the back of the classic car. It was in amazingly good shape. I, as usual, went in the front and sat on the bench seat with our new altruistic friend.

The typical driver to rider conversation ensued, "Been standing there long?" "Not long", "Where are you going?"

"To San Diego, to see my Uncle."

"Where are you from?"

"Paul is from DC, Johnny and I are from Washington."

"Seattle?"

"No, Othello in the desert."

"There's a desert in Washington?"

"Yeah, eastern Washington..." Somewhere along the way of the slow talking pleasantries I noticed we were being passed by car after car, that's when I looked down and saw she was driving 35 topping out at 40 MPH. The speed limit was 60 plus if you gauged it by the other drivers. This was going to be a long trip for a short way. On her seat next to me looked like a freezer bag with bird seed in it. She noticed me looking quizzically at it. She picked it up and waved it around.

"I made this granola," she said proudly. "You can have some if you want some." We were so hungry that we could have eaten the bag it was in.

"Thank you I don't mind if I do." I made sure I got some first and Paul second, Johnny last; we were not going to have a repeat of the coke incident! It was my first granola and it was good. It was starting to get dark again when we made it to her exit.

"You guys are welcome to spend the night with me if you like and I can feed you."

"Wow, that would be great, but we don't want to put you out and cause you any trouble," I said.

"No problem." She fed us and made us a place to sleep in her two room efficiency above a garage. She was very nice and even though she was on the heavy side she carried it well under her muumuu. Her long straight brown hair, framed her warm and friendly face.

She went into her bedroom and left the door open. We turned out the light and laid down in our place on the floor and couch. Just as my eyes were getting heavy we heard her say, "You all don't have to sleep out there, you can come in here." We looked at each other each deferring to the other (sort of like when I was on the cliff above the lake with two other friends, you go, no you go and so on). I think all of us were feeling a little obligated since she gave us such a long ride, fed us and gave us a place to sleep. Johnny got up and said with a dutiful tone and a silly grin, "I'll go", and then marched into her room, leaving the door open. We heard some whispering going on and then in a matter of minutes, "You two can come in here too." Paul and I looked at each other and lifted our eyebrows with an unspoken question as to what that might mean, and smiled. "No thanks we're tired and just want to sleep. Thanks for the invitation." The next morning, we were on the road heading south again. Nobody asked any questions.

Cousin and Caves

The highway turned into a country road surrounded by orange groves, I was in awe. I'd never seen oranges on trees before only in stores on shelves and in bags. Then off to my left were these ruins overgrown with a worn sign whose paint was pealing but the lettering could still be read. It said something about the ruins being "The Mission of San Juan Capistrano," that every year the swallows return there by migration. And then, something about raising funds to restore the mission, but from the looks of the sign and the overgrowth on the brick and mud walls, they were a long way from restoration. I tried to get Johnny and Paul's attention, "Hey guys this is that place they wrote that old song about."

"What song is that?"

"You know about the Swallows, those birds who come to this place every year at the same time, isn't it cool." They were no more interested than the man in the moon.

I said, "Isn't it a shame it is in this condition...hey what are you guys doing?" They were moving into the orange grove reaching for the fruit hanging ripe from the trees.

"Don't take that," I said looking around for an angry farmer with a shotgun. Then I walked over to the trees and saw what they were reaching for. It was the biggest navel oranges I had ever seen. I too picked one...it was the best tasting orange I had ever eaten. Johnny wanted to take some extra, but about that time a pickup truck could be seen coming down the road toward us. I stuck out my thumb, and told the guys there was a truck coming; they joined me quickly.

The pickup pulled over and asked where we were headed – San Diego, I told the Hispanic driver. "I can take you there." In fact, I think he gave us a ride all the way to my uncles', who had no idea I was coming. I knocked on his door and when he came to answer he looked more shocked than pleased to see me. In fact he didn't even invite me in. He and my father must have had more conversations about me than I knew.

I had just come over 1,200 miles and hadn't seen him since

I was a baby and I wasn't even invited in. He didn't close the door in my face, but he hardly spoke to me. His daughter, Denise, whom I had never met, could see what was happening and came running to the door. She came outside and sat on the steps to talk to us. Her mother, Aunt Pat, warned her not to go anywhere. Denise was a couple of years younger than me stood about 5'2" with long straight blond hair. If she hadn't been my first cousin I would have fallen in love at first sight!

We talked about music, the movement and what we were doing hitchhiking across the United States and up and down the coast. She told us that when the Beatles had come to town her mom wouldn't let her go to the concert and she was really bummed out. But as she was walking down the street, this big black limousine pulled over and asked her if she would like a ride. Yap, it was the Beatles out to see what the town looked like before the concert. She road with them for awhile and they let her out not far from where they had found her.

It was getting late and I asked her if she knew where we could sleep for the night. It was obvious it wouldn't be on her parents' floor. She told us she knew that a lot of people slept in the cliffs on the shore. So we set out to find the cliffs. The cliffs were literally cliffs, made of coarse sand that sat back off the ocean. We climbed down and found coves cut into the sand where someone had laid before. I found a spoon and proceeded to cut my cove large enough for me to lie in. I found that while I lay there the sand kept falling into my face and eyes. I picked up a windblown newspaper and covered my face and fell fast asleep. What I hadn't thought about at the time was what if the cove I was sleeping in caved in? What if it rained and buried me with the rest of the cliff that hung above me? This was California, famous for earthquakes – I could be buried for hours while they dug me out as I lay there with a pocket of air created by the San Diego Times. I would be reading the same paragraph over and over until I was rescued, if I was rescued. I was awakened in the morning feeling the sand in my hair with the sound of a little girl's voice saying, "Mommy, look there's people laying there." "Stay away from those guys," her mom admonished, grabbing the little girl as she pointed at us and pulled her away. I think that was the last rejection we needed to decide this trip was no longer as much fun as we thought. It now was time to turn around.

The trip back to Othello was more exhausting than the trip there, with long periods of time standing on the road while the sun beat down on us before we got picked up. For instance, outside of LA there was a corner with at least eighteen people standing there trying to get a ride. We walked past them. By the time we got back to Oregon, the rides got even harder to catch. In Albany, we stood in one spot for about six hours. That's when Johnny decided to call his mom and she came to get us. It was a 650 mile round trip for her as fireworks went off in the distance, the fourth of July and my mom's birthday. Each explosion seen in the distance seemed to hyphenate my independence and yet accentuate my pointlessness.

10

Maryland Not So Free State

I HAD NEVER HEARD SO MUCH NOISE. NOR HAD I heard of such an insect as a Cicada, their tymbal vibrations were so noisy they intrigued and irritated me. We didn't have them climbing our trees in Othello (of course, we didn't have many trees in the desert, those that we had were bought and planted by someone) and I had never heard or seen these noisy insects in the forests around the Cascades or Seattle. Yet here in Bryans Road where Paul's family lived, they were everywhere, and I do mean everywhere. You could be driving down the road and a thud would hit the windshield and you would look up and see two red eyeballs stuck to the window from the bug that had just blinded himself like Hazel Motes, in Flannery O'Conner's recondite story. And, there were these fields everywhere with this large leafed plant. In the middle of them were barns that looked like someone had pulled every other board out from the bottom, in them hung the tobacco. Back home we grew potatoes mainly, and then sugar beets and some corn. Truly, Maryland was a marvel. There were also those green glowing bugs that like to fly about three feet off of the ground at night flashing as it went. One moment right in front of you, the next three or four feet farther flashing away. Not to show my ignorance again I proclaimed knowingly, "Look at all those fire flies."

"They're "Lightning Bugs," I was corrected.

"Oh," I confessed, "we don't have any of those where I am from, either."

"Well have you ever had a Crab Cake," I was asked.

"I've never had a crab," I admitted, "in fact I've never seen a crab."

A cake was something with frosting I couldn't imagine... "You're in Maryland now, you have to have some crab," Linda informed me matter-of-factly. Linda was Paul's girlfriend; she lived in Indian Head just about five and a half miles south of Bryans Road. Paul and I had left Othello shortly after getting back from California, we got on Route 90 and headed East. I don't remember too much about it, but that we got to Maryland in hardly anytime at all traveling day and night. We had hitched again the whole way.

Southern Maryland was very different from Othello and DC. For that matter, many there had never been to DC and had no desire to go, which to me was remarkable considering Bryans Road was only twenty-five miles from DC, thirty minutes away on a good day. Southern Maryland had an accent on "Southern." In fact most spoke with a pseudo-southern accent unique to the area and used phases such as "Y'all" and "Say what?" And, the further you got back into the woods the thicker the drawl, in places like Pomonkey, Nanjemoy and Pisgah, whereas the tease went "they had to pump in the sunshine". These days that is probably not so true. Now more people speak with the same dialect than they did back then, some forty years ago. I know our erudite education system would love to take the credit, but I attribute it to the Simpson's and other popular TV shows.

There were a lot of crew cuts there. Paul and I were the only "long hairs" in Charles County at the time, which made us stick out like nobody's business. But little did I know how many were making it their business. One day when I was hitchhiking to Indian Head I was picked up by a "crew cut" who had a gun on the consul between us. I looked at the gun and looked at him and then tried to make small talk.

"Thank you so much for picking me up and giving me a ..."

"Shut-up," he yelled and then looked at the gun and said, "don't you try anything."

"No sir. I will not try anything I just wanted to thank..."

"Shut up," he yelled louder. So I thought it best to comply. After all, we were only going five miles.

"Have you ever been to a barba?" he asked forcefully.

"What?" I asked politely.

"Shut up," he insisted.

"I am sorry, Sir, I didn't understand what you were asking?"

"A barba, a barba," he repeated as his face got redder.

Finally I figured out what he was asking. His comments pertained to my hair. "Have you ever been to a barber," was what he was trying to say in that Southern Maryland accent.

"Oh, I believe in this free country." That had his attention. "And everyone should have the right to free speech and the ability to wear their hair the way they like to. I used to wear my hair like..."

"Shut-up, shut-up," he said coming to a screeching halt.

"Get out, get out," he demanded.

I was sure if I hadn't, the blood vessels in his face would

have sprayed all over me. I got out and bent over to thank him for the ride, but he wouldn't let me get the words out of my mouth. His tires spun spitting gravel as coarse as his words were at me and he drove away. I wondered later what his real intentions were in picking me up, as I stood there on the side of the road. Was he planning on shooting on some back road because I represented something he didn't approve of or was he trying to scare me into running full speed ahead jumping into the first "Barba" chair I saw? I didn't know, but I'm pretty sure my composure and politeness threw him off and maybe kept me from getting killed.

I walked over to Linda's "rowhouse" another term I hadn't heard of till now. She lived there with her mom and two sisters, she being the oldest. Paul wasn't there, but that was OK, we three had become close friends. She compared us to a *Jefferson Airplane* song, "Triad" from the album "Crown of Creation". She had long straight blond hair (as did a lot of girls those days) and was crazy for Paul. They would go on and get married and have a baby boy, but the marriage wouldn't last. One day she told me some friends had invited her to ride along to this music festival in New York. I asked her if they would have room for me as well, she said she would ask and she was going to meet them on Rt. 210 at 10:00 a.m. I was there and waited for over an hour. She had gone without me. And when she came back she was never the same, she had gone the way of Syd Barrett. She claimed to have seen Jesus at Woodstock.[9]

This was not the first time I had been in Bryans Road. The last time was with Leon who took me to his parents place when they were not at home. He said his father was a poet and was published and was getting ready to retire from being a government worker. Leon had picked up some tickets to see *Steppenwolf* at Merriweather Pavilion. The seats were on the grass and halfway through the show he said we should "rush the stage". I didn't ask what that was because he stood up and said as we ran for the stage at the right moment everyone else will follow! So came the "right moment" and he stood up and I followed close behind him. We made it all the way to the stage and looked around. We were the only ones there, everyone else was still in their seats. We nonchalantly looked around like we had lost our place and walked back down the aisle to the lawn. That was quite different from when I had seen *Grand Funk Railroad* in Seattle. They couldn't keep people in their seats and the promoters thought we should behave like we were at the "Royal Philharmonic." They tried to get control over us, stopping the show three times. Making the band walk off the stage and start again, but who could sit down when the band played "Inside Looking Out"?

Bryans Road was a great place and the first time I had ever had a steak and cheese sub was there. In fact, it was the first time I had ever heard of a sub! It was delicious; we didn't have them in Othello either. Paul asked me one day if I would like a job and I said, "Sure what doing"? "Working at the go-cart track," he told me. That's how I met Butch Rider. Butch was a great guy who was an entrepreneur, and he worked a government job at the Naval Ordinance Station in Indian Head. He and his wife were always coming up with ways to make money and the go-cart track was one of them. I worked there during the day and slept at night in the shed where we would store the go-carts on three levels of shelves. Sometimes Paul would sleep there when he wasn't with Linda. Benny Gray, a gentle giant of a man who lived in Pisgah would sometimes sleep there as well. The problem with sleeping there was we would often get drunk on Boones Farm, or smoke some weed. We would get stoned and smoke cigarettes next to gas filled go-carts or their gas cans. Benny carried a gun tucked under his belt and shirt. And sometimes he would lie on the shelf below me that was tiered out bottom to top. After a few drinks, he would fire at the ceiling. "Benny that's not cool, now I can see the stars and if it rains we are all going to get wet," I would remind him. He would fire one more for good measure.

I met a lot of the locals there. They too were good people who were interested in the West Coast hippy Paul had dragged in. There was Kenny, Lucky, Skeet, Berkley, Vince and a host of others whose names escape me now. One day we were all standing around the go-cart track laughing, telling jokes and they were asking questions about me and the West Coast. Someone made a comment about Viet Nam and not dying and a random name came to me and I said yeah like, "Joe Haze" or somebody. Ha, I laughed and looked around. Nobody else was laughing. Their faces were hung low and they began filing out. I looked to Butch who was shuffling his feet.

"What did I say? Did I say something wrong?" I asked him.

He asked me, "Where did you get that name?"

I couldn't remember the name I had said, so I defended myself, "I just pulled it out of the air, why?"

"Joe Haze was Kenny's older brother and the first one from Charles County killed in Viet Nam," he indicated.

I felt terrible, but there it was again. From the time I was a little kid, I knew things that I had no reason to know. I would know when an earthquake was about to happen or when someone was in danger of getting in a car accident. When Kennedy was killed, I had a foreboding the day before. I stopped mentioning it to anyone, but my mother because it was too weird and people looked at you like you were strange, I didn't want to be strange. I wanted to fit in.[10]

The go-cart track was a popular place especially with people from DC. It sat on Indian Head Highway Route 210 at the corner of Marshall Hall Road. Marshall Hall had been an amusement park that sat on the Potomac. A ferry used to sail down the Potomac from DC and bring people to the park, but that had ceased long before I got there. Now just a few rides were open and people would come by car and see the go-carts and stop to ride for a quarter.

We had rules at the track. You only got eight laps for a quarter and then you had to get back in line and pay another quarter for another turn. The lines were long on the weekends and Benny was the manager. Another rule was that you were not allowed to run people off the track, this was not bumper cars and we didn't want anyone to get hurt. This one weekend an African American couple from DC got in line as I was taking quarters. They jumped the line and forced their way to the front. I told them they would have to go back and get in line where they belonged – no doing! They gave me one quarter for the both of them as they pushed others aside and ran in. I hollered, "you owe me 25 cents!" But they were already making the laps, Benny signaled to me to let it go. Then she started running people off the road, and he followed suit. Benny yelled at Paul to pull her out and Benny grabbed him and told them they both had to leave. He walked up to me and said "I want my money back!" I told him, he hadn't paid to ride so he had no money coming; besides they both had broken the rules. I pointed at the peeling painted sign facing the line at the entrance. He looked at me two inches from my face, I could smell the alcohol on his breath, "You're not giving me my money back, OK I'll fix you." He leaped over the fence and headed to his car opening the door reaching for something in the glove box. I knew he was going for a gun. Benny who was also African American and twice the size of this offender walked over and stood next to me. He too could see what was about to happen. As he reached for his pistol in his belt under his shirt, he said, "Just let him leap back over that fence!" I thought we were going to have a gun battle right at the track with all these people standing in line (twenty or more), all over a quarter! About that time, the girlfriend tried to get by me and out the way she came in. I took a quarter out of my apron and placed it firmly in her hand.

"Here," I said.

She lifted her voice, "I got it, he gave me the money," she got in the car and they sprayed gravel and burnt rubber on to the pavement, smoke rising from their tires as they sped away. There was no doubt that Benny would have taken the guy down in order to save me from getting shot. All I could think of was how people can be so petty over so little. Right or wrong just wasn't in their vocabulary. If they demanded it, they thought that was enough; they should get it. It was the way of thugs. Months later, when I was in jail, I heard that Benny got in a gun battle in Pisgah where he lived, and he was killed.

11

The Dealer Man

*E*VERY ONCE IN A WHILE PEOPLE WOULD COME TO the track and offer us drugs. One guy whom I had never seen before, took me around the corner of the shed and showed me some white substance in a capsule.

When I asked what it was he said in almost a whisper, "boy".

"Huh?" I questioned, thinking he was calling me, boy.

"Boy," he repeated.

"What is boy?" I asked thinking I had a good street knowledge of what was out there. "I've never heard of it."

"Well," he said still in a hush, "cocaine is girl, so ..." he spoke in code as if I should understand.

"So..." I mimicked him. If he didn't want to say it out loud maybe I shouldn't ask. But I had to.

"You mean, 'smack,' 'skag' or 'heroin?'" I concluded.

He gave a slight nod, while looking from side to side.

"What do you do with it? I mean I have never tried it before and isn't this stuff addictive," I hammered him. "Besides how much do you want for it?"

He sighed, and looked frustrated at this novice. "... shoot it," he said "or snort it, whatever you want."

"Can you just swallow it?" He was getting real impatient with me.

"Do what you want with it, it is five bucks."

I thought what the heck; I've tried everything else why not? I saved it till after work and swallowed it with a soda and nothing happened. I felt like I had gotten ripped off. I never liked to be down anyway, I thought it is just as well. I had given up drinking, for the most part if I had to choose, for the same reason. I didn't like the way it felt or how it made you sick.

Na, I'll stick with acid you know, "Turn on, tune in and drop out" wasn't that the mantra? LSD was mind expanding, wasn't it? Isn't that why Nixon and Hoover didn't want you to do it? "Timothy Leary's dead! No, no he's outside looking in..." sang the Moody Blues. Actually, he got fired from Harvard for the controversy surrounding his experiments with LSD. Isn't that him at the foot of John and Yoko's bed?

One night after we stacked all the go-carts back on the shelves, someone came back from the liquor store with a bottle of strawberry Boones Farm. I drank to be sociable and passed it around. Paul then pulled out a couple of hits of "Purple Haze", while we smoked a joint. When it became a roach the acid had kicked in. Paul and I started walking and laughing as we went, everything we said or did was funny. That is until he asked me what had happened to the little spade kid. "What spade kid, Paul, there is no spade kid?" I said as I started to freak out a little trying to figure out what he was talking about. Was it him or was it me? Did I forget about a kid we were walking home or was Paul playing mind games with me? No, Paul was too nice a guy to play with my head for the fun of it. He really thought we were walking home this kid. I always tried to maintain some control and sanity when I went on a trip. Paul was losing it this time that was not good. The fun was over, I had to pull it together and keep an eye on him, not an easy task to do since we had mixed wine with pot and acid.

Phone Calls and Phony Flattery

It was about this time that I started getting phone calls from a girl who called herself Ellie. She talked like she was really shy and coy. She said she had seen me and she thought I was cute – she loved my long red hair. I would talk to her for as long as time allowed when the track was slow. Once it picked up I told her I would call her back. She said no she would call me, and she did every day. Every once in awhile, she would put her hand over the receiver and talk to someone, I thought it might be her mom. After awhile I really think she started to like me for real and didn't like what she was doing, because the conversations started getting shorter, especially when I started pressuring her to come to the track so I could meet her face to face. Or I insisted I could meet where ever she wanted to. I felt like a rock star with a shy fan. Then she told me about this friend of hers who just got back from Nam and was looking for some weed. Could I get him some? I always wanted to be helpful especially for a soldier. I wasn't a dealer so I didn't know where I could go and get some. Normally, it just came to me. I finally got my hands on a nickel bag. When she called I told her to tell her friend to stop by, and I would give it to him. He wanted to meet me at the gas station across the road from the go-cart track, in the men's room. We arranged a time and I walked over to the station and met this man who seemed particularly nervous.

He had short dark hair and a mustache that he kept messing with. I just gave him the baggy of pot and told him not to worry about paying me for it. It had only cost me five dollars anyway, besides he had gone to Viet Nam and fought in a war that I had not, it was the least I could do. He insisted on paying me, at first giving me twenty. I gave it back and said it only cost me five dollars. At his insistence I gave in and took the five dollars.

About four weeks later as I was lying on the shelves, I saw flashing lights through the holes in the ceiling, and then a knock on the door. There were about three police cars. "Gentlemen come out here," the voice spoke on the other side of the door. "You are coming with us," it was just Paul and I. It seemed my admirer was working with an undercover cop who had trouble keeping his mustache on and I fell for it.

We were locked in the old jail in LaPlata, the building was behind the court house just opposite the old "hanging" building – no longer in use. Paul and I were put in the isolation cell used also for juveniles. We didn't know why we were there, someone said something about drugs. But, we would know what the charges were when we were arraigned, "Possession of an illegal substance, intent to distribute, sales of cannabis sativa and conspiracy to sell," or something like that. "What is cannabis sativa?" I asked someone.

We could get five years for each count that would be twenty years for $5 of marijuana. It was considered a felony offense for each count. We were front page news! We were the first drug busts in Charles County and the efforts of a new drug enforcement officer who was eager to make a name for himself. "You were my first arrest," he would tell me beaming.

The cell had three metal beds in it and glass broken out

of the one window with the bars on the inside. The door was metal with a slot where they would slide the food trays in. Paul's parents refused to help him. I knew mine wouldn't help so what was the use of trying. Besides if I made bail, where would I stay, I couldn't go back to the go-cart track.

There wasn't anything to do in the cell – nothing. These days there are TVs not here, not then. One day I found a book under my bed; it was there to keep the bed from rocking since the floor was uneven. It was a "Good News for Modern Man," a Bible in modern language. I started reading the book and began with the Book of John. I guess the guy in California, who bought us the groceries comments stuck with me. I read to the third chapter about being born again and how God so loved the world he gave his only Son. I started feeling funny like I was high. This warmth of love came over me, and I knew what I was reading was true and powerful! It was the most spiritual experience I had had since I had that dream when I saw the stars sing. I didn't know what to do with it! I tried to explain to Paul what was going on and he just shook his head and rolled his eyes. He couldn't figure me out and I'm not sure he wanted to.

Butch came to the window and asked Paul if he was going to get his parents to make bail for him, he told him they wouldn't. Butch told him he would get a loan on his house and do it. He apologized to me. He said he didn't know me well enough to make that kind of commitment. I told him I totally understood it was about $1,000 each. Paul was released, that left me by myself. I still to this day do not know how he got involved in this with me. Guilty by association, I don't know. They moved me out of the isolation cell into the communal cells with a young redneck truck driver who had apparently been picked up for amphetamines. I would be there for two months.

Every week some Bible believers would come and stand outside our cells and preach an evangelical message concluding with an altar call. Since we couldn't come forward, we were asked to raise our hands and pray a prayer with them asking Jesus to come into our hearts and save us. Every week I did, I think I was the only one and nothing seemed to happen. I didn't feel a thing, but they seemed quite pleased with themselves.

Then came the court date, two months after that fateful night at the go-cart track I was standing before a judge. After my name and charges were announced, I was asked to stand up. The judge looked around the room. I don't remember anyone being there but the stenographer.

"Do you have a lawyer?" he said loudly as if to bridge the gap between me and him some thirty or forty feet away.

"No sir, I mean your honor," I said with equal volume coupled with humility.

"Would you like the court to appoint you one?" he resolved.

"Your honor, I don't know what good that would do. I mean I did give that policeman the cana..., cana..." I struggled to remember the legal name, finally I gave up and said marijuana.

"I mean, if I am guilty what good would a lawyer do?" I concluded honest to a fault.

"Do you understand the charges?" he said looking over his reading glasses without blinking.

"I think so your honor. I trust you to make the right decision." Wrong thing to say because the right decision for him and me were not necessarily the same thing. For me it meant "have mercy on this dumb kid", I had turned nineteen in the county jail. For him it meant, as the newspaper would say the next day, "He had intended to make an example out of us."

Then he talked rather rapidly, "I suspend all charges except, possession of an illegal substance. Forthwith, I sentence you to eighteen undetermined months in the state penile system beginning with time served," or something like that. What stuck in my mind was "undetermined," what did that mean? Did it mean I could get out in a month, or two or what? I would find out later it meant nothing "just something these older judges like to say." I would also find out that the Maryland legislature had already reduced possession to a misdemeanor and it would go into effect two months after my sentencing. He knew that but he wanted me to carry the felony charge on my record. Only after giving my life to the Lord did I write a letter to the Governor asking for my right to vote, own property and own a fire arm, otherwise, my rights as a citizen returned to me. Two years later, he would grant me complete Executive Clemency, my records would be expunged, much more than I had asked for.

I would be moved from the county jail to the penitentiary in [11]Baltimore the very next business day. The Baltimore Penitentiary was the second of its kind in the United States. The first was most likely in Philadelphia. It looked dark and foreboding like an abandoned castle left behind by Count Dracula. Having come up from La Plata by way of the beautiful Baltimore Washington Parkway now to this place in the heart of the town, to a dirty building in what looked like an old rundown city. It was my time in Baltimore and the area we passed through by the harbor was not pretty. The building itself looked like it had never been washed in the 160 years that it had been there. Black soot lay thick on the dingy grey blocks that made up its walls with guard posts stationed at the corner and the gated entrances.

The officers that transferred me there exchanged a clipboard with the prison guards. I was led into the admission area where I was stripped, hosed down and powdered for bugs, I guess. Then after I dressed, I was led to a barber chair and given a buzz cut. I was glad for that, going into the penitentiary population with long red hair would not fare well for me as I was soon to see when this young man was submitted without cutting his shoulder length hair. Everyone was looking at him in the chow line. Some were whistling and making cat calls while the security guards stood and laughed. I heard later that he had gotten pushed in a closet where someone had their way with him, it made me sick and angry. The next day his hair was cut.

As I walked to my cell, which was on the third floor of a battery of stacked cells, five or six levels, I had to walk through a group of inmates talking and playing music on radios loudly. At the top tier all I could see were hands and arms hanging out through bars. I asked the guard who they were and he said, "That is death row. They are not let out for any reason except when their time for execution was due," he informed me. I held my supplies: soap, towel and a change of clothes which consisted of a jump suit. "Stand here," he said looking down the row on the second tier. "Stand back," he yelled and grabbed a crack and twisted it about a third of the way. Then he took me to cell 340, unlocked it; I walked in. It was about six feet wide and ten feet deep, with bunk beds attached to the wall. My cellmate was a fellow named Raymond, a local Baltimorian.

The noise level was amazing. Everything echoed, bouncing off the exterior walls. And when each tiers' doors were opened, it sounded like giant steel springs being sprung as the cells came open or closed, together clanging and then banging, echoing throughout. This would be my home for two more months until I got assigned to a permanent place to fulfill my year and a half sentence, I was inmate number 110636.

I probably should have been afraid, but at the time I wasn't, I don't know why. Raymond and I got along fine. I slept on the bottom bunk he on the top. We both wrote poetry and compared them, reading to each other quietly. He was a stout guy, who looked like he could beat anyone who gave him trouble. I certainly didn't want to get on his bad side.

One thing that always intrigued me was that those who were jailed in Baltimore and had lived in the city all their lives had never ventured outside its beltway. They liked to ask me questions about what it was like "out west." Most of them hadn't heard of Washington State (geography not being a strong suit), only Washington DC. I often had to say I was from Seattle, they had heard of Seattle, but had no idea where it was. When I told them about Othello, they would often wrinkle their faces trying hard to fathom such a place. There were no TVs in the penitentiary and *Grays Anatomy* or *Frasier* hadn't hit the air waves yet. It also amazed me how many had been in there numerous times. Some would get out and go right out and commit some crime so they could get sent back. The controlled environment provided for them a sense of twisted security they had never known either at home or on the street.

One day we got let out for chow and as I walked around to the stairs there was Paul standing there cornered by one of the black guys who worked in admittance. At first I thought, "Oh, Paul has made a friend." So I tried to walk on by, but just as I did, I heard this guy tell Paul, "You're mine, you're getting assigned here and you are going to be mine." I slowed down and listened. I heard Paul attempt to reason with him intellectually and was getting nowhere. This guy kept pressing in on him. I don't know what came over me, but I got angry and went crazy and stepped in between them pushing this guy off. I started screaming at him about how Paul was my friend and you are not going to "have him" without going through me first and believe me you don't want to do that because you will live to regret it! Now, I was the same guy that got his butt beat bad by a Mexican kid as a freshman in high school. At this time, I weighed 140 pounds soaking wet. But there must have been something convincing in what I said or my demeanor, because this guy backed off, studied me for a minute and walked away without saying a word. When I asked Paul if he was okay, he just shook his head and said, "No not really." Paul was taking this prison thing harder than I was.

12
Wired and Church

I FOUND THE BEST WAY TO SPEND MY TIME OUTSIDE
my cell was volunteering for studies or going to Church, or AA.
The one study I remember was where they had me seated in a
booth with wires attached to my head and chest, and then put
a wired button in my hands with a screen in front of me that
showed slides of various scenes. As quick as I pushed the button
was as quickly as the pictures changed. I would see a mountain
scene with a beautiful lake, "click" a picture of a sports car, I
would look at that for a moment then "click" a naked pinup girl,
"click" then mutilated bloody body, a quick "click" out of that
and a country road would show up and so on. I believe that it
was some sort of psychological study that said something about
you by how long you lingered on each picture and how your
heart rate and breathing reacted, today they would call it an
R-rated movie or a new series on TV.

I registered as a Roman Catholic, as I had done in the
Army, even though I had never been confirmed Catholic. I felt
drawn to the Catholic Church because of the awe I sensed
in their churches. My grand-parents and my cousins were
Catholic, plus I had a girlfriend in Othello who was Catholic

and attending a Catholic girl's school in Spokane. So I was Catholic and when asked if I would like to have a priest visit me I said yes. I would like to have a visit from anyone anytime. I got a letter or two from my girlfriend and one from my sister, but no others, and even they stopped coming in short order. So I started getting weekly visits from this seminarian from St. Mary's in Baltimore. He would visit me in my cell, his name was Frank McGrath. He being on the outside of the bars with the door closed; me on the inside. He asked me if I wanted anything and I said yes a Bible, remembering my experience in the county jail. He brought me a beautiful Douay translation of the Catholic Bible. I read it and came up with questions and the next time he came I would ask him the questions. Sometimes he knew the answers, other times he would write them down and ask someone and then bring the answer back to me. I could tell he had a good heart and was sincere, and why shouldn't he be? He was going to become a priest. This relationship went on for most of the time I was in Baltimore, then one day he said he would not be back. I don't remember him telling me why, but I was soon to be transferred too and spend Christmas and New Years in Hagerstown, MD.

Hagerstown had two prisons not far from each other, one a minimum security facility, the other a maximum facility like the penitentiary. The maximum facility was rock walled with guard stations on the corners with men with rifles. The minimum one looked like a community college campus with double chain-link fence topped with razor wire, and guard booths. I was assigned to the minimum security one and given my own private cell on a cell block with an activities room, with a TV. This facility, I found out, had had a riot the year before and the inmates had taken over the prison with a list of demands. Now they had no tolerance for troublemakers. Rumor had it that if you were difficult you were sent over to the maximum prison and often disappeared in the graveyard unmarked behind it. One such fellow got visitors and when they couldn't find him they said he had gotten transferred, but they never found him. It seems his transfer got lost in all the paper work, but you know how rumors are.

Things always seemed tense even though there was much more to do. There was a library and a gym where they showed big screen movies. I remember seeing *100 Rifles* starring ex-football star Jim Brown and Raquel Welch. I was given a job, where they would bus us over to the maximum security to work in the cannery making apple sauce. Their major product was state license plates and road signs.

I never saw much of Paul after that, I don't remember if he made the trip there or not, but I made a new friend, Tony. He and I were in for the same thing "possession of marijuana" and we were about the same age. He was from Greenbelt, MD. We used to go to mass together and sign in under fictitious names: Clark Kent, Bruce Wayne, or Mickey Mouse. I guess it was our way of keeping the rebel thing going in a passive way. He would make fun of the priest finishing the wine at the Eucharist. "Look," he'd say, chuckling to himself, "beads of sweat are breaking out on his forehead." Apparently, his experiences with priests were not that good he had no respect for them.

I liked being in a cell by myself, the solitude appealed to my melancholy side. I laid on my bunk and read books I got from the library and listened to the *Beatles* new album "Abby Road."

Listening to it on the intercom station made me lonely wishing I was back out on the street with my friends from Othello. The *Beatles* were our favorite group. In fact when we all heard that they had split up there was a sadness that hung over us that I thought would never end. Then one day Johnny said, "You know we can always look at it this way: now we have four as each go their individual ways, where there had been only one." He was right that seemed to give us hope. Also on the radio/intercom was a new album by the Canadian group *The Guess Who* called "American Woman." I loved that title song with a great guitar lead. I had always had a thing for music that had long guitar leads in them. Jimi Hendrix from Seattle was my favorite, then Alvin Lee from *Ten Years After* and of course, Eric Clapton.

I studied Marxism, Socialism and Ayn Rand. I like what she had to say the most. She wrote about the individual being willing to stand against the world for principles he believed in, willing to be ridiculed and ostracized no matter what the cost or the loss. I'd read, listen to music and stare out the window which faced toward the west. I'd watch the beautiful sunsets as the sky would turn orange with black streaks in it. It was breathtaking and winter was upon us. By spring, I would be paroled back to Washington State. Six months in jail seemed like a big chunk had been cut out of my life. In fact I felt as if more than time had been taken from me. I needed something to fill the gap and give me purpose in life. I wanted something to stuff in there to stop the bleeding. The innocent idealism was slipping into a dark cynicism.

My friends and family seemed to have forgotten me. I am sure they thought it the other way around. My sister Pam, was the only one who seemed to remember me. She had sent me a sweatshirt with a hood for Christmas, and she would receive my calls collect from jail. I was counting the days till I would go before the parole board. When that day came I stood before them, answered their questions carefully which were basically centered on what I would do if they would release me. I told them I would go home to my family and friends, in Washington State, if that were possible, they concurred. What would you do then? I would get a job and stay out of trouble. We'll let you know what we decide.

I soon found myself on a plane back to Spokane, courtesy of the State of Maryland. My sister Pam and her boyfriend Keith met me at the airport. And within two days I was supposed to report to my parole office and would do so for the next twelve months. First I wanted to go in town and see my girlfriend, who was at a Catholic girls' school. At first, she was obviously reluctant to see me. I thought maybe her school was like a prison and she couldn't get out. She informed me that that was not the case. Then I thought it was because she thought her mom would find out. She never liked me no matter how polite I was, I can't imagine why. I can be very persuasive when I want to and I finally talked her into meeting me at the Catholic Church across the street from her school. We sat up in the balcony and talked. But I wanted more and she resisted kindly. My persistence gave way to more than I'm sure she really wanted to do. I look back on that now with regret. She was kind and maybe still felt something for me, but never wanted to go that far, especially in the Church. I finally realized that whatever we had was over in the time I had spent in Maryland. I heard someone clear their throat as if they were having trouble speaking. When I looked I saw a timid priest standing at the top of the entrance to the balcony telling us we needed to leave. I don't know how long he had been there, but his cheeks were red and his eyes wide. Later, my close friends told me that she had been seeing Tom Valdez while I was gone. At first this made me angry, but the more I thought about it the more I understood.

Silos and Missing Missiles

My Dad met a man who worked in salvage at the Moose. He indicated he needed someone to work with him who was young and strong. He could use my help to do salvage work on one of the Titan missile silos in Royal. As a result of the peace talks the missiles were removed, and millions of dollars of metal in countless tunnels sat there for the taking. That's what he did, hauling it out to take to the scrap yard.

I moved into the warehouse where he had taken up residence on the site, gave tours of the tunnels to my friends and threw parties. The silos were like being on a *Star Trek* ship. The halls were round with metal grates as walkways. There were control rooms, galleys and sleeping quarters. Then there were the silos themselves, large tubes some two-hundred feet deep. You could drop something from the landing and then listen for it to splash; it seemed to take forever. The splash at the end was the water that was filling the silo since they had moved out and shut down the sump pumps; it would eventually become filled with water. At the top of the silos were huge doors that were made of thick concrete on rusty hinges.

In giving the tours, especially if there were a lot of girls, I would take them through several tunnels and then tell them to stand still and watch how dark it was when I turned off the lights. It was pitch black and the stillness scary. You could easily imagine an alien creature breathing down your neck. A few seconds was all it took and then someone would demand I turn the lights back on and take them back to the surface.

The parties were unrestrained because if the police arrived, there was a locked gate they would have to get through and besides, the nearest police station was twenty miles away in Othello. We knew they would never make a special trip out to this abandoned silo. Some parties went on for days; loud music, obscene crepe paper messages written on the walls, numerous girls, unlimited alcohol and drugs. I felt more lost than ever. At this point I didn't care anymore. Nothing had meaning to me. The missile base "job" lasted a couple of months and then this guy got tired of pulling metal out of the hole and decided to move on. I moved back to grannies.

One day my Dad called on me to do some art work for his friends at the Moose, my Dad never called on me for anything, so I told him I would. When he came to pick me up I had to say I didn't feel too good. Truth was I was too stoned to be able to do anything productive, let alone some art work. I felt terrible for letting him down. I could see the disappointment in his eyes. This feeling was new for me. I always felt justified in my actions since he didn't like me anyway. This time he was asking me to do something that I could do. He probably bragged to his friends about my artistic ability. I wanted so much to show him that I did have some worth, but I couldn't because here I was stoned again and miserable.

Mom and Dad left for the weekend and we were hanging out at the house. That's when Keith and Pam came in.

He asked if some of my friends and I would help him unload some drugs.

"Where do you want to go to sell it?"

"Spokane."

"Sure why not?" we answered. The fact that I was on parole from prison for drugs didn't seem to faze me. I was emotionally lost.

We got to Spokane, and he found somewhere to park. We all split up into pairs, took a half a dozen "hits" and hit the streets where the long hair freaky people were. We walked up to them and kind of bumped them and whispered, "Acid?" "Mescaline?" All the while not looking at them in the eyes. After about the third or fourth rejection I began to see a pattern. The freaks had become the "Jesus People" and were no longer interested in what we had to sell. They turned the selling process on us! And asked us if we would like to try what they had. What they had to offer was a new life in Christ.

That's when I saw her, the girl with the poufy hair, plaid shirt, patched jeans and piercing eyes that seemed to tear back the layers of my soul's façade laying me bare, hungry and strangely uncomfortable. Her questions made me think and search for answers I thought I knew, but at this moment left gaps in my reasoning. All the while a longing in me grew for what she was offering, "A personal relationship with Jesus." And she spoke as if she knew him, personally, not as some abstract concept or historical study. She didn't look away the way we did when were whispering our wares. Something real was beckoning me from behind those eyes and my resistance was waning. I wanted what she had. I needed what she was offering. Something in me was telling me that everything I had ever thought about Jesus was missing the essential ingredient, Him! The hole in my heart was longing to be filled, that part that I had been looking for, without knowing it was the missing piece. Although I never knew her name, what she may never have known is that from that moment on there would be no turning back until I found it. "Jesus loves you" were the last words I heard, and they stuck in my head, my heart.

Part II
The Charismatic Stream

"We are called to demystify the gifts of the Spirit and
we are called to put the ministry of the Holy Spirit back
into the hand of the church! The ministry of the Holy
Spirit is for every man, woman and child in the body of
Christ. All the gifts of the Spirit are for all of us!"
John Wimber

13
Just Say "YES"

STEVE ANDERSON WAS SOMEWHAT OF A LONE bone. You would think someone who could play his triple pick-up Gibson Les Paul guitar with its five foot high Rickenbacker Amp like Jimi Hendrix, would look the part too. But Steve never tried to "fit-in". In high school he was quiet and often melancholy and wore his hair relatively short for the '60s. He dressed like someone in the Penny's catalogue.

We really got to know each other when we both worked at the Cimarron Restaurant. I started as a dishwasher and graduated to setting and making up the salad bar. I also made Chef Mel's award winning cheesecake that he had developed when he had worked at the famous *Silver-Dollar* restaurant in Seattle. The recipe was for sale he told me for $300. Steve graduated to short order cook. I never quite made it, though I tried. He and I were never close friends, but we knew and liked each other. So you could imagine my surprise when I got a letter from him in which he beckoned me to become Christian. In it he described me to a tee. He said he knew I had some kind of knowledge of what it meant to be a Christian; I just needed to give into Him to fulfill my purpose in life. The letter said so

many nice things about me that it was faltering and obvious
that he thought more highly of me than I thought about myself
at the time. I tucked it away and held on to it as "the ruin fell"
and the pieces came together by divine appointment.

The idea to see Steve the day of the failed Spokane "business
trip" hadn't even crossed my mind until Keith ran after me in
front of my parent's house and tried to convince me to do drugs
instead of doing Jesus. It was his accusation that I was headed
to see Steve that motivated me to go. I really didn't know where
I was going at the time, but there was a stirring in me. After
he said, "I know where you are going to see that Jesus freak
Steve." It was like a light came on! Yes that is exactly where
I wanted to go! And as I pulled away from Keith and walked
across town, I didn't know what to expect or even why I was
going there. As far as I knew I was only going to see a friend.
Keith had called him "that Jesus freak, Steve" but Steve was
no more "Jesus freak" like those we had left in Spokane than
he was Jimi Hendrix. He didn't fit the mold for that either and
I knew I had to see him.

When I walked into his room on the second floor of Granny's,
I was met with the most exuberant radiant person I had ever
seen. It certainly wasn't the melancholy Steve I had known up
to that point. He was talking ninety miles an hour. His face
was lit up with joy as his eyes danced. He was talking about
Jesus as if he knew Him and how he was sure I would come. He
handed me a *Good News for Modern Man* (the same version I
had found under my bed stand leg and read in jail). He opened
it up to the Gospel of John the fourteenth chapter and said,
"Read this, it is all here." I read, *"Let not your heart be troubled:
you believe in God, believe also in me. In my Father's house are*

many mansions: if it were not so, I would have told you. I go to
prepare a place for you. And if I go and prepare a place for you,
I will come again, and receive you unto myself; that where I am,
there you may be also" (John 14:1-3).[12] I read and he talked and
talked and while he talked and I read, I kept hearing a voice
inside me saying "just say: YES."

"Yeah," I said softly.

Steve stopped talking and said, "What?" I looked at him not
realizing I had said it out loud.

"Yes, I mean, I do believe in God and I believe in Jesus,
what I didn't know is He has a place for me – to be with Him,"
tears welled up in my eyes as that warm feeling came back
to me!

"Look," Steve said. "Let's get together and study the Bible."

"How about tomorrow," I said.

"Let's pray," he said, "Lord thank you for bringing, Rob
here today and making him my brother. Be with us Lord as we
read your word."

I walked home on a cloud; my heart was overwhelmed and
about to burst. I was loved and falling deeply in love with my
Lord and Savior. I couldn't think of anything else. This was
November 4, 1970, the Christmas shopping season was starting.
Christmas was different to me – it had meaning, and it spoke
to me deeply. It was about the birth of Christ and the whole
world had been celebrating it for almost 2,000 years, most of
the time not realizing the significance of this holiday. Every
time I watched the TV and Christmas was mentioned whether
it was "The Little Drummer Boy" or "The Gift of the Magi" or
"Santa riding the Norelco triple head razor," I wept. I wept from
November to January as a deep cleansing was taking place.

I picked up that crayon colored Bible given to me as a baby and began to carry it with me everywhere I went. And everyone I met I shared my faith with and asked them the same question the girl on the corner had asked me, "Do you know Jesus?" And "Jesus loves you." Steve and I met every night "to get high on the word." I couldn't wipe that silly Jesus smile off my face! My friends knew something drastic had happened to me, one such was Tony Hecker (Shelly's boyfriend) who walked up to me as I was talking to several people about Jesus.

"Rob you've really changed," he declared with an astonished look on his face.

"Tony," I paused and asked, "do you like me better now or the way I was before?" He thought for a moment. I thought sure he would say he liked me better before I accepted Christ, because we smoked dope and dropped acid together. But, he surprised me by saying, "I like you better, now."

I thought to myself "me too."

Instead I said, "Tony you too can change by asking Jesus to come into your heart."

"No, no," he said turning from me before he changed his mind as he held up a hand as if to block anything coming from me to take hold of him. He quickly walked away.

First Visible Vice Down

Pam's boyfriend Keith was the only one who didn't seem to like what had happened to me, he was cynical to put it mildly. I was still a cigarette smoker. I tried quitting BC (before Christ) so many times that it was ridiculous to even think about it. I had littered the highway many times with packs of cigarettes, vowing never to smoke again only to buy another pack at the next stop. I had been smoking since I was thirteen. My mother was part of the cause, she had a philosophy: "If you're going to smoke I don't want you doing it behind my back." The problem with that was that meant having another source to "bum" cigarettes off of and to "borrow" a pack from my parent's carton. My Dad was never happy to "lend" but my mother thought of it as more of a rite of passage. She was always eager to have me take the next step on the ladder of life, as she knew it. When Keith told me he had a "Christmas" present for me and tossed me a pack of Kool's I knew what he was really saying. He was mocking my faith, "You're now a big holy Christian but you can't even give up cigarettes." I knew through his mocking the Lord was speaking to me about cigarettes hurting my witness. I prayed, "Lord you know how impossible it has been for me to quit smoking. Now if you help me for the sake of my testimony I'll not open this pack of cigarettes that Keith has given me. I'll carry it around as a testament of how real You really are in my life." I carried them around for at least two months and never once after that had the desire to smoke them. The Lord had delivered me from smoking. Whenever I felt them in my pocket, I was reminded that the Lord had truly given me a new life in him and I had the power to live it through Him.

In only a matter of weeks I thought if I have changed, I should look like it too. I cut my hair, took off my patched jeans and put on my corduroy slacks, with a cardigan sweater. The more I thought of things to change, the more things I gave up, my record collection, my stereo that I loved. Steve gave up playing the guitar. I began to judge my spiritual maturity by how much I could give away. I knew nothing of the Desert

Saints at this time. I now believe this was necessary for me to make a complete turnaround[13].

Christmas came and Steve and I decided that we would attend every Christmas service we could possibly get to, starting with the Baptist church, the Presbyterian Church, the Assembly of God, and the Lutheran Church and finally ending up in the mid-night Mass at the Catholic Church. Everywhere we went we were happy to be in the Lords house to celebrate His birthday. Steve had icicles hanging off his mustache, me off my nose but the two of us were not cold. The warmth of His Love was pulsating in our hearts.

The nightly Bible study meetings in Steve's bedroom at Grannies outgrew his room and his makeshift altar which he would light candles on. Soon, we were meeting in the living room and our converts kept coming. Steve and I took turns leading the study. It became obvious that we would need a bigger room. I went to that Lutheran church I had attended with my family and asked the new pastor if we could use space in the church for our Bible study. He graciously gave us whatever we needed. At the time, we took turns reading a passage of the scripture. Each one of us would take a verse, read it aloud, and then say what it meant to us. There were no wrong answers, this was personal. After one said what it meant to them, the others were allowed to add their thoughts. I always encouraged each one with their contribution. Having a good theology was not important, but to have a great relationship with the Author was. We sat in a circle and then we would discuss what we read after finishing the verse. Often times someone would come who struggled with reading out loud. Not wanting to make them feel uncomfortable I would preface the reading with, "If you want to pass when it comes to your turn to read, that is okay just defer to the person next to you." I thought it was more important that they receive what the Lord had for them by just being there, than making them uncomfortable. I wanted them to come back.

The problem was the circle we sat in. It just kept getting bigger! At one point, I counted upward in numbers of 200 young people, all in one circle! It was crazy, but we had our own Jesus Revival going on.

Then came the requests to speak at the denominational churches, and police rallies. I shared what the Lord had done to save me from drugs and alcohol and from prison to praise. What I saw in most denominations was that the adults saw me as an anomaly and they looked and talked to me as if I had nothing to offer them. Othello was a small town and I knew a lot of their problems. I also knew that the Lord would alleviate them if they would only receive Him to do so. "That's nice that you finally got your life straightened out," many would say as they patted me on the arm. I would answer it wasn't me that had "gotten it straight" it was the Lord. But I could see that many of them simply didn't get it. They had formulated their own concept of "religion" and were very comfortable with it and had no desire to change it.

I knew what had happened to me wasn't just for me and my friends alone. And even if they had not been "that bad" they were not that good either. No amount of good works could merit the Kingdom of God, it was a free gift. And, it came with surrender to the King of the Kingdom, a surrender which began by admitting that you were not good enough for it. What could I say? Jesus had a plan for their lives? Could I tell them Jesus loved them? That meant nothing to most of them. Love was a concept that had to do with romance and to most romance was meant for long ago as a young person. No, that would not make an impression on them. Could I say to them that Jesus had come and died for them that they might know Him, not just know about Him? No, I could only share the joy and exuberance I had for the Lord and hope that my excitement would rub off on them, but very few got it. I began to feel like there was something very wrong with the organized church. I heard someone say it was as if they had been baptized in lemon juice. They all looked so unhappy and aloof. I didn't understand it.

I made visits to churches on Sunday, normally with a friend or two. I was hungry for all of the Lord I could get. I didn't care what flavor He came in, whether it was Baptist or Catholic. I remembered that one Catholic church which had turned us away in California, because of how we looked. And then there was this Independent Baptist Church in town. Frank Booth who had been coming to our Bible study said it was his parents' Church, and was a good "Bible believing church". I thought all churches believed in the Bible how could they be a church without it? A long haired friend and I went on Sunday. The message was full of a lot of biblical references and he seemed to have memorized many of them, this impressed me. As he preached he seemed very excited and angry, while he waved his Bible from the pulpit. It seemed to me he measured what was right with his church by what was wrong with the other churches. At the time I didn't know if he was right or not, until after church when he ran to the back to shake hands with us as we were leaving. I stuck my hand out and he looked me straight in the eyes and said, "I'll shake your hand but I'll pretend he is not here," he nodded toward my long haired friend. I couldn't believe my ears! Didn't Jesus have long hair? If he showed up in this church would he pretend he wasn't here, maybe he just did.

After our next Bible study, I asked Steve, "Since we are now Christians, shouldn't we go to church somewhere?"

He said, "yeah, maybe we could go to his parents' church."

"Oh," I said excited, "where do they go?"

"They are Episcopalian and go to the Episcopal Church," he said matter-a-fact.

"What's an Episs-caw-pail-leon?" I struggled to get my tongue around it.

They met in a Methodist church in Othello, but had a church of their own, St. Martins in Moses Lake. They seemed happy to have us there. They didn't have many young people, most were in their forties and fifties or older. The Priest, Fr. White and his wife welcomed us with arms wide open. Before I knew it, I was being confirmed by the Bishop of the Diocese of Spokane and made a licensed lay reader. I loved reading the word with as much exuberance as possible, as one translation of Peter said, "as the Oracle of God". I spoke as if it was real and alive, not as if it was something written long ago that had grown tarnished over the years. Everyone in the Church liked the way I read and they seemed to get excited too. Fr. White asked me if I ever thought about the ministry. I thought I was in the ministry. He said would you like to become a Deacon? I said yeah sure, but what about a Priest, why stop at the Deaconate? He thought and said let me look into it. I had no formal training, I hadn't even graduated from high school; I had gotten my GED. He came back to me about becoming a captain in the Anglican Church in Canada. That would mean, as he described it, on-the-job training for two years and then I would go to seminary before becoming a Priest. After that I could come back to the USA to be rejoined to the Episcopal Church. That all seemed like it would take a long time before I was made a minister. I wanted to be in the Lord's will so I didn't rule it out. He said he would see what he could do. In the meantime, we kept having our Bible studies.

I was hungry to read everything I could get my hands on. Moses Lake had a Christian bookstore, and I loved to just walk around and look at the titles. Sometimes by just looking at them the Lord would speak to me concerning an issue or a teaching. I was like a sponge for the Holy Spirit. I picked up one book about St. Francis of Assisi. I love his simplicity and love for the Lord, and the fact that he had nothing and yet he became the very icon of Christ. I read Watchman Nee's *Normal Christian Life* and though I didn't understand everything I read, he spoke to my very core. I also bought this one book by an Episcopal priest called *Nine O'clock in the Morning*. It was written by Dennis Bennett. What Dennis Bennett was talking about here was quite different and had me curious. I wrote him a letter which I thought he would get fairly soon since we both lived in Washington State. I wanted to know more about this thing called the Baptism in the Holy Spirit. But, I never heard from him until two years later when he wrote me and said he was rearranging his office and he found my letter between the wall and the back of his desk.

St. Martins had a good library in the narthex. Many of the books had been donated by the former Rector who mysteriously left the church. One Sunday, while I was waiting for my ride back to Othello, I was going through the books when I saw this little paperback book squeezed between two hardbound books. I worked my fingers between the books to get a hold of it and pulled it out. It was titled *The Gift of the Holy Spirit* by J. E. Stiles and in the front cover was written by hand the name Gene Ford. He had been the former priest who was the Rector before Fr. White. When I asked Fr. White who he was, he asked me where I had heard that name. I showed him the little book. He said, "He almost split the church and decided to leave." I found out later he was asked to leave by the Rectors Counsel. This only made me more interested. How could this man "almost split the church"? Did it have something to do with the Holy Spirit? Wasn't the Holy Spirit the third person of the Trinity? Dennis Bennett had talked about the power of the Holy Spirit. If this was God, I couldn't wait to read more about it. I took the book home and I couldn't stop reading it.

He said that if one asked the Holy Spirit to fill us he would come into us. All we had to do is pray and then believe he had done so, and to thank him. I prayed and said, "Lord fill me with your Holy Spirit." Then I said, "Thank you Lord for filling me with your Holy Spirit." He said in the book if we had prayed that then it had happened, just as the Lord had indicated it would. And he said that with the Holy Spirit came the gifts of the Holy Spirit. One gift was also a sign and that was the gift of Speaking in Tongues. He said that everyone who received the Gift of the Holy Spirit was given Tongues as a sign that the Holy Spirit had been poured out upon him. I spoke to the Lord, "If you have filled me with your Holy Spirit I now have the ability to speak in Tongues." I didn't even know what tongues sounded like. I had never even heard anyone speak in Tongues before. So back to the book: He said that the Psalmist had written "I opened my mouth panting eagerly waiting thy commandments." I then stuck out my tongue and panted much like I had seen a dog do. I was so eager and I was panting for the Lords commandments and Tongues. As I did, I let my eyes follow onto the next thing that the book said. It indicated that when a person is new to the Baptism in the Holy Spirit he is like a new baby that is merely learning how to speak, so very often the Tongues he speaks is like baby talk. And remember this is the Holy Spirit's language not necessarily ours. St. Paul says *"...though I speak with the Tongues of men and of Angels...",* so tongues can be either of this world or the one to come. It also says, *"...my spirit prays but my mind is unfruitful."* That means what comes out of our mouth can be a heavenly language that I do not understand. But I don't need to because, *"Likewise the Spirit also helpeth our infirmities: for we know not what we should pray for as we ought: but the Spirit itself maketh intercession for us with groanings which cannot be uttered"(Rom. 8:26).* I found out later that "uttered" meant "articulated" in the original language, otherwise the Holy Spirit will pray through us in a language that only He understands with sound that comes from the depth of our spirit because only He knows what we really need. I began to groan and then speak in a baby talk. I thought, "Oh that was kind of neat." Little did I know how wonderful this gift was, *"He that speaketh in an unknown tongue edifieth himself..."* (I Cor. 14:4a).

14

Close Encounters
the Third Kind

I WAS IN LOVE WITH THE LORD, HE HAD TOUCHED me and I would never be the same. "You have put salt in our mouths that we may thirst for you," commented St. Augustine. I was hungry and thirsty for everything and anything that the Lord had to offer. I was in church on Sundays and in a prayer meeting every day of the week. I wanted everyone in the world to know I was a new creation and that they too could have the same wonderful joy I was experiencing. I couldn't conceive why anyone wouldn't want it.

[14]The Holy Spirit is the third person of the Holy Trinity but He is not in third place. He is equal to the Father and the Son, the Three in One (as established by the The Athanasian Creed[15]). I knew God the Father as much as I knew God the Son, the Son revealed Him to me in the scriptures, and in the Lord's Prayer. But I didn't really know Him, God the Holy Spirit. And little did I know there would be so much opposition to Him. But why wouldn't there be? If everything the church taught and the scriptures had written about God was true then everything it had

to say about a Christian having a real enemy was also true. An enemy who hated the very image of God and would do everything to deny us access to the power of God that came from the presence of this third Person of the Trinity, power to overcome and defeat this enemy in our lives and the world around us.

I read this little book by Stine about the *Gift of the Holy Spirit* for the rest of Sunday and into the beginning of Monday. I couldn't put it down until I had consumed it. Gene Ford had left me a treasure in the wake of his departure. If the gift of the Holy Spirit was for me, I wanted it. The book said all I had to do was ask for the Holy Spirit and the Lord would give Him to me filling me, baptizing in the Holy Spirit[16]. I had nothing to worry about, because it was the Father who would give Him to me and if I ask for a fish would he give me a snake? If I asked for bread would he give me a stone? How much more the Holy Spirit to those who asked for Him[17]? I knelt down beside my parents couch in the living room and I asked him to baptize me in the Holy Spirit. Then the book said if I had asked, then I have received. It was that simple, so all I had to do is thank Him for the Holy Spirit. "Thank you, Jesus, praise you Jesus," I said, "Thank you for giving me the Holy Spirit."

Then the book said, if I have received the gift of the Holy Spirit I also have received the gift of tongues among other gifts[18]. The early church spoke in Tongues as the Spirit gave them "utterance,"[19] which was an old fashioned way of saying "the ability to do so". I now had the ability to speak in tongues, but I had no idea what that meant. I had only heard of tongues in a derogatory way from what my mother had said. What I would learn was tongues were another way of saying "languages" which are unknown or unlearned by the speaker.

Accordingly, they could be tongues of men or of angels[20]. Stine said in his book that one way to begin was first to believe you had the gift and then he quoted the Psalms, "I opened my mouth, and panted: for I longed for thy commandments." [21] I look back on that now and it sounds funny, but I was following the book to a tee. So I panted, and panted, I felt like a dog. Then it indicated that sometimes tongues sound like baby talk. In fact what I didn't know then but know now, is the word for tongues is sometimes referenced as *glossolalia* taken from the Greek, meaning to babble. If the Lord wanted me to babble like a baby, I could humble myself and do that. The gift of the Holy Spirit was like anything else in the Lord. It was cooperation with Him. I would make the sounds and He would make them into words that He understood. [22]If I pray in an unknown tongue my spirit prays but my mind would be unfruitful[23]. He that speaks in an unknown tongue speaks mysteries[24] and he that speaks in an unknown tongue edifies himself[25] or else he "builds himself up in the faith". Tongues are the only gift in the Spirit that is for self enrichment. If it is used in prayer it becomes the vehicle by which the Holy Spirit prays for us according to our actual needs, not our perceived needs[26]. So I began to pray in this baby language, and it moved smoothly into this unknown tongue. I thought to myself, "Oh, that is nice," but nothing more – until later that evening.

Pentecost at the Prayer Meeting

The Bible study that night was a typical one. We all sat in a circle and read a passage from the scriptures and then discussed it. After the study in the fellowship hall of the Pilgrim Lutheran

Church, as was our practice, many of us concluded the night by filing into the sanctuary and kneeling before the altar for closing prayer. Normally, we would just wait until someone began to pray as they felt led. This night we waited and then I thought, "Okay, I'll do it" and I began.

"Dear God," I started in my most formal voice, but immediately I thought to myself "that's not right!"

I started again, "Our Father..." also as formal and holy sounding as I could, but I was stopped again, "that's not right either!"

Then it hit me, he was more than a formal God who was distant and unapproachable, no he wasn't just "Our Father" He was "my" Father.

I began again, "My Father, my Father, HE is my Father," now that knowledge was penetrating my soul from my spirit and I choked up. No longer able to speak I could only weep and weep. What felt like liquid love began to flow over me. I thought I would melt right there into a puddle of love. I collapsed as I knelt.

The two girls who were sitting on each side of me began to ask me, "Rob are you okay, why are you crying?" I think they thought I had completely lost it!

I said, "Yes, I am okay, in fact I am more than okay. The most wonderful thing is happening to me. I feel love being poured out on me."

I paused and spoke, "I think it has something to do with what had happened to me, this afternoon," as the realization began to dawn upon me. I rose from my seat and stepped out of the pew where I was sitting as I continued to speak, "It is called The Baptism in the Holy Spirit."

"I read about it in this little book today...." my voice trailed off as my thoughts continued.

"You can have it too, it said it is sometimes given through people putting their hands on you, would you like me to put my hands on you and see what happens?"

"Yes," said one kneeling on the steps near where I was standing. I put my hands on him, and he began speaking tongues, immediately. I was amazed. I made my way around the room repeating the same scenario.

Then before I could get to people to put my hands on them they spontaneously began to speak in tongues. The sanctuary was filled with this wonderful sound of people speaking in tongues. Tears were flowing down their faces and some with laughter, it sounded like we were no longer alone. The room had filled with angels praising God!

It was about that time at a side door to the sanctuary that I saw Mike Vogel looking in wide eyed. I said, "Mike come in," he came in and as he did I said, "Mike kneel down, you can get this too." By this time, I too was laughing and crying with great joy. I helped Mike kneel down, and he did so politely but, he stood up again. I said, "No, kneel down" and he did part way and then got right back up. This time he went back out the door before I could get a hold of him again. The next time he came to the door ready to duck out if I came to get him, he said as he signaled with his hand, "Bill, come on." He was there to pick up Bill who was his brother, who had been at the Bible study and now was having his own personal Pentecost experience. Bill answered, "Just a minute," with the joy of the Lord all over him. Mike appeared in the doorway one more time not crossing the threshold, merely peeking around the corner into the room again, urging his brother's exit. Later Mike told me, he told Bill on the way home, that he thought, "This could be of the Devil." Bill told him through his Jesus grin, "I really don't think so, it feels too good."

I don't know how long I stayed there that night, but I know I was the last one to leave because after everyone had gone, I just sat there. I never felt closer to the Lord than in that moment. I could almost see Him sitting next to me with His arm around me. In fact, it became a regular thing for me to come to that chapel and just sit there quietly alone in the presence of the Lord. One of those times, I was sitting there praying and I began to feel a gentle breeze flow over my face and then circle around it. Suddenly, I heard an audible voice which I thought came from behind me, it said, "Be careful what you pray." I turned around thinking someone had come in and sat down quietly behind me, but there wasn't anyone there! Then I heard it again, this time I knew it had come from within me and it came with the impression that the Lord was pleased with me and he *wanted* to answer my prayers. My prayers needed to be careful, that is full of care that they were what the Holy Spirit wanted me to pray. I knew how important it was to allow the Holy Spirit to pray through me in an unknown tongue because I could manufacture ideas on what to pray with my mind, but I couldn't be sure they were what he wanted. Allowing him to pray through me in a language that transcended my knowledge eliminated that problem.

On tapes I was getting from Virginia Galusha, [27]Chuck Smith talked about the Baptism in the Holy Spirit. He said one day he was praying for a young man to receive the Gift of the Holy Spirit and when he did the young man kept saying one word over and over and Chuck said he thought to himself what is this? Come on, just get on with it. That is when a man from a foreign country came by and spoke, thinking out loud, "he is saying thank you, thank you, in my native tongue." Chuck said he silently prayed, "Sorry Lord." So I knew the Jesus People where Spirit-filled, if they were nearby I would have joined them, but the closest that they were was in Spokane and that was 120 miles away. The Spokane Jesus People[28] were not associated with the Calvary Chapel Jesus People.

Our nightly prayer meetings grew smaller, but more powerful. We started having adults visiting us. A couple of ladys started coming and they brought a visitor from Sweden, who seemed to understand English well enough, but was unable to speak it that well. They seemed to enjoy the Bible study, but only came once a week and then left right after, not joining us for prayer afterward until one night.

We all went into the sanctuary to pray; we began as usual in English, and then transitioned into tongues. Our tongues had grown quite sophisticated in so much as you could make out sentences and paragraphs as we prayed. Elsa, the Swedish lady, as soon as she heard it began to glow with joy as if she understood what was happening. I went back to her and her escorts and asked if she knew what was going on and if they too wanted to be baptized in the Holy Spirit. The two ladies escorting Elsa waved me off with the show of their hands and got up and took Elsa out. The next time they came to the Bible study they were not smiling only Elsa was. Afterward, there appeared to be some discussion as to whether to join us in the sanctuary or not. When they did it was as it seemed under protest from the escorting ladies. When we started to pray,

Elsa began to weep and weep, her escorts were very upset at her and almost picked her up as they took her out. They never came back. I went to their house to do a pastoral visit shortly after that, but was told Elsa didn't want to see me. I was never quite sure if it was Elsa or her escorts who didn't want her to see me. It remains a mystery to me today just what happened.

It was also at this time that Corinne Michaels and Gladys Parham started coming to our Bible studies. Ms. Parham was related to Charles Fox Parham[29]. He was at being of the outpouring of the Holy Spirit of the modern Pentecostal movement at the turn of the century. Corinne was a beautiful Spirit-filled lady who sang in the Spirit. It was the most beautiful sound I have ever heard. It was almost spiritual opera! It felt as if heaven broke open and glory spilled out when she sang. We all liked kneeling beside her when she sang, so hopefully some would splash over on us.

I was hooked. I had to be where this Holy Spirit stuff was happening. I had a meeting with Fr. White at St. Martins as he informed me that he had everything in order for me to become a priest through the Canadian Anglican Church starting as a Captain in service. I told him what had happened to me as a result of finding the former rector's book. That I had been Baptized in the Holy Spirit, and now spoke in Tongues. He looked down with a disappointed look on his face and said very quietly, though no one was around that he too, spoke in tongues. I said very excitedly "You do, how come you never talk about it?" He mumbled something about not wanting to offend those who didn't speak in tongues. To me he sounded like he was ashamed of this gift of God. I didn't understand it and I didn't want to judge him for it either. He had been good to me. He got me confirmed in the church when the Bishop came down from Spokane, and he had me licensed as a "Lay Reader," now he had found a way to make me a priest with the Episcopal Church by way of the Anglican Church. "But," I told him, "I wanted to pursue this gift and be with those who sought after the move of the Spirit." He hung his head again and said "OK, if that is what you want I am not going to try to talk you out of it." I know he had put a lot of work into getting me into the program to make me a priest. I felt bad about that, but I knew my heart and had to know more about the move of the Holy Spirit and I had an idea where I could go to find out.

The Assembly of God Church is where I met Pastor Dale Johnson. He was a good man. He and his wife came over from Seattle. They were Spirit-filled, but their service seemed like a Baptist service with the Holy Spirit thrown in for good measure. I wasn't sure about them. Then there was the "Revival Mission," on Main Street across the street from bars. I and another brother went to their service and found it was made up of four people, two elderly couples. One was a preacher and he was tall and thin and he spit as he preached. His wife was big and heavy and seemed to be the boss. The other couple was very kind and seemed frustrated with the preacher and his wife. They had been praying for revival and the outpouring of the Holy Spirit. I am sure they didn't even think the answer to that prayer had come through their door with these two hippy looking kids, but here we were. The skinny preacher asked if he could lay hands on us and pray for us, I said sure. He prayed and prophesized, when he did I thought he was mad at God! He screamed and shouted and worked up a sweat on his brow as he lifted one and lowered the other with pensive look. It seemed as if he thought we should be doing something, but I had no idea what that might be. The kind looking couple seemed to be miffed when the big heavy lady at the piano started going on about "Jesus Only" as if she was looking for a fight. The nice couple got red in the face, but didn't respond. They invited us to dinner after church at their house, and told us we could come with them to Moses Lake to a United Pentecostal Church. I had no idea what that meant, but it had Pentecostal in its name so I wanted to find out. He warned me that they were "Jesus only" too. I thought that meant they didn't like Buddha, or Mohammad, just Jesus, which I certainly could agree with. There was something very sterile about them and their service, it was as if the life had been squeezed out of it like an orange for juice, the juice was gone only pulp was left. The women all had long dresses and long hair and the men all had short hair and white shirts with no ties. I am sure we looked strange to them in our jeans and T-shirts.

The Spirit did not bear witness with my spirit. It was amazing to me in these days, when I had no theological training just a love for the Lord, how sensitive my spirit was to identify with what was right and what was not right. Or as I would say today, what was Orthodox Christianity and what was not.

I was seeking out "Pentecostal" type churches. One church we visited frequenting was Bethel Tabernacle[30] in East Wenachee, Wa. This was a trip of over 90 – 100 miles from Othello. It took at least an hour and a half to get there-- a round trip of three hours and the service lasted two to three hours. We didn't care because if the Lord was moving, we wanted to be there. The place on a Sunday night was packed out, standing room only. We always tried to get there early to sit as close to the front as possible, "close to the spout where the glory pours out". The Pastor was an anointed man who moved in the word of knowledge and prophecy[31]. If I got a personal prophecy there or not, I do not remember, but I do remember all of us being filled with the Spirit when we got home.

One night after such a trip, I had a vision when I lay down on my bed. I have never had such a vivid manifestation before or since. I closed my eyes and saw myself being transported through space, it jolted me. I sat up in a panic, "What was that," I said out loud. Then that quiet reassuring voice within me spoke to me and said, "Do not be afraid. Only watch and see what I am going to show you." I lay back down and closed my eyes and saw myself moving through space again, this time I came to rest at the feet of Jesus as he sat on the throne. I sat up again, my heart was racing, but this time my thoughts were, "What am I doing seeing something like this?" I knew how unworthy I was to be seeing what I was seeing. But, again that reassuring affirmation came to me and brought me peace to let it happen. I saw who I knew to be the Lord Jesus on a white throne high and lifted up as if I was small at his feet. And over him and around the back of the throne was a pulsating rainbow, neon like. The colors ran together like the Aurora Borealis only even in pattern around the throne and streaking out like the sun. The Lord looked at me, and I felt love and grace at His glance. And then He looked to his right and from behind the throne from out of the rainbow marched a multitude of people, and faces on the front row that I recognized, in particular Mike Vogel, Bill Vogel and many others from the Bible study. And behind them a multitude that I knew in my heart but did not recognize, as if they would be people I would come to know at a later time. The Lord looked back at me. I sensed he was pleased. It was then that I was released and I sat up and walked around the room praising God in the Spirit pondering through tears the vision as to what it meant. What I did know is that somehow I was connected to them and they to me.

When I tried to share the vision at the Lutheran Church after our Bible study I did so reluctantly not knowing if I should. But why shouldn't I? It was true and wonderful and maybe someone could help me understand it. What I found was people either doubted me or resented me for some reason. Thereafter, when I shared it, I did so only sparingly and when I did it was through many tears and sometimes sobbing. Because of the emotional impact of the vision came back to me and always made it difficult to speak of.

That nice elderly couple from the mission called me up not long after this and said they were going to give up the mission and did I want to use the facilities. This happened right about the time I had been praying for a new place to meet instead of the Lutheran Church. Not that there was anything wrong with the Lutheran Church, it was that oftentimes we couldn't meet there because they were having something going on and the further I got into it the more I wanted to distance myself from any denomination. I told them I thought the Lord was leading me to form a coffee house outreach and that that location would be perfect. I also told them that I thought the Lord wanted us to call it "The Way".

15

...so that if he found any there who belonged to The Way... Acts 9:2

The waves rippled gently off the pebbles on the banks of the Columbia River, "the mighty Columbia" wrote Woody Guthrie. The sky was crystal blue and the cliffs of basalt lavas red in the desert sun cut and shaped by the last ice age as we walked the ancient shores. Arrowheads, petrified wood and beautiful agates littered our path as a handful of us hiked together to enjoy the presence of the Lord outdoors. Some were skipping rocks across the choppy water getting one maybe two hops. It was then I spotted a piece of driftwood about three feet long with a slight hook at the end, a nub from the former branch worn away by the constant beating of water and rocks in the river. I picked it up, it had some purpose to play, what I didn't know. A few feet down the river I picked up a second piece, this one straighter than the first and longer, at least four and half feet long. I carried them both, and then I placed one across the other and noted what a beautiful rugged cross they would make the centerpiece of The Way.

We removed the wall in front of the windows and scraped off the "Mission" lettering from the glass and in its place I wrote "The Way" in rounded lettering that was popular among Haight / Ashbury storefronts. We painted the walls a light blue except at the end, opposite the windows, that I painted white and placed the now flat black cross from the driftwood I had found. And in the drop ceiling I mounted a blue spotlight that would remain on always making the cross shadow the length of the wall, a stunning effect from the street. In the middle of the wall (the length of the room) I place a huge copy of Richard Hook's Jesus. Then I asked Frank Booth if he could get his hands on some large spools which we covered with plywood and decoupage. Frank, his older brother Charlie and his father owned an electrical contracting company rightly named for Othello, "Farmers Electric".

I placed a small table with a basket on it for anyone who wanted to make an offering next to the door to the prayer room at the back of the main room. It was also a passage to the rear of the facility that had living quarters of a sort. It lacked a few essentials like running water, heat and air conditioning, but I lived there for a short time, when the weather permitted.

It was about this time that Phil and April Hansen joined us. He played guitar and they were both art school majors. Now we had a worship leader and artists who could put verses on the tables and outstretched hands on the windows. We continued our nightly Bible studies and prayer meetings. Before we got our tables and chairs in place, we just sat on the floor cross legged, in a circle. One night we were sitting there with visitors. When we got to the part where we just prayed in the spirit, I was praying in tongues with my eyes closed. I got the feeling someone was watching me. I cracked one eye slightly open, and there wide eyed next to me was a young lady with tears in her eyes, and she said, "Where did you learn such beautiful Hebrew?" When I explained the Baptism in the Spirit and speaking in tongues she too received the gift.

Miracles just seemed to abound. Money was never an object. When it was needed, I just went into the prayer room and prayed passing the empty basket on the way in. When I concluded praying, very often I would come back out and there would be cash in the basket. Where it came from, God only knows. Never once did I see or hear anyone come in, it just appeared there.

One time I was counseling with someone in the prayer room when I heard the front door open, I came out to greet whoever had come in and it was a very large American Indian. He started to say "What is this...", he paused looking at the cross on the wall and the picture of Jesus. I said, "This is where we worship Jesus." At the name of the Lord he fell out on the floor and his eyes rolled back and he started foaming at the mouth while he was shaking violently. I told the person who I had been in counseling with to run and call an ambulance while I bent over him and began to pray. I rebuked the evil spirit in the name of Jesus and suddenly he stopped shaking, his eyes opened and the foaming ceased, I gave him a towel to wipe his mouth off. About that time, two police officers came in and asked what was going on. Behind them came his family members. He looked at the police and then at his family's wide eyes and got up and walked out. The ambulance pulled up as he exited. I wish I had a chance to follow up with him, but I never saw him again.

"M&M's"

Othello was a rural town that catered to the agriculture community around it. For such a small town it had a lot of churches in it. The religious community was made up of one third Catholic, one third Mormon, and the last third a mix of various Protestants: Baptist, one independent the other Southern Baptist, two Lutheran churches: one American and one Missouri Synod, two Pentecostal, one Assembly of God and one Hispanic Assembly; Church of Christ, Presbyterian, Methodist, and various versions and cults. So it was inevitable that we would get approached by Mormon Missionaries.

I was in the back praying when the Mormons came in and were invited to sit down. One of the members of The Way came to get me and I came out and greeted them.

"What can I do for you?" I asked.

"We come to ask you to repent and be baptized in the name of the Church of Jesus Christ's Latter Day Saints."

"Oh, why would I want to do that?"

"Because the Mormon Church is the one true church, commissioned in these last days to restore the faith to the world before he returns," they said without blinking.

"But, I am a Christian. I believe in Jesus Christ as my personal savior. He lives in my heart and we are trying to live by his word, the Bible."

The missionary took the Bible and threw it on the floor and said, "This means nothing if you don't have the whole truth."

"Look, we are going to leave you this book and just look at it and pray about it and we'll be back in two weeks and you can let us know what you think about it."

I said, "I'll look at it," and he handed me *The Book of Mormon*. It had been red lined with passages that told you to turn to the next page and in the front it gave instructions to "pray and see if these things are true." I did and when they returned, I met with them again.

"Did you read the book we gave you?"

"Yes I did."

"Did you read the underlined verses?"

"Yes I did."

"Did you pray about it?"

"Yes I did."

"Well what did you think?"

I said, "I prayed and asked the Lord if this is of You."

"What did he tell you?"

He said, "NO."

"No?" they asked as their faces paled. "You won't reconsider?"

"No, I did what you asked. I read it and prayed and the Lord told me it wasn't of Him. So if it is not of Him I don't want it."

"What did you do with it?"

"I burned it."

They nearly fell off their chairs. The paleness in their faces turned red and they became speechless for the first time.

I said, "If it is not of the Lord then it is "another gospel" and in Galatians the scripture tells us that if we or an angel bring you another gospel, may he be condemned to Hell!" (Good News for Modern Man) "That is why I burned it."

They got up stunned, walked out and never came back.

Now I had no formal theological training, but I was Spirit trained. And when I prayed about the book of Mormon I turned to my spirit which is centered in my being where His

Spirit dwells. I listened to that still small voice within, that intuitive speaking in my heart. I heard as I quieted myself very clearly, "No this is not of Me." I didn't need a lot of intellectual knowledge. I just needed Jesus, and he was protecting me and guarding me from harm.

It was also about this time that I knew I needed more tools under my belt. Not that the Lord would forsake me. Nor that he would, in that still small voice, leave me out in the cold. If there was more to know to study to show myself approved, I would need to go to school. After all, I had dropped out of high school. I started asking around where I might go to school to become a better minister. The name "Elim Bible Institute" kept coming up, so I contacted Elim and told them my situation. When they got back to me, they said they would make a way for me to be able to attend school there. Money was not the object, but calling was, and they had prayed and felt I should come. I was registered for the fall term, but I was on the west coast and they were in New York on the East Coast. How would I get there? And what would happen to the ministry of The Way while I was gone? Was it time to give it up?

The fellowship continued to grow. Some pastors brought their youth groups there some from Moses Lake. One Assembly of God pastor brought a busload to our Saturday meeting. We couldn't continue the way we had at the Lutheran Church. We couldn't read the Bible in a circle, it didn't work. The more people that came, the less people wanted to read and discuss it out loud. So our services became more traditional with me teaching from the front.

Steve and I used to tag team when we led the meetings at the Lutheran Church but now he had taken another path.

Corinne Michaels and Gladys Parham went to Moses Lake a lot to attend a [32]"Local Church" meeting on Sunday afternoons. I thought the Local Church had some good ideas such as sitting around in a circle around the Lords Table, which they did every Sunday evening. When a person felt led, he would walk up to the table and take of the elements. In the meantime the congregation sang hymns spontaneously, and "pray read" the psalms. Pray reading seemed forced and contrived to me and the oddity of the service didn't sit well in my spirit. Even though I embraced the teachings of Watchman Nee foundationally and tried to emulate them, I could never embrace the Local Church as my own.

I loved The Way and the work it was doing, there was a certain innocence about it and a purity. But the longer it existed and the more it did, the prouder I became of it and who I had become as a result. I was no long the kid shaking his fist at the sky telling God to prove himself. I was no long trying to measure up to make friends, and I no longer had to impress my family or avoid them. One night as I was locking up for the night I heard the Lord speaking to me, in my spirit.

"Rob, look around." I turned from the door, and at first saw the window where I had painted the name, "You did that didn't you" the Lord said.

"Yes, Lord I did," I said out loud.

"Look at that wall with the picture of Jesus on it, you did that didn't you?"

"Yes," I said again feeling a little prouder.

"And the cross on the wall, you made that and hung that light over it, didn't you?"

"Yes, Lord I did that. Looks good doesn't it?"

"And even the placement of, and idea of the spools for tables that was you too wasn't it?"

"Yes, Lord," by this time I was starting to see he was going somewhere with this dialog and I was starting to get concerned.

"Why, are you showing me this, Lord?"

"Why? Because this is all you isn't it?"

"Yes, Lord but..."

"It is you and not Me," he said. I was stunned, and I recognized a not so subtle pleasure of self-reliance lingering in me from the observation just pointed out to me. Then the Lord dropped a brick on me, "I am going to take it all away from you." I felt awful because I knew it was true. What I had accomplished here was more me than Jesus. Because He loved me He was going to remove something that had the potential of getting in the way of my relationship with Him by feeding my pride. This was a lesson I would be learning over and over again.

Moving Out of "The Way"

Three guys came to The Way, they were close friends. They were collegiate and certainly not street wise hippy types. They were good young men from good families. Gregg Baldridge, Jim Hysjulien and Clint Bridges came together to The Way and they wanted to be baptized in the Holy Spirit. The four of us went into the prayer room and got down on our knees. I showed them what the scriptures had to say about it and instructed them accordingly. Then I laid hands on each of them and began to pray. I told them to ask for the Holy Spirit and then thank Him. They prayed thus "thank you Jesus, praise you Jesus" over and over. We went on for about an hour. Gregg was the first to start praying in tongues and was ecstatic and got up and left. Jim was soon to follow and then left. Clint was there for the longest time and after three hours of praying I told him I was going to leave him alone in the room. About thirty minutes later he came out of the room, speaking in tongues with his hands in the air as he paused only to tell me in English he had gotten it! He headed out the door with his hand over his head. He was praising God in the Spirit. He told me later he drove around that night just praising God for a long time before going home, one hand on the steering wheel and the other in the air, he couldn't get his hand back down, it was stuck there.

I was going to the Assembly of God by this time. I became a member and was baptized by immersion, not understanding Sacramental Theology[33]. Pastor Dale was supportive of the ministry of The Way. One thing I noticed right off at the church was that prophecy seemed quite prevalent there, especially among certain ones. I earnestly desired all the spiritual gifts, to be used by the Lord in anyway and every way he could. I prayed, "Lord I would like to be able to prophesy that is a gift that I have not yet manifested." It became a regular request over a couple of weeks. One Sunday, a pause came in our worship and I listened for a word to come forth, but nothing came. Then I prayed again, Lord use me to prophesy. When I opened my mouth and these beautiful words of encouragement came forth, lasting for what seemed like a few seconds but was actually a few minutes. Then it stopped and I smiled and opened my eyes as I said thank you Lord. But as I looked around at all the pews, and there was no one there to be seen. Where were they, they were there a minute ago? Then it hit me, they were all lying prostrate on the floor! What had I said? Whatever it was, it must have been powerful enough to make everyone get on their face before the Lord. I was so surprised.

Gregg and Pastor Dale seemed to hit it off. And they had some ideas to improve The Way. There was a house that was available up on the same street as the Assembly of God. This would take us out of the business district and away from the bars, no more drunks falling in. But, I thought that was why we were there to reach out to the lost, lonely and down hearted. Greg thought where we were was dumpy, and it was, but I didn't mind. The house had bedrooms in it which meant I would have a place to live, that was a plus. And it had a bathroom and a kitchen, also a plus. To top it all off the Assembly of God would pay our rent. Okay, how could I refuse? I was told that I would still be the one in charge, but after what the Lord had told me I knew that would not be true. In fact, everything became a battle, with Gregg[34] calling the shots, and Pastor Dale behind him. I was always wondering what was going to come up next. I felt like I was in the dark until a decision had already been made. I was no longer necessary. The ministry wasn't fun anymore. I was tired and worn out. I began to pray for the Lord to move me out of there. I didn't want to have to fight to get things done and with the conflict, the anointing seemed to lift. We were not getting the crowds we were at our other location mainly only Assembly of God people. I started turning some of the leadings of the group over to Greg, since he wanted control. I asked him to lead the Bible study at times. That way I wouldn't get in trouble with the Lord either. But the conflict both spoken and unspoken started to take a toll on me and I began in a short time to struggle within myself and burn out. My prayer for the Lord became: "Lord either change me, or change those who oppose me, or Lord move them or me on." In the midst of that I got a phone call, it was from Butch in Maryland.

16
Life Lessons

*T*HE TRUCK LUMBERED OVER THE STREETS INTO the neighborhood like an elephant through the African plains. In the back of the truck the generator roared blocking the sound of the engine in the front, but not drowning out the droning, sickening sweet tune, that maniacal music-box that played in one's head long after the day was done. This "Mister Softee" truck was Butch's latest venture and I was his "manager" of this new business venture, as he described it on the phone. I informed Butch that I was no longer the same person he knew when he had last seen me, and I had worked for him at the go-cart track. I was now a Christian and my life had changed. If that didn't bother him, I would be happy to return to Maryland and work for him on this new project. In fact I told him he was an answer to prayer and indeed he was.

I lived with him and Carol in their home in White Plains some ten miles from Bryans Road and the former go-cart track. Why Butch would call me some two plus years after I had left Maryland as a parolee, I had no idea. It had to be the Lord. Some of my old friends looked me up at Butch's, one was Vincent Dalio. Vince had lived at the trailer park with his mom and sister across the road from the go-cart track. I led Vince to the Lord and started an exploration to find a fellowship within a week of my arrival. Vince also asked around as did Butch as to where there was a "Jesus People group."

Prayers, Poems and Promises

Alexis was a tall brunette married to a Naval Commander who with her husband lived on the Naval Base in Indian Head. The group was comprised of about a dozen committed attendees, with another dozen or so stragglers who would come and go. Alexis sat Indian style on the floor with the rest of us, the smile on her face and her manner gave the appearance of her being near the same age as the rest of the group. But, most were in their late teens or early twenties, whereas Alexis was in her late thirties or so by my best guess. The commander was a little older and a professor at the Naval Ordinance Station. Most called him "Prof" and he looked the part with light graying around his ears and the back of his neck. He was soft spoken, whereas she was effervescent. Prof called Alexis his teenage wife. They both loved the Lord and if I was to guess their religious leanings, I would say Baptist, even though their church was the base chapel which blurred the evangelical lines.

Even though my age was only a couple of years older than most of them there, my studies and experience were years ahead. I sat there and took a deep breath. I was relieved to be just one of the sheep. I told them when they questioned me about my background and asked me to share my testimony. I shared about prison for possession, and the Jesus people and how they influenced me. I shared about The Way and my shepherding, but most of all I shared how happy I was to be here with them as just one of them. Alexis then hit me with a brick. She had been praying for me to come she said! She and Prof were moving in a few months and they needed someone to take over the group for them. Tears welled up in my eyes. It seemed that the Lord was not through with me yet. And though I was relieved to not have the responsibility, I was happy to have a fresh start.

After the meeting and the Bible study was over, it was time for snacks and soda and for listening to music. Of course, my hobby and passion after the Lord had always been music. I couldn't play much more than a few chords on the guitar, but I had a great appreciation for the latest that was offered especially if it was Christian or had a Christian connotation. Virginia had given me tapes from Calvary Chapel not just teachings but Jesus Music. Groups like the *Children of the Day, Love Song, The Way, Mustard Seed Faith* and *Sweet Comfort.* I loved the new sound, indicative of a new movement, the Jesus Movement. This night I heard something that was only slightly emblematic of Jesus music; it was John Denver, "Prayers, Poems and Promises." The hit song from the album was "Take Me Home Country Roads" with the lines "almost heaven West Virginia." Only later would I find out the song was written tongue in cheek, not by John Denver but by the members of the *Starland Vocal Band* in a flat in Georgetown, DC.

The Green-Wood

Darlene Norton at the Othello Assembly of God left me with a prophetic word that would change my world, challenge my belief, and shake me out of all idealism I had pertaining to the faith. As everyone was saying good-bye my last Sunday there before leaving to return to Maryland, she smiled at me and said as if I wasn't there, "He'll be back and he'll be bringing a bride with him." I was no more prepared for what was in store for me than I was a heart attack.

Sandy was a pretty young girl who was a regular with the group on the base. She walked with a slight limp accented by the inch and a half lift in her shoe on the right leg, which carried visible scars. The scars she received when her leg was shattered from being hit by a car as she walked on the side of the road carrying her skateboard. She was thirteen at the time and would spend two years in the hospital at a vulnerable age of development and one susceptible to emotional scars to go along with her physical ones. She lay often sullen and under a dark cloud, only relieved by pranks she could play on hospital staff. Her mother stayed by her bedside always trying to console her while her father drove a cab, both being past the age when having children is the norm. Sandy was their only child. Most thought her parents were her grandparents, she once told me.

The group continued to grow and Alexis and Prof moved as they had indicated they would. At first most came out of curiosity to see the guy with the long hair from the "West Coast". But eventually they came for the love and the joy they found there in Jesus and for a time of paring as many found their husbands and wives in our mist. It seemed love was in the air. In a matter of months we had enough people to fill the Assembly of God in Glymont for the wedding.

Warnings were everywhere and ignored, I had determined I knew for certain what God's will was. I had the prophetic word from Darlene. I had the faith to believe for the relationship. After all I had attended the Basic Youth Seminars[35] several times. I knew what to do to make it work. How could it fail? All I had to do was my part and then God would do His part. I had followed the correct order as I had always done to the letter. I had gone to her father and asked for her hand in marriage and he gave me permission. He said whatever she wanted she could have, he only wanted her to be happy. One thing he did I took as peculiar was the way he spoke to her, it was in sort of a baby talk. To him she was still that little girl in the hospital. Another warning came from her best friend, Marcia. She asked me to come over so she could talk to me only hours from the scheduled wedding. When I did, she very delicately tried to tell me that Sandy wasn't ready to be married. What she didn't tell me was that Sandy was still living promiscuously. While we were engaged and up to the night before we were to be married she was sleeping with other guys. While I maintained we should wait until we were married, it seemed I naively overestimated her Christian maturity or didn't want to consider it. The final warning was when Sandy herself came over to Butch's to tell me she thought we should "put the wedding off". I gave her all my persuasive reasons why we shouldn't put it off, while at the same time we walked through the woods across the street from Butches house. I reached up to a pine tree limb hanging at eye level to pull a pine cone from it; it didn't budge. It was green and would only come by sheer will and I would not be dissuaded. She saw me struggling and reached down on the ground and picked one that was easily retrieved having fallen by its own volition. At that moment the green one was stripped from the limb leaving a long wound in the severed branch. I tied them together and gave them to her; it was settled. One was ready to be picked and tied to the other, one was not.[36] Her Mom who was not fully convinced of this relationship, signed for her to be married, she was seventeen and I was twenty-one.

Nothing really changed for Sandy except she now had this guy sharing her bed and her parents. Her Mom and Dad liked me, but they could see that the relationship was a struggle to say the least. I continued to lead my group Bible study which was rapidly growing into a church. Sandy's participation became sporadic now that she was "expected" to attend. And more often than not, she would opt out at the last minute leaving me with a troubled demeanor throughout the meetings. She was determined to live as she had prior to the marriage coming and going as she saw fit. I saw this as violation of our fidelity to one another. After all we were no longer two but one. I expected her to be at my side. But the difference in opinion didn't stop there. I was "hyper religious" (which we called "On Fire for the Lord" back then), which meant to me at the time – don't smoke don't chew and especially don't run with boy's who do. But it went beyond that. I didn't listen to "worldly" music, I had given away my record collection that were not Christian, no alcohol, no cigarettes, very little if any TV, and then there couldn't be the hint of anything immoral or anti-spiritual on it. The list kept growing. She on the other hand, didn't understanding why anyone would give up any of those things. Couldn't she see how awful all that was? It finally dawned on me maybe I needed to meet her at that level, and then she would see how "sacrificing and Christ-like" I was and then the Lord would help her to see how ungodly those things were. I would do my part and God would then do His part as I wanted it to be.

That's when the *Rolling Stones* came to town. She wanted to go and I being the "loving" husband would take her. She would then get a good clear picture of how worldly and ungodly it was, I plotted. As we were shoved through the turn-sty at RFK stadium, a very real fear of being trampled to death if we fell, came to mind, and once in our seats the whole stadium was moving under our feet with screaming, bouncing fans. I was sure it would collapse into a mass of twisted metal and broken bodies. As I was contemplating our demise, fireworks began to rain down on us from above. Two tiers over us were fans tossing them into the crowd below. Surely these episodes would impact her opinion of this display of hedonism. But, when I looked over at Sandy, her face was lit up as elation came with the pounding sounds of "Beast of Burden." My plan had obviously failed, she was having the time of her life as I sat getting angry, an anger which I could not allow to be expressed because it was not a Christian virtue, so I stuffed it.

When I had gotten engaged, I informed Butch that I didn't think I could make it on an ice cream truck drivers' salary. I would have to get another job where I could provide for a wife, and hopefully children. I started working construction as a carpenter's helper. It was then she informed me that she didn't want children, something she hadn't told me when we were dating. If she had, I wouldn't have heard it. After all, once she had them, how could she not want them? Children were a gift of the Lord, happy was the man whose quiver was full of them.

Finally, I decided that maybe a change of place would make a difference. My family hadn't met her and she hadn't met them. I would take her back to Othello. Maybe getting her away from her family who treated her like a child would help her stop acting like one. It would be the first time she had ever been away from her Mom and Dad for any reason, other than being in the hospital. I reassured her whenever she wanted to go back to Maryland she could. With that reassurance we boarded a plane and flew back to my home town.

We stayed with my parents for about two weeks and I reconnected with the group I had left there. The Way no longer existed by this time, which was okay with me, even though the memories of the things the Lord had done there lingered in the back of my mind. Mike Vogel had a trailer and we moved into it. We were finally living on our own and things seemed to be working out. Sandy seemed to be adjusting to married life like never before. My plan was working.

I got a job working for Frank Booth as an electricians' helper. Frank and I had good fellowship as we drove all over the Columbia Basin wiring homes, climbing poles, wiring pumps, schools, and commercial properties, both new and old. The ministry took a back seat to the marriage, but wasn't ever far away. We went to the Assembly of God. I introduced her to Darlene who had prophesied concerning her. And the people made over her, not only trying to make her feel welcome but included. I think they thought she would bring the same intensity to the work of the Lord that I had as my counterpart, but that was not who she was and she felt that pressure. This contributed to her feelings of displacement. What I didn't know at the time was that when I went to work with Frank she would get in the car and start to drive the near three thousand miles back to Maryland, at least once a week. I, of course, was oblivious, lost in my idealism except for darkness I could see creeping over her. Then several of the guys from the group in Maryland started showing up on our doorstep.

17
Getting Back

WE WERE ALL SITTING AROUND THE TABLE IN
the kitchen area of the single wide trailer. There were six or
seven of us, all I know is we were all hungry. Vince had come
from Maryland with Don Varney and then followed others. On
the table sat a meager portion of gravy in a bowl and a partial
loaf of bread. I counted the slices and sighed. There wasn't
enough to make one round, let-alone satisfy the hunger of each
of us young men squeezed in around the table. We took hands
and I prayed thanking the Lord for his provision. And then
I deferred to my brother on the left, as I passed him the loaf
and then the bowl of gravy. I figured if there was any gravy
left when it got back to me I would just eat that. And I would
sacrifice my portion for the others, even though at the time I
was the only one working. I would just trust the Lord to give
me strength. I don't know exactly when it happened, but the
joy of the Lord fell on that table as we each shared what God
was doing in our lives. We were laughing as the loaf made its
way around the table to me. I reached in the bag, forgetting
my original count. My fingers found a slice and as I put it on
my plate, I thought to myself that I must have miscounted. I

passed it on to Don on my left, who took it and placed another slice on his plate. I covered my slice with gravy from the bowl and passed that on. We ate and we laughed and the bread and bowl made the rounds until we were all passing because we were full!

When I was convinced that nobody wanted anymore, I sat the loaf and the bowl back on to the table and then it hit me what had just happened! Everyone stopped talking, noticing the look of surprise on my face and they listened as I spoke with my voice quivering.

"Do you guys know what just happened," I asked.

"I counted the slices of bread in the bag when we first sat down to eat and there was not enough to make one round around the table, but look there is still bread left in the bag."

Someone asked me if I was sure.

I said, "Yes and look at the bowl of gravy it is at the same level it was when we started."

"Wow," was all anyone could say as disbelief gave way to amazement.

Because I didn't have to throw all my time into saving my marriage I had more energy to give to my studies. Two books in particular and one magazine really spoke to me at the time. The first book was Watchman Nee's *Release of the Spirit*. I bought it thinking I was going to learn more about the Holy Spirit's outpouring through the gifts. But instead the Lord knew exactly what I needed and that was to understand the purpose of conflict in my life, both in my marriage and my ministry. The Lord wanted to break me. His precious gift of the Holy Spirit was locked within my spirit[37]. And in order for Him to get through to me He had to work through layers of self centered promotion and preservation. At the heart of the matter was who I was and always had been, an insecure self-loathing individual needing approval. I had grown comfortable living like this and learned how to cover it with a Christian facade. The Lord needed to break through this in my life by shattering my self reliance and dependence upon my perceived spiritual accomplishments. Now Watchman's book does not go into that kind of personal detail but rather an overview, for instance: he talks about when he was explaining this process to someone while they were having tea. And on the table sat a plate with biscuits or cookies, Watchman reaches down and takes a biscuit and breaks it, but then slides the pieces back together. Then he tells his fellow observer, "See how the biscuit appears to be whole? Now watch how it yields to the hand that broke it," and he touches it and it separates without resistance. "That is what the Lord wants to do in our lives, make us vessels that yield to the hand of the Master." He goes on to say that the Lord uses "the Cross" in our lives for the purpose of breaking us, so that he can use us. And the cross or our crosses are things in our lives that we powerless to escape or fix, but that we have to bear. In bearing them something of us has to die. Now this was not a message often heard in Charismatic circles. No they were more often about what you could get from the Lord than what you were expected to give. Suddenly, the difficulties in my life had meaning and purpose designed to create in me a new heart as I was to humble myself under His mighty working so he could be expressed in me and through me without resistance.

The other thing that the Lord used to speak to me at the time, was a magazine called "New Wine". It featured articles by Bob Mumford, Derek Prince, Don Basham, Ern Baxter, Charles Simpson, sometimes Ralph Martin and others. Virginia Gualusha had given me Mumford tapes early on and I was a member of his tape of the month club. These guys taught the Charismatic Church maturity and depth because they could see the anemia in people running from church to church and from this meeting to that conference, never getting plugged in to the local Church. Juan Carlos Ortiz observed that the Charismatic Movement was miles wide but only an inch deep.

"New Wine" sought to bring maturity and a deeper long lasting understanding of Gods purpose for his Church and his people. The second book was also by Watchman Nee, called *Spiritual Authority*. In that I came to understand how God had placed his authority in men. All authority belongs to Him whether it is the policeman, or the politician the pastor or the parent. The source of their authority isn't them, it is the Lord. And that He watches over his authority and holds accountable anyone who uses or abuses that delegated authority. If one is in a position of authority he had to be under authority. It is how God designed it. Spiritual Authority wasn't to rule over someone, but to cover someone with love, protection and prayer. I knew this is what I needed, up to this point I was a lone bone on my own! I prayed for days and fasted as I sought the Lord, where and to whom I might turn to as my spiritual director, someone to walk with me. David Easterly was an Assembly of God pastor located in Warden. He had been a great supporter of The Way and had brought his youth group to participate on occasions. I called David and asked if I could meet with him. This began a wonderful relationship that was much needed.

Explosive Situations

I was making enough money now as an electrician for Frank and "Farmers Electric" that we could move out of the trailer into a house for rent. The house sat at the other end of the block from my parent's house on the same street. We owned a decent car and things were looking up, for me. Sandy could see that I was getting quite settled on living here for awhile, not something she had bargained for. I started going to the Assembly of God in Warden on Sunday mornings and to the Assembly of God in Othello on Sunday nights. The rest of the week I was in Warden for men's meetings and whatever was going on.

The trailer still housed people from my group, one of whom was Bill Vogel. One day, after work Bill came home to find Joyce Danielson there. Joyce was recently a part of the group. She had gone to school with some of those in it and loved the Lord and had a heart to serve. She had stopped by to bake a cake for the guys. Bill told her that that was fine but if she didn't mind, he was going to get in the shower. So, she went about baking the cake and he got in the shower. Some time midway during Bill's shower, he heard her knocking on the bathroom door asking him how come the oven wasn't getting hot. He told her the pilot light didn't work and that you had to light it at the bottom. She had no sooner left the door when he suddenly thought, "Oh, no!" At that very moment he heard an explosion that rocked the trailer. He ran out wrapping a towel around himself as he did only to find the front door laying out in the yard about twenty feet from where it had been attached and Joyce crawling on the floor, her eyelashes and eyebrows burnt completely off! She had turned the stove on and in the process of waiting for it to get hot, it had built up a substantial amount of gas. When she had stuck her head in to light it with a match, it exploded. Thank God she was all right except for the misplaced eyebrows and eyelashes and the now short curling hair that outlined her face.

Sandy and I had had a rough start that had not yet found a smooth road through a peaceful valley. I had been living under the illusion things were getting better and that her quietness was a sign that she was finding contentment. I couldn't be more wrong. Idealistically, I believed that "love conquered all." I just had to be loving and in the end, He would win her over. Now in Othello, because I thought that my kind, gentle and steadfast approach had been affective, I let my guard down. Her aggression became passive; sex was the first to go, and then homemaking began to wane, and finally church was cut out. I knew without church and the Lord at the center of our relationship, there wasn't much hope. After several "not feeling good," and promises to go "next" time I was getting ready to go to the night service in Othello and saw that she was not. At first, I tried to encourage her, encouragement gave way to pleading, pleading to begging, begging to demanding. It was at this stage that she knelt down and put her face in mine and wrinkled it up as she spit out an obscenely so vulgar it would make a sailor blush. Apparently she too had been harboring pent up resentment that she could no longer contain as she spew her frustration back at me.

Something in me reacted without thinking, and I slapped her. She had always been so frail. Her skin looked translucent, sometimes so much so that dark rings were more often than not around her eyes. As soon as I slapped her, a black eye formed immediately. I felt awful, I apologized profusely. I told her I didn't know why I did it, I just snapped. She now decided she wanted to go to church and she would wear it like a badge. It was her way of getting even with me. I was ashamed, but I felt like this was what I deserved, I was my own cross.

I talked to David about it. He didn't condemn me or scorn me, he listened. I told him about the whole relationship up to this point. He asked me if she had ever been this far and this long away from her parents, and I told him, "No I didn't think so." When I went home I asked her if she wanted to go home and visit her parents. I thought that maybe she would go home and find everything was not what she had remembered it to be and then want to come back. I took her to the airport and told her to call me as soon as she landed and let me know she got there okay. I counted the hours and when I figured she had gotten back to DC and made the ride to her parents' house. I waited for the call that never came. When I finally couldn't wait any longer, I called her parents house and asked if she made it okay. Her mom answered the phone and I found out she had made it but she didn't want to talk. In my optimism, I thought she was just worn out from the long trip and needed to rest and she would call me when she was ready. That never came. She finally had me where she wanted me, 3000 miles away. But I was a Christian, and the Lord was explicit about divorce and I had taken a vow before God "until death do us part." God had a thing about vows, so then did I. Besides, if I did exactly what I was supposed to do with the marriage, He would make it work in spite of what either one of us wanted, right? I just needed to read more books about it; get more counseling and be more self-sacrificing. After all Christ had died for his bride, the Church, if I did anything less than that, I hadn't done all to make it work.

It took about four to six weeks of waiting to talk to her and then begging her to let me come back, "Just give me another chance." After promising to let her live her life without my interference, she agreed to let me come back "and give it a try." I look back on this and I wonder where I would have been if a return to Maryland hadn't been in the cards. Most likely I would have given up on the idea of the ministry. Whereas now, I was thrown back into the work of the Lord by the request of those who had been a part of the group before I left.

I started leading a Bible study at Lucky's (who now called himself Luke) and Bonnie Lane's house, not far from Sandy's parents' house. It was at one of these Bible studies that a group of guys from Oxen Hill came down to see what was happening. One was Harry Neumann who had been raised in the Pentecostal Holiness Church and was very turned off by Christianity. In fact, he was currently considering the premises theorized in the bestseller, *Chariots of the Gods*. This is a book which postulates that man is the product of panspermia. The idea that the world was seeded by an alien race which have over the centuries visited the earth to check up on how their offspring were doing. And, that various sources have documented their visits, recording them by filtering the events through their frame of reference in time; one source was the Bible, and Ezekiel's flaming wheels. The Lords anointing was on me for this discussion and I just kept pointing back to the need for a personal relationship with the Savior and God the Father, who created us for His purpose and plan for our lives. I led each one in "the Jesus Prayer" and they received a new life through the conversion. The next week Harry brought his Catholic girlfriend Pat Carl. I had never met another Carl who wasn't related.

Pat was a German Carl on her father's side and her mom was an English war bride. When her parents were first married and her mother came to the United States, she didn't know how to cook and had never seen some of our American delicacies such as watermelon. Her father who was a practical joker, brought it home and she asked what she was supposed to do with it. He told her she was to soak it in the bathtub overnight and to place it in the oven first thing in the morning. He stopped her, just as she was opening the oven door. Pat told me one time she was making a meatloaf when the pages of her cookbook stuck together. She had done everything up to putting it in a pan, but when she turned the stuck page it read "now place a banana in the middle and bake," which she obediently did. Pat later became a Home-Economics teacher. Pat and Harry gave me a ride home after the Bible study. In the driveway of my in-laws house I led Pat to the Lord. She lit up, her eyes aglow.

18
Deliverance

*E*VERYONE SAT IN MY LIVING ROOM LOOKING A little dismayed but not shocked. They were my Board of Elders. The group had grown and now were meeting in three different locations. I had hoped each location would multiply and establish its own identity as a church. Maybe they would have, had I given it more time. I followed the pattern of the "Little Flock" of Watchman Nee's, the "Local Church" and named each accordingly: The Church at Bryans Road, The Church at Oxen Hill, and The Church at La Plata. As it turned out, most of the people we saw at each location were people who made the trip from place to place. These were wonderful committed people and we were drawing people from as far away as Bowie. That is why what I had to say to these elders was hard.

My world was closing in on me. My doctrine which was based on *Sola Scriptora,* "the Bible Only" made the narrow way narrower, more constricted. We had done away with "worldly holidays" such as Christmas and Easter. Christmas was a pagan holiday. Easter was the name of the goddess of fertility. There was no room for hyperbole, everything had to be taken literally. I remembered a dream Brenda Booth told me about:

She saw two groups of people and in the dream she asked who they were. She was told that the large group was the "elect" and the smaller group was the "very elect". At the time I didn't see that as a warning, but thought that it meant that we were the very elect, so much for humility. Salvation was based on a decision, an act of the will, "to invite Him in and be Lord of your life," until then God was on the outside looking in. What I would find out is not only was my salvation the product of "Pelagainism[38]" but most of evangelical thought was *lived* as if it believed in it, though if you had asked us we would deny it. Perfection was achieved by "right living". God could help but only if "you" really wanted him to. We would judge people in the church by their fervency in the Lord, how much they prayed, came to church, tithed, served, etc. And the standard was even greater if they were in "leadership". The more we knew the more I could see the faults in so many groups: the Catholic had "the traditions of men", the Baptist although they might be saved, rejected the gifts of the Holy Spirit so they may have been apostate, the Pentecostals were holy rollers and their extreme expressions were too full of worldly emotion, the Charismatics were too shallow and had no valid concept of the Church life. The more I thought about it, the more I felt I understood what the Lord had said that, "Had the days not been shortened there would be no flesh saved[39]." After all these, were the last days according to Hal Lindsey and Chuck Smith. I had heard someone say, "I believe in thee and me and I am not so sure about thee."

My doctrine concerning myself was placing a strangle hold on me, it was *too* perfect and demanding. I was fasting twice a week, spending at least an hour in prayer daily, reading my

Bible daily, keeping a journal, and condemning myself for every fleeting thought that was not Christ centered. I envied Martin Luther for his bleeding knees, Francis of Assisi for his poverty, and John the Baptist for his camel hair coat turned inward and his lunch bag of bugs. I was as much a protestant ascetic as I could be, without the flagellations. And my greatest source of self condemnation was that I was unfit for the ministry because I had failed to bring my wife to a fervent relationship with the Lord. Her church attendance was still sketchy at best. I was failing, and I was disqualified to be a pastor according to 1 Timothy 3:4-5[40]. I had been carrying this around ever since I had gotten married and now it was starting to take a toll on me. I wasn't living what I preached. My home wasn't in order. If I couldn't lead effectively in my home, how could I in the Church? If it is not working domestically, don't export it!

I loved being a pastor and working for the Lord more than life itself. I had to ask myself, had the ministry become an idol to me? Had I really learned the lesson the Lord had tried to teach me at The Way? Was I the reason my wife was not living for the Lord? Was the Lord preventing her from serving Him to teach me a lesson? The solution was simple. I had to give up the thing I loved most in life. I had to let the vision die so that He could resurrect it. I had given up my home, my job, and my dignity so many times begging her to make the marriage work. Now it was existing in name only. I would have to do nothing less than what Christ had done for the Church, I would lay down my life for Sandy so that she would then surrender to the Lord and he would restore everything, like Job. I would make the ultimate sacrifice by giving up "my ministry". I would have to step down from being the pastor of this "Local Church". We knew how to talk grace, but we didn't know how to live it. It was unmerited favor, but we had to earn it, as we sang, "I have found favor with the most high God and Jesus is his name." How did we find it, by living for the Lord as an act of our will. We would never say that we could do it without his help, but we lived as if we didn't need his help as "obedient children".

As I told the elders that I wasn't qualified. The look of doom came over them. I had told them that one of them could step up and take my place as pastor because I had not gone to seminary or to Bible College. At this point, we were not a part of any denomination so I didn't have a source I could turn to and have a "graduate" sent over to take my place. But from the look on their faces I could see that this wasn't going to happen. But what else could I do? I had to let it die. It was called "The death of a vision" and I was convinced that this was the answer.

The voice of reason and sanity was with Mel McNerney. She and her husband Mark lived on the second floor of the Carrico Building across the street from the courthouse in LaPlata, we lived on the third floor. One of our home groups met in their living room and I often had dinner with them. Mel cut my hair and spoke reason and encouragement with me like a good friend and hair dresser would. It had kept me going without completely losing my mind. This enabled me to keep smiling and rejoicing in the Lord, while an unknown resentment was seething beneath the surface.

At first it just came out in flare ups when Sandy and I were talking. Then when the silent treatment began, I started experiencing fleeting thoughts. Thoughts I determined were demonic because of the anger they envisioned. I had learned deliverance from Derek Prince and become quite proficient at calling out demons in others and myself. But what I didn't know was you can't "call out" resentment that was nursing hatred. I didn't like what I was seeing in myself. This was not the person I wanted to be or believed I was, but the dark thoughts made me believe I was capable of the unbelievable. As usual, I studied harder to try to find a way out. I was reading a book by Don Bashan called "Deliver Us From Evil" and thought I should seek out help from him. I called him and asked him where in the Washington, DC area I could find someone who could help me. He gave me the number of a former Naval Lieutenant Commander, Bob Wright. Bob gave my number and information to John Metcalf an editor at *National Geographic* Magazine, recently commissioned to start a church in Bowie. I met him at his office in DC. He listened while I talked, the more I talked and he listened the more uncomfortable I became. He held his cards close to his chest. I seldom could tell how he felt about what I was saying. In fact when I finished I waited for him to tell me what to do and he just looked at me.

Until I asked him, "What I should do?"

He said one word, "move".

"Move?"

"Move where?"

"Move closer to Bowie and the New Covenant Church and get involved and see what happens," he said. At this point I was ready to try anything.

"Oh," he said as I was leaving his office, "How many from your church do you think will come with you?"

I hadn't thought about it. "None, or maybe one who lives near Bowie."

Time went by and nothing seemed to change with Sandy.

I deepened my studies and worked on my bachelor's degree. Finally, when I was expressing my frustration about the "Church life" not changing anything with her. John agreed to meet with Sandy and talk to her. He concluded I had been too easy on her and that I needed to be more forceful because she didn't respect me. He even suggested that I spank her and said he had spanked his wife and she thanked him for it. Now John over the years had been my salvation in personal matters because of his practical down to earth approach to faith, just the opposite of my esoteric tendencies. But, I really had a difficult time wrapping my thoughts around this direction. The result was she not only didn't thank me, she now expressed how much she hated me and him. This was not working.

The church was getting into Shepherding. I was assigned to someone much less experienced than me, but he had gained favor by his "submission" whereas I had become "trouble" by my constant questioning and challenging. The person I had been assigned to instructed me that I needed to stop asking questions and looking for answers that had Biblical support. Literally to "stop reading your Bible and just listen to me". I went to John and told him what I had been told, he just shrugged his shoulders as if to say, "Well, do it." It was then I went over his head, a move that took a long time for him to forgive. Bob Wright said he didn't believe me, though I had no reason to lie. He said he talked to John and that he didn't believe I was told that, either. That left me alone in the wilderness again. I decided I would commit, what was considered at the time a grave err, to leave New Covenant Church and to look around. I ended up standing in a long line that went around the block in Catonsville at this Episcopal Church called St. Timothy's, where God was moving mightily in the Holy Spirit through Fr. Philip Zampino and the healing ministry.

Although I loved the work the Lord was doing at St. Timothy's, it was a large church and I couldn't see how I would fit in. I was a minister, I wasn't a priest. From my early experience at St. Martins in Moses Lake, I knew it would be hard if not impossible for me to move into ministry there. And besides, I lived in Crofton and the Church was in Catonsville, a long haul for someone who traveled into DC and Arlington, Virginia every day.

I decided I would go back to New Covenant in Bowie and see if I was wrong about it. I was in constant confusion about what I was doing with my marriage anyway. One Sunday morning I was met at the door to the Church by John literally blocking the way. He was determined in no uncertain terms not to let me in. I was shocked and dismayed. What little amount of remorse I had felt about leaving faded away like a mist on a sunny morning. I decided I would go to the Greenbelt church where Barry Wood was pastor. When I met with Barry and told him what had happened I could see that he understood, even though he didn't comment one way or the other. He asked me if he could arrange a reconciliation meeting with John, would I be willing to come. I said I would. It was neutral ground and he was very diplomatic. We reconciled and I was back in the Bowie church the following Sunday.

At this time, Sandy's mother had moved in with us after the death of her father. She was always helpful and stayed out of any disagreement that came up. My brother Tim came to live with us, and I got him a job working for me at an office building I was managing. I was going to enroll him in the churches school so he could finish his High School. He was excited about the possibility. But he came to me one day to tell me he thought he had to go back to Othello. When I asked why, he said that Billy, Sandy's mom, was picking on him making it hard for him to feel comfortable living with us. I hadn't seen this coming. When I confronted her, she neither denied it nor confirmed it, which told me it was true. So I bought him a ticket back home. My heart ached when I put him on the plane. There were twelve years difference between us; I had left home three years after he was born so I never knew him until now. I had lost my opportunity to get to know him better.

The churches were growing and I was longing to get back into the ministry again, but every time the opportunity came up I was passed over. John taught one of my college courses. It was a class on preaching the word. I thought I would do well because I loved to teach and had done it for years before, but when I got my grade it was barely passing. Several of the other class members were only months old in the Lord and they got rave reviews and promotions to lead home groups and got selected to become elders and pastors. When I asked why I was being passed over and what did I need to do to measure up? I was told my problem was my wife, my home was not "in order". There it was again, I had to be my wife's salvation and she mine.

My sister Pam and her son came to stay with us. Sandy wanted to take her out on the town to see the sights and go to some clubs in Annapolis. I was all for it. Pam I thought would be good for Sandy and enjoy seeing things she had never seen before. But the going out became an every night affair and they got home later and later. I stopped waiting up for them because

I had to get up early and go to work. Finally, Pam told me she needed to go home several months later. I said I understood and hated to see her go. It was nice having family with me.

Sandy continued to go out at night to "see friends". I soon put together that the friends were male friends who had picked her up in bars and taken her to their home. When I relayed this information to my sister Pam, she reluctantly told me that this was going on when Sandy took her out. She told me that she often had to sit in the living room of someone's house while Sandy went in the bedroom with a new male friend. I was hurt and angry, why didn't you tell me I asked her and she informed me that that is why she had left because "she didn't want to get in between us" since she saw Sandy as her friend. I was aghast, she was my sister, my flesh and blood and she couldn't let me know how unfaithful my wife was?

19
Living Dead

THE WHEELED TRASH BARROW FLEW BACK ACROSS
the mechanical room while I screamed. Hot tears bleared my
vision as I screamed again and swung with all the pent-up fury
I had stored over the years.

"Didn't I do my part?"

"God, where were you?"

"I have given up everything for this marriage, I have
begged, bartered, bargained, humbled myself and humiliated
myself."

"I have moved, given up jobs, given up ministry, family,
friends even my very life." I thought I had loved my wife as
Christ had loved the Church, I died for her and now I never
felt more dead.

"But what did you do God?"

"Were you laughing at me?"

"Everything I had been taught and learned was if I had
done my part you would do your part and work in her, instead
I have found I am left with nothing."

I screamed again and again and took the broom handle
in my hand and beat the trash can from one side of the room

to the other. I was working the night shift that had rotated to my turn every three weeks. The 650 ton chillers roared over my screams. There would be no one else there till seven in the morning. I had all night to get it out.

I had lost. I had lost everything. What did I have left? Why didn't I just end it all? I had obviously learned nothing. All of those years of studying, praying, attending this seminar and going to that counseling session for what – nothing? My marriage was over and my ministry was over. My marriage had become my ministry and now I had nothing to show for my faithfulness, my dedication and sacrifice. It wasn't a love lost it was a life lost. No, I was not deluding myself into believing that I had somehow lived a spotless life. I knew my shortcomings and failures which were only magnified now in the refection of this divorce. I had finally caved in and gave her the divorce she had been pushing for these seven long years. And to top it all off she hadn't even showed up for the court proceedings. Her mother did and she told me she was there for me.

Sandy took me for everything I had, car, house and all, I had nothing, zero, nada. Normally, I wouldn't have had to give up my half of the house. The year before when we came close to a legal separation, I told her I would give her the house and drew up a paper to show how sincere, kind and loving I was. All the time thinking she would take that as proof that I really loved her and that she would be foolish to walk away from such a wonderful, generous guy! Ha, the joke now was on me as she pulled that paper out at the deposition. I was shocked that she would be so selfish. Why I don't know, it shouldn't have surprised me if I hated her, but I didn't. She had held on to it for the last year. Otherwise she had never given up on the idea of divorcing me, not even for a minute. In fact if truth be told she had always had it in her mind that marriage was disposable and divorce was optional, not like me who thought it was holy and for life.

I decided I needed to protect myself, albeit too late and for what little benefit it might achieve, by counter suing. I would sue her for adultery, and she would not deny it. It did me no good except for personal justification. Had not Jesus said that that was the only legitimate reason for divorce? Forgiveness was a one way option and she didn't ask for it or want it, but I would give it because I needed to for my sake. Because this wasn't so much about her as it was me and my failure.

All I had left now was the smallest portion of faith and it was hanging on by a thread, a thread like a spider web that clung to me rather than I to it. What I thought I knew was gone, all I knew now was He was God and I was not. In spite of everything that I did not understand, this I was certain of. My faith, everything I thought I knew and understood was now in shreds. Where would I go and what would I do now? I, at my very core, understood why God hated divorce. He hated it because of what it did to people. Something was torn inside, ripped apart that I hadn't even realized was there. It wasn't even an emotion, or an intellectual assessment, no it was deeper, it was spiritual and yet natural, it was more like a breathing covenant. Not a piece of paper but something that had flesh and blood in it and now it had been strangled and laid dead like road kill. I hated divorce too. I thought at this moment that if this was my lot in life, I would remain single for the rest of my life. A void had opened up before me. I had spent so much time, energy and emotion trying to get this right. Now I had nothing left, no vision, no direction, and no purpose.

I realized I had been walking on the edge of this chasm for a long time. I had forced the issue, I had "made" it work, albeit not well. A darkness had covered me for a long time as I had lived an illusion of faith, and now all I had left was the darkness that forced me inward "a dark night of the soul". I had read St. John of the Cross's masterpiece several times, understanding it a little more each time, having picked it up at the Catholic Information Center that was across the street from one of my buildings. Now I was living it.

Ironically right next door to the CIC was a porn theater, talk about a contrast! The choice was never more obvious, light vs. darkness. Every morning as I bent down to turn the dead bolt in the front door to open the building my eyes were forced to look at that theater. I chose to use that moment to pray against it for it to be closed. Not many years later, I would be walking down that same street, no longer responsible for that facility and was reminded concerning this petition. I looked around for the theater but all I found was its façade, the prayers had been answered and the building had been gutted.

Homeless Bound

The severed vassalage left me with my Honda which exceeded 100,000 miles on the odometer. She got the townhouse, the furniture, MG Midget (another foudroyant gift) and I kept the income from my job. Alimony was a negotiated determination in the State of Maryland. John and Sharon Metcalf invited me to move in with them until I was able to find a more permanent location. I didn't bring much with me, my clothing and my Stereo with my record collection which I shared with Phil.

Phil was John and Sharon's youngest. We became fast friends, brothers of sorts. I being his elder brother, music and the Lord became our common denominator.

This was short lived as a group of college friends from Frostburg started coming to church and moved into what became a group guy's home. I and my music moved into the converted garage. I had hoped I would get close enough with John that I would become a deacon, next in line for the pastorate. This never transpired. I was invited to become an "observer" of the "leadership" meetings. I was told I should keep quiet and that I couldn't have a say in the decision making. But, the new group of college friends were invited to participate. I didn't understand this in John's thinking. These guys were, as far as I could see, novices, fresh out of school and not seminary. They were all wonderful guys and oftentimes they would come into my room to ask me spiritual questions and we came to respect each other.

It was about this time I got a call from my mother and my younger sister home in Othello. My older sister, Pam, had gotten in a car accident and was in a coma. She had gotten thrown out of the car she was driving and the car rolled over on her. Her eighteen month old and her seven year old children were thrown away from the car. The car had rolled over her head and lay on top of her while the gas was leaking. There was swelling on her brain.

The car was hidden from the road as her seven year old son, Philip, who had fractured his hip, managed to climb up to the road and flagged down a passerby in the pouring rain. The passersby happened to be Christians who pulled her out from under the car, which could have burst into flames at any moment. They then flagged down a semi-truck, who radioed for an ambulance to take them to the hospital. My mother told me that the doctors were unsure she would make it. My sister Shelly called me not too much later to tell me that the doctors had told the family they needed to say their good-byes. I was nearly 3,000 miles away with odds like this she would be gone by the time my plane got to Spokane, and I had driven to the hospital. I told Shelly I would pray.

I got the call about six that evening and went right to prayer pacing the floor, swinging my arms, and lifting my hands to heaven, sometimes dropping down on my knees or laying on my face. Sometimes my voice was quiet, other times I shouted. I knew I had to work in the morning getting up at five a.m., but I couldn't stop praying, my sister's life depended on it. Everything in me told me that. I was supposed to storm heaven and draw the sword against the evil one who wanted to take her. Then hours of prayer later after three a.m., I broke through. The weight lifted and Assurance wrapped His arms around me. Pam would not die, she would live. I heard a familiar voice in my spirit. I called my mother and it was after mid-night there, she answered the phone immediately. I told her Pam was going to be alright, the Lord had assured me. The next day Pam opened her eyes. The swelling on her brain had started going down overnight. She would tell me later that she had entered a tunnel of light and it was beautiful, even though she wanted to stay. She was told she had to go back and she returned to us.

More Coffee House

I don't remember how we got connected it was probably through a local group called The Sons of Thunder. I had asked them after a concert if they had an interest in some of the stuff that was happening on the West Coast at Calvary Chapel groups like the *Children of the Day, Love Song, Mustard Seed Faith,* and *the Way* to name a few. They said they were. I had all these albums and would loan them to them if they would like since they had never heard them. Their lead singer gave me his address on Connecticut Ave in Bethesda. I said I would drop them off. Vince and I made the trip, and I took my stack of albums in hand and went up to the door where I thought I was supposed to go. I had lost the address. I knocked and knocked and no one came to the door, so I opened the storm door thinking I would put them in between the doors but there were too many albums. I tried the main door and it was unlocked – nobody leaves their door unlocked in DC or its immediate suburbs. I thought this had to be a trusting Christian who had to leave and knew I was coming by. I placed my treasured albums inside leaning against the wall, next to the door.

The next time I saw him, I asked what he thought of them and he looked at me like I had just dropped out of a tree. He didn't remember me and never saw the albums I had left inside somebody's door, a house I know I would never find again. We got to talking and I told him about my background with coffee houses and he said he knew someone who might be interested, his name was Scott Wesley Brown. I knew of Scott as a local musician who had a self-produced album. I thought it was very good for a beginner. The only place to buy good Christian music outside of George Beverly Shea and the Bill Gaither Trio was a small Christian Book Store in College Park on Campus. They had concert information posted and some Jesus Music, but they were really not much bigger than a closet. I asked if they knew

SWB and how I could get a hold of him. They said they did in fact. He had a new album that had just arrived called "I am a Christian." They gave me his phone number. I called him and spoke with his dad who was his manager at the time and told him what I was interested in doing. He had Scott called me and we met at the Key Bridge Marriot in Arlington. Scott told me he wanted to put together a company that would have the backing of a few churches to bring in artists into the Washington area. I told him we had thirty churches at the time and I would see if they would be interested in backing this ministry. John was interested when I talked to him and suggested Barry Wood join me on my next meeting with Scott. That was the beginning of Maranatha Ministries in the DC area. I met some of the artists this way.

One time before Barry McGuire was going to go on stage, I was in the men's room and heard some mumbling coming out of the next stall. I was washing my hands when Barry walked out. I guess I must have looked puzzled because he looked at me and laughed and said, "That was my prayer closet, where I was putting my song list together". We both laughed and he walked out and was introduced to the hundreds waiting to hear him. Another time I had gotten to a Nancy Honeytree concert a little late. The warm up band was just finishing up, I headed in through the door to the auditorium and ran right into Nancy (whose albums always feature her last name). I was star stuck and tongue tied and I said, "Oh so sorry Honey Tree", she looked at me and chuckled, I felt stupid. Apparently she liked to slip in the back after the lights went down and watch the warm up group. I soon backed out of Maranatha, and let the more experienced handle it, as I felt like I really had done all I was supposed to do with getting it set up.

While I was at the "guys" house we got a request from a young man and his sister who were starting a coffee house in Bowie. Bruce Miller thought I would be the right man for the job. I was reluctant because of what had happened at The Way and I didn't want to get involved in anything as large as Maranatha again. But I told him I would certainly check it out and let them know. I really didn't want to be in the coffee house ministry all my life. My heart was and is as a pastor. We were to meet in Kip Gannett's and Meg Gannett Friedman's parent's house.

Powdered Sugared Fingers

It was an eclectic group to say the least, there were people from all different churches. I introduced myself to Kip as having been sent from my church, New Covenant. Kip had been good friends with the guys at the house through high school and was excited to see me. He took me right over to meet his sister, Meg, who had just sat down to feast on one of the powdered donuts that sat out as refreshments for the group. I reached out to take her hand as Kip introduced me, something in my manner gave her the impression I was going to take her hand and kiss it. It had powdered sugar all over it as she reached out to me and then took it back apologizing for the sugar she gave it to me anyway. She looked up from her seat on the couch, laughing somewhat nervously.

Kip opened the discussion with laying out a rough idea of what he wanted to accomplish and then let others contribute their thoughts for the same. Most sat silently so I decided to chime in to assist him. What I thought was a fundamentally benign effort as laid out in the "Great Commission" and that of reaching the lost for the Lord. Two girls on the opposite side of the room asked what I meant by that. Taken aback, I was at a loss for words. I thought all Christians would understand that thought.

I explained, "You know, bring people to the Lord so that they can be born again?"

They talked among themselves for a minute and then fired back, "Well we have a problem with that term."

"What term is that," I asked puzzled.

"Born again," they clarified.

How can anyone have a problem with that term I thought naively. "In John 3:3 Jesus says to..."

They cut me off, "We believe we are born again in our Baptism." I thought how could they believe that? Don't they believe in receiving Jesus through praying the sinner's prayer?

I asked them, "Where do you go to Church," trying to find a reference to bridge the gap. Kip quickly jumped in trying to play interference before the discussion went further downhill. As they said, "St. Pius" and then responded that they were not sure they could be a part of a "so called born again group" the very term offended them greatly. This was not going well and I wasn't helping. It was as if we were all from the same planet but we were not speaking the same language.

20

Just Like Starting Over

THE TAPE "DOUBLE FANTASY⁴¹" WAS CONSTANTLY looping in my Accord, I especially liked "Watching the Wheels", because in some ways that was what I was doing. "I no longer played the game." Oh, I was certainly living for the Lord. I just wasn't looking anymore for anything from Him. I had given up on the idea of marriage and it didn't look like ministry was in the cards anymore. And I was OK with it. For the first time since giving my life to the Lord I had no ambitions.

I felt like what my friend Frank Booth used to say, "I just wanted to be the nail that holds up His picture." I had given up, or what Andrew Murray called "Absolute Surrender" and I really was at peace with myself and the Lord, finally.

So what was I doing sitting with John and Meg after a home group meeting telling him we both thought the Lord was leading us to get married? It felt surreal.

John turned to Meg and said, "Are you ready to be married to a pastor?" I nearly fell off my chair. I don't know what I was expecting, but none of this fell into the category of prescience.

"The funny thing about it," Meg responded thoughtfully, "is that my mother told me not long ago that she thought I should marry a minister. I laughed," she continued shyly grinning. "I said, right Mom how's that going to happen? I'm Catholic." This was so weird it had to be supernatural. I had finally reached contentment as a single non-cleric young man. Now, I was being encouraged to, not only get married, but John was suggesting that I was minister material. And, I an evangelical / charismatic was asking to marry a Catholic whose Mother had prophesied concerning the event. Only God could have put this all together.

Meg and her parents were Catholic charismatics whose group, "Friends of Jesus," participated in the laying on of hands to bless us at the wedding. One of whom was a Catholic Deacon. The wedding was officiated by John Metcalfe a charismatic evangelical pastor, taking place at St. Stephens Episcopal Church in Crofton. Talk about an ecumenical cacophony! The seeds of the three streams were ever present.

Meg and I walked the aisle side by side, got to the altar, and turned to the congregation and began the ceremony by asked for forgiveness for the failure of each of our first marriages. Meg's two beautiful children Wendy and Jesse then followed as flower girl and ring bearer. We ended the ceremony kneeling together to take communion. It was February 14, 1981, Valentine's Day[42].

Okay, about this time you are either bored to death, asleep, or scratching your head asking yourself what does all this have to do with "one man's journey through the three main streams of faith into one mighty river?" Proverbs 16:9 says "The mind of man plans his way, But the Lord directs his steps." I had forever tried to come up with a plan that I thought the Lord had for me. Just as I thought I had it all figured out, it would fail. I took that as my failure at work, when all along it was the

Lord directing me into his plan. At least he used my stumbling to get me where he wanted me to be. Every step of the way the obstacles I had been fighting and standing against "having faith," "claiming the Word," were resisting the Lord. The Lord was more concerned about what he could do in me than what I could do in Him. Too often I had thought I "knew" what he wanted me to do when I was just getting in the way of what he was trying to do "in me". His purpose is in the process.

Drawing Lines in the Sand and Surf

Meg was not only my wife and partner in ministry she was my disciple. She was like a sponge, she soaked up everything she could concerning the Lord and His plan for salvation. At this juncture you could be thinking you married a Catholic so you became one. Quite the contrary, I spent a good deal of time teaching Meg how much in error the Catholic Church was. And I was convincing.

We worked side by side and it was wonderful! However, by now you have an idea about me and my idealism. I thought I could be a good husband and father, but I had no real frame of reference. I adopted her kids and claimed the one she was pregnant with when we got married, as my own. The only way I knew how to be a father was clinically by what I read from more books, magazines, and listening to teaching tapes. I was terrible. I knew I didn't want to be like my father was to me and yet there was too much of him in me. This was my problem. Where he was hard and aloof I was hard, engaged, but overbearing like him. I really loved these kids, but I expected too much from them and their mother. I didn't take time to understand how difficult it would be for them. I needed to friend them first before I could father them. I needed to take time to show them how much I cared before I imposed on them rules even I had trouble living by. I should have eased into it but, instead I was like a Crusader pillaging and plummeting a village.

I was taught that the wife is to submit to her husband[43] and the children to obey their parents[44], for if a man does not know how to rule in his own house, how will he take care of the church.[45] That was my mantra. I expected them to accept me as "Dad", but didn't realize that was a title I would have to earn. And then it would never supersede who their natural father was to them, it couldn't. Adoption wouldn't automatically make us family but legally in name, time and love would only do that. During the week at home, at school and at church we were the Carl's, but every other weekend Wendy and Jesse would be the Friedman's. Their natural father would also remain there for them[46]. Adults can be so petty and proud about these sort of things. I was more than unrealistic, I was hard and difficult on everyone. It created a tension that was constant and no one should have to grow up with that. I am just proud that they turned out so well, in spite of me.

Ministry wise, things started happening. When we prayed for people, they fell on the floor under the power of the Spirit. I had heard but never seen anyone "Slain in the Spirit" till one Sunday when Meg and I were asked to pray for Emily. We were meeting in an elementary school in the "multipurpose room" whose floors were asbestos tile on concrete, hard. She wanted prayer and so John asked me to pray for her while he continued to lead the meeting. I asked Meg to pray with me and as I prayed I closed my eyes. Then I reached up and touched her forehead and felt her leave my hand. I opened my eyes just about the time she hit the floor and bounced. I didn't know what to do next, so Meg and I just left her there as we crawled back to our seats looking as if we had done something wrong.

People got healed, filled with the Spirit and we got a home group that grew and wouldn't go home after the meeting. We often went to bed after the 'home-group meeting' and left them to themselves in our basement because I had to go to work early in the morning.

John had us now attending the leadership meetings and attending the Mid-Atlantic Leadership Conference's annual meeting at Gettysburg. There we met and sat under the teachings of Jaime Buckingham, Bob Mumford, Derek Prince, Ern Baxter, and David du Plessis just to name a few, so many that I can't remember them all by name. At one of these conferences we were at a work shop when they asked for anyone who needed prayer to come forward. Several people came forward, Tara our youngest six or seven at the time, followed them up. Meg nudged me to get her but something in me thought to wait. When the leader asked her what she needed she told him, "I want to pray." She had been accustomed to coming up with her mother and I to pray at church so she didn't see any reason why she shouldn't pray here. Sometimes when she prayed people fell under the power of the Spirit; it was no different here. The Lord had planted in her the seeds that the enemy would want to steal away, but the Lord had a hold on her.

The Charismatic Movement centered on teaching, whereas the Jesus People had been centered on evangelism. The Charismatic Movement was what happened when the

Pentecostal Revival began to overflow to the denominations. In the beginning, you could barely tell the difference between the two. In fact the terms were used interchangeably. But, there was an obvious difference; the result was a more cerebral, respectable movement. With the Jesus People our fervency was based on reaching the lost, bringing them to the Lord, getting them filled with the Spirit, and reading their Bibles. But, with the Charismatics it was about getting them to Church, and getting them to pray the prayer and then get them in a class about the Holy Spirit. Little was talked about relationships in either, they happened naturally or not at all. The denominational church had been talking relationships for a long time, but decentralized the Lordship of Jesus, leaving the gifts of the Holy Spirit and evangelism out.

Six years into our marriage, Meg got pregnant and it looked like she was going to keep it[47]. But as the pregnancy continued, complications evolved. She had an ectopic pregnancy which was growing. The doctor informed us that if something wasn't done, I would lose both of them. There was nothing to do but for him to operate to save Megs life. Now, at this point in our relationship with things beginning to happen in the ministry and the kids getting older, I knew it wouldn't be too much longer and we could devote all our time and efforts to the work of the ministry. Maybe we could even start our own New Covenant Church since we were so good at drawing people in. I had mixed emotions about having another child to take care of, especially since I knew what a lousy father I was. But at the same time, I always wanted to have children and never doubted I would. Having one of my "own" was desirable even though our youngest Tara was every bit my "own". She was even born with red hair and green eyes (both changed as she grew). She had mine and Megs' personality and I didn't have to share her with "another Dad". I was conflicted when the doctor told us that the baby wouldn't make it to full term, but would only take Meg and its life as it grew. I didn't want to go through this emotional teeter-totter again especially as we moved further into ministry. I asked the doctor if he could, while he was "in there," tie Megs' other tube so we wouldn't have to go through this again.

I said, "Why not? Nobody would know."

He just pointed upward and said, "He'll know."

The operation took longer than we thought it would and I spent the whole time praying for Meg in the chapel. I prayed for forgiveness for myself and repented of placing what I thought was His will above that which he would make known. After it was over the doctor came into see me and he looked a little wide eyed and frazzled. Then he told me it went well and the baby though trapped in the tube was perfect in form for its age. I thanked him and told him I had prayed for him. I don't know if he did tie the "other" tube[48] after all, but Meg never got pregnant again. I soon moved into my forties and she, not long afterward, followed.

Meg ended up spending almost two weeks in the hospital while the nurses went on strike. She was fed food that was inappropriate for her type of operation. The result was her system shut down. Further problems ensued with the strike. She had no one who would change her sheets, linens or bathe her. Meg was miserable and when she complained, things just got worse. The head nurse got an attitude and stormed in and out.

In the meantime the kids were on their own. Wendy was sixteen and had a car so I could depend on her to pick up her brother and take care of her sister while I was at work or at the hospital with Mom. They felt like they had a "get out of jail free" card and basically went and did what they wanted to without supervision. I was never sure of what was going on and hoped they were being responsible. For the most part, I look back on this and I think they were, but at the time it seemed like they were never where I thought they should be. I wasn't eating right or getting enough sleep worrying. I don't know how single parents do it, especially with a wife in the hospital who is not being taken care of properly. I thought I was losing my mind, and started having panic attacks.

Nobody from our church came by to see her or to ask if we needed help. I think I only got one call from John during this whole time. I could be wrong, but I don't remember many family members going by the hospital or asking if they could help with the kids either. The one person that did come by was Jack Cox, a New Covenant Pastor from Severn. I had only met him at leadership conferences and talked to him and Mary a little then. He was a pastor of the highest caliber. You knew he cared and when Meg finally got out of the hospital and had lost almost thirty pounds weighing around 104, we knew it was time to make a change.

I never took "making a change" lightly or cavalierly. I had to know it was God before doing. Bob Mumford's *Take Another Look at Guidance*[49] was my basis for knowing the will of God in a situation:

1. The Word of God (objective standard)
2. The Holy Spirit (subjective witness)
3. Circumstances (divine providence)

We were, sent out from Bowie to help John with a hurting church in Glen Burnie whose pastor was no longer with them. The church was wounded, he had been a wonderful man who they had come to rely on. Most of them were former military and the church had been established on Fort Meade. When he left we were not allowed to ask why, where or what, because "if you're not a part of the solution then you are a part of the problem.[50]" Otherwise, don't ask if you don't have anything to do with the issue. I respected that mentality; it showed deference toward the individual and stopped rumors from spreading with half-truths. It gave an individual the opportunity to get some things straightened out without the interference of someone who thought they "knew it all". John didn't talk much anyway and sometimes he didn't answer you at all when you questioned him. He took the "pastoral confidentiality" seriously.

I went to him and asked him to release us to Jack. Severn was closer than Glen Burnie and it looked like Bread of Life was going to fold eventually. Those among us who were sent out to help with the church and were candidates for becoming the new pastor, it looked like none of us were going to be appointed. Plus, our kids were going to a Christian School near Severn where they would have friends to sit with in Church. We felt beat up from the Bowie shunning and the Bread of Life delay and now the loss of our unborn child and the trauma Meg had been through. It was time for a change. The stream, in spite of the pebbles or because of them, was moving us onward again.

21
The Twelve

RODNEY HOWARD BROWN SUDDENLY BURST
from the stage in the auditorium, hit the floor running, passed
the pool set up for baptism, down the aisle beside where Jack
and I sat, out the back door screaming as he went. Suddenly,
he burst back in through the center aisle, back up to the stage
turning and staring at us all with sweat running down his face
and his eyes bugging out. He was fresh from the Lakeland,
Florida revival he had brought from South Africa to evangelize
the United States he informed us. Jack and I left that meeting
with more questions than we had before we went in. I picked up
a VHS tape from a meeting he had done to learn more.

Jack had Meg and I started coming to his home group
for about six months and then turned it over to us. Rather
than meeting in our home, which was a long way from his
house where it had started, we decided to start meeting in the
church building. That proved to be a good midway for most of
the people. Jack had me sharing the word on Sundays as well.
Meg began to move in prophesy even more than she had at
Bowie and it was always right on as confirmed by Jack and the
elders. I started giving more words of knowledge. The church

was growing. There were twelve home groups, and two services with two hundred or so at each service at its peak. This was a big difference from the fifty that had met in the school building. The new building seemed to make a difference. Bowie had never had 100 and Bread of Life far less than that.

I began to pray for those I called out with a word of knowledge and some fell on the floor coming under the power of the Spirit. And others were completely healed and or filled with the Holy Spirit. Many healing testimonies started coming in: people healed of cancer[51], infertility, and the common cold! We were being encouraged and fulfilled. In the freedom we were given, we were growing and prospering in the ministry the Lord had gifted us to do.

For Father's Day, Meg and the kids took me to an Oriole's game at Camden Yards, about half-way through the game there was a rain delay. At the same time my pager went off (this was before cell phones) and it was Maria from our home group. She sounded both strained and emotionally drained. She told me her van was left running in her driveway while she ran in the house to get something she had forgotten. Somehow, the van came out of park and began to roll with the door open. Her toddler fell out of the van and it rolled over his head. She was at Johns Hopkins Hospital and he was in critical care. I told Meg and the kids I was going to the hospital and would be back as soon as I could. Tara began to cry. This was a special event for her Daddy and now he had to leave! I reassured her that I would be back ASAP, besides there was the rain delay on the game.

When I got to the hospital in the waiting room sat her whole family and her mother's Catholic priest. I led the group in prayer while I waited to go in and pray for the baby. Maria came out finally and said that we, the Priest and I, could go back to pray, but we would have to go in one at a time. The Priest said, "You go first," and I did. When I entered the room, it was very crowded. The doctor and nurses were working on the child who lay on his back, so small. Maria stood opposite the doctor on the other side. A couple of nurses scurried to follow the doctor's instruction. I simply reached up and touched the toddler's forehead and prayed "Lord touch this child with your healing power." Immediately the child opened his eyes and looked at his mother and sat up saying, "Momma." He was healed. The doctor's eyes widened and the nurses turned around and looked amazed. I walked out and announced that the child would be all right and went back to the game, which hadn't started until I got back.

It was also about this time that I got a call from my mother who was very upset. She said Dad was talking about leaving her, that he said he didn't love her anymore. He loved another woman. I told Mom to let me pray with her. As we did, I received a picture of this overweight woman suddenly grabbing her chest and falling to the ground. I didn't tell mother what I saw, but asked her what the woman looked like. She described the woman I saw in the vision. I simply reassured my mother that it was going to be okay. I told her that something was going to happen within the next couple of weeks that would change everything (I don't like to give a timeframe because it is too easy to be guessing rather than be hearing from the Lord. I actually thought it would be within the week.) I asked her to keep in touch and let me know what happened. I didn't take the vision literally, but knew the Lord had showed me that he was going to remove this woman from my father's life. My Mom called me back *in a week* and told me Judy had a heart attack and died instantly. This is exactly what He had shown me.

The home group continued to grow, Meg became a Sunday school teacher, and Jack asked me to become one of the elders that would make twelve. They were a wonderful group of men and were supportive of what the Lord had been doing through me. That is until the home group outgrew the fellowship hall one night and we moved it into the sanctuary. I counted seventy people in the room. This was the only time it happened and never again after that. The word got back to the elders. And one of them accused me of trying to build my own church within the church (whatever that means). I didn't understand, wasn't that what we were supposed to do, grow? I don't know if he thought I was trying to build an army and to take over the church with a coup or what? He accused me before the elders and then said I should step down and give up my group. I looked to Jack for direction and got none, I was stunned. Then Ray and Bill spoke up for me. Ray Burkheart and Bill Thompson could always see what the Lord was doing and were supportive. This was the first time and would not be the last.

My accuser went on and said he didn't believe in the "Word of Knowledge[52]" or the healings that would take place from my ministry. He talked about when he was a kid in a Pentecostal church where he witnessed the false healing of teeth and other bogus things he had seen. But all I could think about was I thought we were a Charismatic church which meant *we believed* in gifts, didn't we?

I look back on it now and think he must have seen me as a threat to be the next one to become a pastor[53], since I had been one, and he would be passed over. John used to have a saying that your ministry would make room for you. Mine had and now it was being crowded out, again. I wouldn't fight for it or try to defend myself. I would leave it up to the Lord. The Lord had made things right when I had been wronged before, I didn't want to get in the way of His line of sight.

The home group continued to move in the power of the Holy Spirit. One night I brought out the Rodney Howard Brown tape I had picked up when Jack and I had gone to see him. During the message, Rodney brought some Church leaders up on the stage to give their testimony. When he did the strangest thing. As they were speaking, they began to get drunk in the Spirit, some fell out laughing and others froze in place, like they were in suspended animation. The tape itself was anointed. When I stopped and began a conversation with the group to find out what they thought of it, they began to experience the same thing. They were falling out in the Spirit, laughing and freezing in place.

That next Sunday I asked Jack if I could bring up anyone from the home group who wanted to give a testimony. He said I could. But when I did right there in front two hundred people in the Church, the same thing happened again! As they were speaking they froze, started laughing or fell out drunk. I was astonished and amazed. But, I looked out from the stage and many of the people were confused. They were not sure they believed what their eyes were seeing. I tried to explain what was going on. It seemed to be a move of the Spirit that was happening in many revivals both in the past and·in the present. That next elders meeting, my accuser was lit up. The result was I was asked to give up my home group.

I began to wonder if the Charismatic movement was coming

to an end. It seemed Severn Covenant was opting for becoming a respectable Bible Church. The calling out by way of Knowledge continued, but it felt like I was being throttled down. First they ask me to move over to the side as I prayed for people but when people kept manifesting signs of the Spirit I was asked to move to the back of the Church. Meg's prophetic words became less frequent. Finally someone suggested I minister in the fellowship hall, not in the church service. I would not hide the work of the Lord. I stopped moving in the gifts because they were unwelcome. Jack suggested I start a Saturday night service. I was willing to give it a try but nobody came.

I started looking for other ways to serve Him but could sense the flow of the river beginning to lead us on. I had been very interested in the Christian College started by one of New Covenant's pastors after he had gone to Oxford to get his D.Phil. I received my Bachelor's degree from this college and was a part of the first graduation class. Meg earned her Bachelor's degree and took over the duties of leading the whole Sunday school program. She started a training program and developed a curriculum she would later use in a college course she taught.

I began working on my Masters while I led the college at Severn Covenant, teaching classes on different books of the Bible. I soon became more involved in the college and served one year as its Dean of Students. Dr. Comfort was excited about my progress and arranged for me to go to Oxford,[54] the same college he had gone to, with a full scholarship for my PhD. All I needed to do was spend four weeks a year at the college campus while the rest of the work would be done by correspondence. I had arranged to get the time off from work at the bank where I was the Facilities Department Manager. At the last minute, they changed their mind. I was heartbroken, but figured where the Lord closed a door there would be one opened somewhere else. I found a way to work on my Ph.D. through correspondence and graduated with honors. I worked on Christian Psychology not only because I was interested in it but because most people in the Church failed to see mental problems as real issues. Many in the evangelical church at the time thought all problems could be solved by the power of the will and prayer. If there was a psychological issue it had to be demonic, behavioral or the parents fault in some way. I thought I could bring insight and light into the church through this ministry.

Agape Deficit

Tara was always the sweetest, kindest, most loving, generous person I knew (and still is). She was not just a daredevil but she virtually was fear - less. When we were praying for someone at the front of the church or in front of a crowd at the leadership conference she would boldly come up front and begin praying for others too, or she would trot clear across the neighborhood to knock on some new family's door who had just moved in to ask if they had anyone her age who could come out and play. At first we took this as just precocious for her age. She only saw the good in people and refused to see anything else.

The rejection became more deep seated. She knew from an early age that I was not her natural father. She never had contact with him and he was unreachable by our efforts. Some of the kids asked her why her natural father never came to see her and added, "What's wrong with you?" When she was a young teen she started running away, her Mom (and me at first) trying to track her down, sometimes all night long. And when we did would find her with the wrong crowds. I thought she was seeking some kind of friendship since those she had tried to be friends with had shunned her.

When she came home on her own, after running away, very often I'd sit with her and tell her how much we loved her and asked if she could tell me what was going on. And she would tear up and answer, "I don't know." From the look in her face I could see she really didn't know. She would apologize and we would pray together and then not long after that she would do it again. Another time she told me she liked the feeling she got from running, it was like a high. The church didn't understand, not just the other kids but the adults as well.

While Tara continued to try to cope and find herself, one Sunday she came to church in Goth array with her head shaved and one strain of hair dyed purple. It was like the parting of the sea, her seemly "best" friends scattered and the adults just stared.

You don't need facts, just the assumption to convict someone especially those in leadership. Bob Mumford has said, "I have made a painful discovery in my journey – wherever the most Scripture was preached, it seems that I have found the least amount of *Agape*.[55]"

Before long I was being asked to step down as an Elder. Ray Burkheart and Bill Thompson spoke out on my behalf again, others remained quiet. The reason was that my house was not in order, Tara's shaved head and black clothes was the proof. There was no "brother we want to stand with you and help you and Meg in this difficult time." It was cold and hard.

When I told Meg that I had been asked to step down, she was livid. She could not believe they would do something like that but she too had experienced the "love" of the brethren and just bit the bullet. Now this was the last straw. One of the elder's wives saw that she was "upset" and tried to give her a hug. To her it felt like a knife in the back that was being twisted, and let them know in no uncertain terms she was not in the mood for a hug. They saw it as her just having a problem, it couldn't be them.

I had enough experience now to know that when God can't get your attention with a still small voice he would speak louder. I stepped down, trusting Him to lead or make it right. He led. Dr. Comfort who had founded the New Covenant Church at Queenstown and the Christian College, had also experienced the "agape" of the church, when he got "voted out". That would have been okay for him except the college existed under law in the state of Maryland only as it had a Church for a covering. Now he had no church and he was left out in the cold. That's when he called me and asked if Meg and I would be willing to sign papers of incorporation to form a new church on the Eastern Shore to enable him to continue the college. We prayed about it and the timing was good. We would help him start, ironically, "The Love Church" as he called it, and move to the Eastern Shore. Our days in the Charismatic, Evangelical Church were on a course of converging into another stream that would form one mighty river. We didn't know it but He did. What man meant for evil God meant for good.[56]

22

Full Circle, Sort of

$\mathcal{T}$HE DEER DANCED IN AND OUT OF THE LINE OF
trees across the field of winter wheat while Meg and I sat on
the front porch sipping cold drinks as the sky turned several
colors of red, orange and pink.

"Those are crop circles I tell you," she said insistently.

"No I don't think so," I said trying to keep the sarcasm from
seeping though the sound of my words as the smile on my face
betrayed me. We were discussing the patterns in the wheat that
lay amidst the standing wheat. They appeared random rather
than in concentrical patterns as seen in England.

"I tell you, those are from mysterious means! Maybe even
aliens like that movie *Signs* with Mel Gibson." I couldn't tell if
she had gone from serious to kidding me.

"I heard on the radio, they are caused by deer making paths
in the wheat and or by whirlwinds as we called them back in
Othello."

"I still say they were made by aliens."

We had found this home after searching for a year. It was
only five miles from the Delaware line but seventy-five miles
from downtown DC, where I worked, and we loved it. It was

over 100 years old and had been restored by the former owner. It had a Jacuzzi for two upstairs, an old barn that had been made into a garage and a fallen pecan tree had been made into an armoire for the TV in the living room, with book shelves on either side, and it was beautiful. In the backyard, walking through the screened in porch to a very private deck with the house, garage and hedge surrounding and enclosing it from all peering eyes. Stepping down from the deck were paths that led to the pool surrounded by beautiful flowers. The path wound around the above ground pool through the daylilies on one side and ten foot high Rose of Sharon on the other, next to the fence and next to our neighbors shed.

"Who died?" the voice came from over the fence as Mr. Butler squeezed in between the green house and the dog pen. Mr. and Mrs. Butler were the very picture of "Americana" with his overalls and with her grey hair pinned up. They were in their late 80s, but you would never know it.

"Huh," I turned around to respond. "Oh, you're talking about our Celtic Cross?"

"Yep, who'd you bury there?"

The cross stood four feet high in front of our covered swing wedged in between two flowering crabapple trees. Meg and I liked to sit there in front of the cross to have our quiet time praying and meditating on the Lord and watching the birds in the magnolia tree in the opposite corner. It was the perfect place to get alone, as long as no one was peeking over the fence or the hound dogs were not baying.

Mr. Butler was a wealth of information regarding the history of the house and the area. "I would never have gotten married if it wasn't for that house of yours there," he said.

"How's, that," I asked.

"My wife moved into that house. That's how I met her. I grew up right in this house next to you here."

"Really," I was intrigued since I was three-thousand miles from my home.

"Yep, I was shy."

I couldn't imagine him being shy, since we had been talking since the day we moved in, maybe it was the house.

"I remember the very first "Victrola" I had ever seen. It was in that house. You had to wind it up, we didn't have electricity then. I remember when we first got electricity out here. They had it in town, but not out here."

Town was Denton, five miles in from Hobbs where we now lived. Denton was a town that would make Othello look metropolitan, and it was the county seat. Othello had had a presidential visit from Theodore Roosevelt on "Radar Hill" before the hill had radar, a part of the Saddle Mountains. It was there that the Bureau of Reclamation first considered that desert to be valuable for farming. And Denton's claim to fame was a visit from Franklin Delano Roosevelt in 1938. He spoke in front of the courthouse on Labor Day. The speech was broadcast on radio to the rest of the country. Roosevelt was there to support his New Deal programs and also to win votes for his ally in Congress, Maryland Representative T. Alan Goldsborough. Goldsborough lost anyway.

The Love Church met in Dr. Comfort's home which I soon began to realize was by design. Every time I talked about Church Growth and moving the church from its "temporary" location, his living room, the subject changed. The idea of us coming to the Eastern Shore to help him start the church was that I would be made the Assistant Pastor and take over the church while he concentrated on the college. He only later expressed that he had no desire to build another church he had already done that several times, his heart was with the college.

Meg moved right into the role she had at Severn with Sunday school, a role she was a natural for and very good with. But as much as Dr. Comfort tried not to he attracted people. Some of his old members from the Queenstown church started coming. Next thing he knew, he was enlarging the living room to enclose the porch. Some of those people thought that because they knew him longer maybe they should be promoted first. In fact there was actually a power struggle over the Sunday school program and some things were implied that were not true concerning Megs handling of it. I listened to the conversation between her and another lady who thought she should have control over it. Meg was very kind and firm believing that Dr. Comfort had commissioned us to help him. After all he and Shirley, his wife and Meg and my signature were on the document of incorporation. That should carry some weight, right? Wrong. Two things happened simultaneously. One, Dr. Comfort decided that he was going to make Shirley his Assistant Pastor. Up to this time he had taught that women were not to be ordained to the level of Pastor that was a man's responsibility.[57] But one church had stood with Dr. Comfort when Queenstown had left him high and dry. That was The Love Church in Elmira, NY and they were not New Covenant, they were Pentecostal and they ordained women. With Shirley as his Assistant Pastor he would never have to worry about the church voting him out again, there would be no other pastors. The second thing that happened was that word had gotten back to Shirley and Bill (Dr. Comfort) that Meg had caused a rift with the other woman who now wanted control of the Sunday school and they came to our house with the purpose of trying to straighten her out. When Meg got the drift that they were not there to support her but to correct her that was the last straw. She didn't want to get beat up again and rightly so.

We soon determined that we should resign, that we no longer felt needed or wanted. In fact at this point, I was sure we were both done and we would not get our hopes up for any kind of ministry. We would just find somewhere where we could hide. I was tired of trying to find my place to fit in and to reclaim my role as Pastor. Meg was also just as content to just live out our lives as "non-discriminate members" in some church somewhere. But the Lord wasn't about to let us off that easy.

Aglow Fellowship[58] was having their annual Christmas dinner and someone gave up their ticket and offered it to me. I had remembered Aglow from the early days of The Full Gospel Business Men's Association. They had been largely responsible for introducing the "Gift of the Holy Spirit" with speaking in tongues to many of the non-Pentecostal / Charismatic groups. It was at these meetings that I had met Demos Shakarian, Dennis Bennett, and heard speakers like Hararld Bredesen, Larry Christiansen, Costa Deir and Sid Roth for the first time. Aglow started out as the women's branch of the FGBM, with Rita Bennett being a founding member. So I was very familiar with Aglow, but hadn't heard of it in the years since leaving Washington State.

I went and sat at a table with Rusty and Ruth Petrides. Rusty sat next to me with Ruth on the other side. Ruth introduced both of them to me and began asking me questions, the Holy Spirit was all over her. Before long she asked Rusty if he would mind changing seats with her so she wouldn't have to keep leaning over the table to look around him to talk to me. She kept apologizing for talking so much but I really liked talking to her. She seemed on fire for the Lord and at the moment in time I was resigned to become a normal Christian, whatever that meant, I wasn't sure I knew how. Ruth kept trying to get the attention of her Pastor Fr. Nate Southworth, who was sitting at the main table. He was wearing a Roman collar. I asked if he was Catholic and she told me, "No, he was Episcopalian," or at least that's all I heard and could relate to. I went home after the dinner and told Meg we ought to go to this Episcopal Church in Easton. I added, "I know Episcopal Churches, that is the first church I went to when I had gotten saved. It will be easy to hide in an Episcopal Church," I proudly proclaimed.

The church I found was actually meeting in Ruth and Rusty's restaurant, The Crystal Café. The café was set up as a square within a square, with a brass rail outlining the inner square where tables were normally. The outside square was set up with table and chairs along the window and a counter with stools on the back wall next to the kitchen. Whereas booths framed the walls to the left and the right, we sat in one of the booths as far back as we could get in this kind of set up. For Church a "portable altar" sat in the center, outlined by the brass railing, toward the left wall. We were handed a spiral bound service book that had the liturgy in it and a song sheet. As we sang, Fr. Nate moved around the room putting oil on the foreheads of random individuals laying hands on some and praying for them the way we had done. The songs we sang were the same as those we sang in New Covenant. After the songs someone read a passage from the Old Testament, we read a Psalm together and then the reader read from the New Testament an epistle reading. Next, Fr. Nate took his Bible and stood in the middle of us and we all stood with him, which was difficult for us who had settled into the booth, and he read the words of Jesus from a gospel. He then shared a message that was somewhat lacking in continuity, but still full of life coupled with folksy terms. This all was very different from any Episcopal Church I had ever been to, and I liked it. Meg commented afterward that she liked it too.

Ruth made her way back to us and seemed subdued, "You made it." I introduced Meg to her, she shook her hand. She took her other hand and rubbed it nervously as if the handshake had been too hard.

"I'm afraid I talked your husband's ear off at the Aglow meeting," she told Meg.

"No, you didn't," I assured her. "I enjoyed our conversation."

"Well, I'm glad you came," she said. "Have you met Nate yet?"

"No, don't bother him. He looks busy."

Fr. Nate worked his way back to us after talking with at least a dozen people. He stopped us just as we were about to go out the door.

He said, "What are you doing now?"

I looked at him a little wide eyed not knowing what he was asking and didn't answer.

"Let me take you to lunch."

"Okay," I said, looking at Meg for the "go ahead", she nodded.

"Do, you like Chinese?"

"Yeah, we like Chinese."

"We'll go right next door." He pointed at the wall behind us.

"Look I have to pick things up here, you go next door and get a table and I'll meet you there in a minute."

"Okay."

Meg and I walked next door and sat at a table and waited for him to come. When he did, we talked more about what we had just experienced.

"I like it," I said again.

Meg hesitated, "will you be happy just going someplace?"

"What do you mean," I asked naively.

"You know what I mean, just being a member and not having to be in charge?"

"Yeah," I said somewhat defensively. "In fact, I would be relieved to not have to worry about all the garbage that comes with leadership. I am tired of having a bull's eye on my back. No, I am done, finished. I don't need to be a pastor anymore." She looked at me as if she didn't believe me. "But if I was going to be a priest in a church like this, I would like to be one just like this guy." Then it just hit me he didn't know my name and I wasn't sure of his, although I thought Ruth had said it was Nate, Fr. Nate.

Nate stood about 6'2" or so and had grey hair and a grey beard although I thought he must have been prematurely grey. He certainly didn't seem old. He had so much energy and enthusiasm, like a man on a mission. He came bounding into the restaurant, sat down and told the waiter what he wanted and in the same breath turned to me and said, "Why are you running from the ministry?"

I couldn't believe my ears! How did he know? I hadn't even told him my name and now he was reading my mail? I didn't know how to respond. Tears welled up in my eyes and began running down my cheeks as I just stared.

"You, know you belong in the ministry. You can't hide from God," he said.

"Hide." How did he know? I had come there to hide, nobody but Meg had heard me say that. My mouth which was now quivering finding it impossible to speak without blubbering could only produce, "I don't know."

It was happening again! When I gave up at The Way, I suddenly found myself taking care of another youth group some three-thousand miles away. When I gave up on marriage, I suddenly found myself in a relationship with a beautiful young woman with a readymade family as if to make up for all the time I had lost with my first marriage. Now that I had given up on being ordained and working in the ministry, I was being directed again back into it. Was this really happening to me? I had felt like such a loser trying to live an illusion and when I had given up suddenly this person who didn't even know my name, was speaking to the hidden recesses of my heart.

Part III
The Liturgical Sacramental Stream

The Catholic Church possesses one and the same faith throughout the whole world, as we have already said (Against Heresies 1:10). Since therefore we have such proofs, it is not necessary to seek the truth among others which it is easy to obtain from the Church; since the apostles, like a rich man [depositing his money] in a bank, lodged in her hands most copiously all things pertaining to the truth: so that every man, whosoever will, can draw from her the water of life. For she is the entrance to life; all others are thieves and robbers. On this account we are bound to avoid them, but to make choice of the things pertaining to the Church with the utmost diligence, and to lay hold of the tradition of the truth. For how stands the case? Suppose there should arise a dispute relative to some important question among us. Should we not have recourse to the most ancient churches with which the apostles held constant intercourse, and learn from them what is certain and clear in regard to the present question? For how should it be if the apostles themselves had not left us writings? Would it not be necessary [in that case] to follow the course of the tradition which they handed down to those to whom they did commit the churches? (ibid. 3:4).

Irenaeus 189 AD

23
One Mighty River

*T*HE HEAT WAS RISING IN THE ATTIC OF OUR farmhouse as I rummaged through the boxes of books, magazines and cassette tapes. I had saved everything never knowing when I would need them again, or so I told myself. There were countless cassette copies of *The Word for Today* with Chuck Smith, Bob Mumford's "Tape of the Month", Derek Prince *Deliverance* tapes, and conferences with John Wimber, Paul Kane, Jaime Buckingham, and others which we had attended. And then there were plastic magazine holders full of *New Wine Magazine*, *Charisma Magazine*, *Logos Magazine*, *Koinonia*, *Ministry Today* Magazine and *New Covenant Magazine* which I had worked on as a transcriber and editor for John. I was looking for the *Ministry Today* Magazine which I didn't have too many copies of but something in the back of my mind said I had one about this church with a cover picture of its founder and patriarch. I found it! There was Randolf Adler's face smiling on the cover of the magazine.

A Mighty Wind in Chicago

The year was 1977 and the meeting was a group of Evangelical pastors gathering to discuss how they could best reach the lost for the Lord, everyone had a sense of the Holy Spirit's presence and purpose. Everyone had a desire for authentic Christianity based on the early church. Many thought they had attempted that already and found within themselves "something missing" and each being more isolated than ever. But what several found was they hadn't gone back far enough, back to the early 1900s and the Azuza Street and Topeka Kansas revivals, with Charles Parham from Kansas and William J Seymour in Los Angeles and the birth of modern Pentecostalism with evangelism, speaking in tongues and the healing ministry. Some traced their history to the early revivals of Charles Finney and or Jonathan Edwards and still others to the Plymouth Brethren with J. N. Darby or his follower C. L. Scofield. The more they studied the early church and the church fathers, and the disciples of the first Apostles, the more they recognized the early church had a liturgy following in the same line and pattern of both the Temple and the Synagogue worship from whom the Church was born. In fact, even in their Evangelical / Charismatic worship they knew that their prescribed pattern followed every week was technically a type of liturgy. So what was missing that the early church had? What would a New Testament early church service really look like today?

In their search the group divided into three groups: one took the Episcopal Church road, the other the Antiochean Orthodox and last group formed their own group calling it a Convergence Movement of the Evangelical, Charismatic and

Catholic (Liturgical/Sacramental). The Charismatic Episcopal Church was born.

The first problem and one that it carried till recent years was with the name. When they tried to explain what they were, that part of the name, "Episcopal," the explanation became very lengthily.

"Oh so you are Episcopalians," someone would say.

"No, we are not Episcopalians in the sense you think of today." "Episcopalian means ruled by bishops, like in the Bible."[59] I really had trouble understanding this because the logo at the time was also the same as the Episcopal Church United States of America (ECUSA), only the ICCEC[60] had a Holy Spirit dove in the middle. The ECUSA church was also in the heat of a controversy by ordaining professing homosexuals, which any good evangelical would not do. They also ordained women to the priesthood also something Evangelicals, with the exception of Pentecostals, wouldn't do. So many would just assume the CEC[61] was the same as the ECUSA. In fact most, when you tried and succeeded explaining it, would never attempt to explain it to anyone else. It was just easier to say "He is an Episcopalian now."

And they would raise their eyebrows as they exchanged that look, without saying what it meant: I always knew he was a little off.

The other thing I thought was that maybe the CEC had had a rift with the Episcopal Church and broken off from ECUSA starting a splinter version of the church. Many a church had splintered off of the ECUSA, but not the CEC, nothing could be further from the truth. It was truly a new work birthed out of the Pro-Life Movement. The way Bishop Adler liked to tell it was when he was involved with Operation Rescue he noted that when the Catholics and the Protestants got thrown in jail, the Protestants called their lawyers' and the Catholics called for a prayer meeting. This left a lasting impression on him.

Then Bishop Adler at a golf outing with his good friend Joseph Moats a Nazarene pastor, started talking about his study of liturgy. According to Moats, Adler gave him a prophetic word from Ezekiel 22:26, *"My priests have violated my law, and have profaned mine holy things: they have put no difference between the holy and the profane, neither have they showed difference between the unclean and the clean, and have hid their eyes from my Sabbaths and I am profaned among them,"* on a small piece of paper. Moats stuck the piece of paper in his pocket and promptly forgot about it, until he found it there weeks later.

When he read it he lay on the floor prostrate crying out to the Lord "What are the Holy things the priests have profaned that now profane you?" The Lord then gave him seven things: The Lords Supper, Baptism, Confirmation, Penance, Unction, Holy Matrimony, and Holy Orders – the sacraments of the historic church. These thoughts placed within him a spiritual hunger. Being a Nazarene and not knowing anything about the sacraments or the historic church, he wanted to know more, he had to know more. By the Divine inspiration in these men the search led them to form the Charismatic Episcopal Church.

Coasting to Coast

The CEC was having a Convocation, what we would have called a joint meeting in New Covenant. This was taking place in California near San Juan Capistrano and Fr. Nate wanted me to go with him and Venita, his wife. St. Simon Peters Church would foot the bill. How could I refuse! The last time I had been there was when I had hitchhiked through California, and we had stolen oranges near the ruins of the mission. It was amazing how everything had changed. The orange groves were gone! I was confused, nothing looked the same! In fact the place had so changed that even the swallows who used to return to the mission every year now flew to the local CVS drugstore instead.

The mission had turned into a tourist attraction, with a ticket booth, a turn sty, and a gift shop. I bought my first crucifix there, a fairly small one with what looked like a coin in the center. I was told it was a St. Benedict Cross. And the coin was actually a saying by St. Benedict which when translated said, "Step back Satan" on one side. And on the other[62] "Be gone Satan! Never tempt me with your vanities! What you offer me is evil. Drink the poison yourself!" The story behind it goes that Benedict was given poison by his own brethren and when it failed to harm him he said these words! I surely could relate since I had been through the fire more than once by those I thought should cover me with love instead of trying to finish me off! Bob Mumford has said that the Christian Army is the only army in the world that seeks to finish off its wounded!

There were three things I noted about the convocation: There were thousands of people from all over the world and the procession of each was led with each churches banner. We had banners for awhile in New Covenant and we went traipsing up and down the aisles waving them during our "worship time." The second thing that impressed me was there were numerous dancers leading the way, such as I had not seen before. We had dancers like Margarita Chase and Karen Wentz[63] and they were good, but this was like seeing angels dancing before the throne in worship. The third may seem strange to some, but outside the tent before the meetings and afterward there were priests and bishops and men in general smoking cigars in front of God and everybody! We would never have done that at New Covenant. We wouldn't want anyone to stumble, so we said, we as the elders hid it. This to me indicated that there wasn't a religious guilt finding spirit that I could see among them, but instead there was joy, there was real liberty and a powerful presence of the Lord. Father Nate had flown me out there and put me up in a motel and I would never be the same. At the conclusion of each day's meetings, the band led us in singing *Non Nobis Domina,*[64] which means *"Not unto us, O Lord, not unto us, but to thy name give the glory !"*

By March of 2000 Meg and I were received as members in the CEC and St. Simon Peters Church in Easton, Md. The church had moved from The Crystal Café, to The Avalon Theater,[65] a more fitting place for it with its cathedral-like dome. The people of St. Simon Peter were so warm and welcoming and I soon began teaching in classes of Church History and Bible studies among them.

Life in Jesus

Bishop Philip Zampino, whose church[66] I had visited during my hiatus with New Covenant Church of Bowie, was asked to leave ECUSA and St. Timothy's Church, he had built up through the healing ministry.[67] He in turn went on to have a healing ministry, radio program and travel a time with Kathryn Kuhlman.[68] In 1982 the Lord led him to form a Benedictine

Community near Libertytown, MD. It was a community where families lived and shared a farm working the land and serving in the ministry. It had a convent, seminary, a thriving church and a healing ministry where people came from miles around. Bishop Zampino was its founder, abbot and regional Bishop for the Mid-Atlantic CEC Diocese.[69] I cannot imagine having that much responsibility and not stumbling under the weight of it. I know I could not do it nor would I try.

Fr. Nate had me there to stand before the Bishops' Council; they would consider me for the Priesthood. The council was made up of the diocesan Canons: Fr. Larry Hill, Fr. Ed Meeks, Fr. Dennis Hewitt, Fr. Martin Eppard and Bishop Philip Zampino. I waited in the sanctuary on my knees for what seemed like the longest time not having much hope that I would be accepted. They had my resume and my college transcripts. I had by now, a Bachelors in Ministry, a Master of Ministry and recently a Doctor of Christian Counseling Psychology degree. Quite frankly, I was tired of school and going for no particular reason or desirable outcome. In fact, I was just tired period. I loved to learn and to study but ... I was brought in and stood before them. Bishop asked me why I wanted to be a priest. My answer, as best I remember, was that I wanted to do the Lord's will for my life and if that meant serving as a priest then that's what I wanted. I told them my testimony from my mother's prayer in utero to the Episcopal Church to my journey before the Throne of Christ (which I still could not share without choking-up), to the Assembly of God and the Way, to the Local Church and New Covenant. By the time I got finished I was weary and emotionally drained. I explained that each step of the way the Lord had kept me moving forward and not allowed me to quit.

They asked me to leave while they discussed it in prayer to get the mind of the Lord. I walked out of there convinced I had sealed my fate and I was finished. I was such a loser, what was I even doing here? They called me back in. They said YES, that I was accepted to go to seminary. What? What? I was confused, seminary? I thought I was being considered for the priesthood. I felt an inward joy that burst into tears and mental confusion of going back to school. That would mean there still was no guarantee that I would be ordained after three more years of seminary. Nate had indicated he had spoken to the Bishop about me and thought he was just going to push me through to ordination. Fr. Dennis said why are you crying, you've been accepted? I blubbered something having seen the Lord and having a calling and going to school for so many years all at once – it didn't make much sense, but I was in. When I got home I told Meg, she was less than enthusiastic, knowing what I was getting into.

"What? They want you to go back to school? How long?"

"Three years," I mumbled.

"You can't do that. You're on the road going back and forth to work every day. How are you going to be able to go to seminary on top of that?"

"Yeah I know besides I already have nine years of Bible school, seminary, and graduate school."

"What do you need more school for?"

"I don't know. If they think I need it then I guess I have to do it."

"You're crazy," she concluded.

"Maybe I am, maybe I am." My doubts bobbed to the top floating in the sea of self pity. Was this just another way to delay the inevitable, rejection?

24
Formation and the Farm

I AWOKE TO THE DEAFENING SILENCE, THE STERILE smell of the room and the presentiment of the nisus that lay before me. The eastern sun was just beginning to rise and lighten the sky sending forth its beams bouncing gently off of the landscape reflecting through the one window over the other bed, lapping away the blanketing cold left by the darkness just moments prior. We had been informed the night before that we were to rise in silence and make our beds. There would be an inspection. We would not speak to each other as we stood before the mirror beginning our day with the necessary grooming. Our voices were reserved for the praise and worship at Lauds[70] of the Divine Office.[71] The community would be there as the morning announcement rang with the commencement bells in the tower. I whispered "good morning" to a smiling face under the frame of dark blue with white bordered habit. The facial reply was one of stern rebuke, as it was followed by a finger to the lips reinforcing the silent rule. "Sorry," I said realizing my conciliatory comment was too an addition to the first of many mistakes. I almost said I was sorry for saying I am sorry! This could keep going on until I got permanently kicked out! I dipped my fingers in the fount[72] and made the sign of the cross[73] as I entered the nave[74] from the narthex. I genuflected, made the sign of the cross as my knee touched the floor acknowledging the presence of the Lord and slid into the pew, sitting on the "boys" side. I lowered the kneeler and leaned into the pew in front of me folding my hands asking the Lord to hear my prayer and receive my worship.

The purpose of a girl and boys side was never fully explained, but when we began to recite the Psalms in a chant, we would do so antiphonally, one side would say one verse and then the other would respond with the next verse, it was beautiful. Then we returned to the silence. It continued until we filed out of the nave after which we were free to talk. Surprisingly enough the silence had set in coupled with the lingering psalms like a rainbow after a rain in our quiet thoughts. Nothing more than common curtsies then prevailed.

Breakfast was prepared and served by the Nuns and women from the community. The men from the community were plowing the gardens, feeding the chickens, doing carpentry work and all that was needed to be done to keep the families going. The Nuns lived in a house attached to the Bishop and his wife's home. Two other families lived together in the large farm house and one family in an apartment attached to the seminarians sleeping quarters. A couple of other homes would be built later. Being there was truly heaven on earth for those of us who would spend one weekend a month attending classes. You could sense the presence of the Lord as soon as you passed through the gates off of the main road and dipped into "Life in Jesus," set in a small valley with the chapel at its center as you passed the pond with the rowboat tied up under a willow tree.

We wore black cassocks with wide sashes, my cassock was large and the sash was too long. When I fastened it with the Velcro as tight as I could, it slipped slowly down till it was wrapped around my feet tripping me. If it didn't slip, I found myself stepping on the seam of the cassock as I walked or especially when I tried to get up from kneeling. I must have been a sight to see as I walked with folded hands tripping, bumping and stumbling into the postulate in front me. We walked single file from the chapel to the fellowship hall where we would be served breakfast by the community and the oblates thereof.

The day was broken up into the Divine Office as previously mentioned with Eucharist after breakfast, then morning class followed by lunch and Sext and then afternoon class followed by None followed by dinner and Vespers then the evening class. Our day was full and filled with prayer, praise and the word. I found that I enjoyed and respected the structure; someone has said that the Divine Office is like a rope that we don't have to think about but to only cling to. It allowing it to pull us up into the presence of the Lord, and that it did. This was quite different for me who had done many teachings saying there should be no structure only the following of the leading of the Spirit. But, if I was going to be perfectly honest every meeting I had ever attended had some sort of familiar structure. There was no such thing as a structure-less meeting. Even the Shakers and Quakers who sat in silence until someone was "moved by the spirit" followed a week after week pattern. If done the same way more than once it became a structure, a tradition you couldn't get away from! So who was right? Which was the "traditions of men[75]," we were warned about and which was of the Lord? The easy way out was to say they all were of the Lord that no one had a corner on it. But what did the Bible say about it and could it be used as the only authority? The more I thought about it the more questions I had.

Liturgy, to me as an evangelical, was a dirty word; it was the epitome of the doctrines of men – wood, hay and stubble[76]. Little did I know, but was soon to find out, in the book of Acts 13:1 it reads: "As they *ministered* to the Lord and fasted the Holy Spirit spoke…" the word *ministered* is the Greek word *leitourgeo* which is where we get the word Liturgy! It means to perform ritual acts, the work of the people. It could read literally: "As they performed the liturgy and fasted the Holy Spirit spoke…" The early church had a liturgy and acknowledged it.[77] Justin Martyr described early church worship in 150 AD that is just fifty years after the Apostle John died and two hundred and fifty years before the identification of the canon of the Holy Scripture. Justin depicted the church service like this: "Then bread and a cup of mixed water and wine were brought to the president of the brethren (the bishop) and he took them and offered up praise and thanksgiving, 'at some length.' When he had finished the thanksgiving, the whole congregation present assented, saying 'Amen' which means 'So be it.' Those whom were called deacons then serve a portion of the consecrated bread and wine to the baptized believers, they call this food Eucharist.[78]

There were two models that the early church followed, the Synagogue worship and the Temple worship. The Synagogue worship[79] was centered on the reading of the Holy Scriptures and teaching. The Temple worship was focused on the sacrifice for sins. The early church followed this pattern as well, albeit not as developed as it is today but of the same pattern. The mass is divided into two parts the first part is the praise and the reading of the Word the second half divided by the sharing of the peace and then the sacrifice of Christ is *"remembered*[80]*"* in the Eucharist (Thanksgiving), sharing the Lords Supper. The Eucharist takes place with the proclamation of 1 Corinthians 11:24. In the early church the catechumens[81] were released from the service just prior to the Eucharist because you had to be baptized and the catechumen often went through two years of teaching before being baptized[82]. This was to help prevent nominal Christianity of which the Lord spoke of in the "Parable of the Sower" and the seed which fell on shallow ground which would fall away during persecution. The grace received from the Eucharist is a privilege, an empowerment and a Sacrament[83].

In archeological finds of early meeting places of the church most have been found with an altar in the center, built into the wall, not a lectern or podium because the Eucharist was considered the center of the worship not the preaching of the word[84]. The canon of the New Testament's twenty-seven books weren't even complete until Athanasius's Festal Letter in 367 and later in 397 at Council of Carthage the canon was established[85].

What did the Church rely on before the Canon of New Testament? They relied on the written word and the spoken word of the Apostles[86] and their disciples. The printing press wasn't even invented for hundreds of years and most didn't know how to read anyway so what did the church rely on? They relied on what we rely on today if we are going to be perfectly honest, *tradition*, the written word and the leadership of the church that has been called "the magisterium," those with the authority and power of the church to teach religious truth. In American and most of the rest of the world in the 21st century we choose who this is whether it is a televangelist who everyone thinks is the greatest, or he or she with the latest revelation and bestselling book or our revered pastor.[87] They become our magisterium. If they say this is the God honest truth, we believe them and our belief system is then established upon what they say and those they may reference. And if the tradition of our church is to believe certain things like no ties or lipstick, we try to substantiate it in the Bible. The Bible remains the final authority and the highest, but how we understand it is directly influenced by both our tradition and those teachers we embrace who influence us.

What the early church did was rely on the traditions (they believed) that were handed down by the apostles[88] and what the church fathers taught (not just the Apostles but those who followed after them) and the Scriptures that they knew to be authentic (by the authority of the bishops).

You see, in most protestant churches the altar has been replaced by the pulpit as the center of worship. A pattern of the Synagogue and have displaced the Eucharist with an inflated importance of The Word. This would have been very foreign to the early church. We need the teaching of the Scriptures and the Sacrament of the Eucharist and the Traditions of the Apostles. This can only be accomplished by going back, not merely to the Reformation, but 1,000 years before that to the Historic Church.

The CEC was about going back to the Historic Church without giving up our Evangelical and Charismatic foundation, the three major streams of the Christian Church into one mighty river of the faith. This was called Convergence Worship.

25
Different Perspectives

IT WAS DARK AND A LITTLE CHILLY, BUT HAD A
beautiful dome and nicely painted art deco outline around
the stage. We had moved from the Crystal Café to the Avalon
Theater where Fr. Nate had worked out a deal with his
cleaning company and Avalon Foundation. One Sunday, David
Abercrombie who would become our Deacon saved us the cost
and humiliation of having burnt down this historic building.[89]
As Fr. Nate's sermon progressed, I noticed the Advent Wreath
behind him which being made up of real greens had dried
over the last four weeks and the candles had gotten shorter
from the ever present breeze that seemed to haunt the place.
Next thing I knew, the wreath was ablaze and I looked around
for a fire extinguisher and saw none. Visions of screaming
parishioners exiting the building flashed through my head.
David was seated behind Nate and I said to David trying not
to panic, the wreath ... and pointed to his left. He looked at
me and said "what" and then moved into action as Fr. Nate
turned, looking a little miffed, to see why we were interrupting
him. David grabbed the bowl of freshly made holy water and
dumped it all on the wreath. As soon as he had picked up the

holy water (which I had questions about) my thoughts were not coupled with relief instead they went right to the question of sacramental correctness. Was it right to use holy water for extinguishing fires instead of exorcizing demons?[90] This thought is similar to another one that came up in seminary: "If a fly flew into the consecrated wine would it defile the wine or would the fly become consecrated[91]?" I was truly inundated with what I knew, what I thought I knew and what I was beginning to know. The Liturgy and order began to gel into deep spiritual meaning.

Everything we did was important because it represented a type or shadow of the Lord somehow. The candles on the altar represented the Old Testament and the New Testament; the one on the right was the Old Testament and was lit first the one on the left was the New Testament and it was lit last because the New can never stand alone. They also represented the Divinity and Humanity of Christ[92], the Divinity on the right (facing the altar) the Humanity on the left. The Humanity of Christ could never be lit without the Divinity, so the right Divinity would be lit first and the Humanity last. They were the first things lit in the service. The light of Christ upon the Altar meant that the service was to begin, and when they were put out that indicated it was over. They were lit before the procession and put out after the recession.

Procession begins with incense leading the way.[93] Incense represents the prayers of the saints rising throughout the ages before the throne of God.[94] Then follows the cross, "Then Jesus said to His disciples, 'If anyone desires to come after Me, let him deny himself and take up his cross and follow Me.'"[95] Behind the cross is the Gospel Book containing the four Gospels[96] bringing the good news to the masses. Behind the Gospel book comes the preacher and priest. They are servants of all,[97] they are last in the procession. The priests[98]and all clergy who serve at the altar wear white as a symbol that Jesus has washed our sins white as snow.[99] Everything in the service has meaning.[100]

Signs and symbols were everywhere I was beginning to see. "The first Christians were Jewish, and they worshiped according to their liturgical traditions. Their worship was rich in signs, symbols and sacraments. This is important; whether we realize it or not, everything dear to us is rich in symbolism. We are a symbolic people. Our wedding rings, our money, our credit cards, are all symbols. Even the pages of our Bibles are linguistic symbols – symbolic of the word of God. God is so great that we would never be able to grasp Him or His love without our Christian symbols. The sacraments use natural things such as water, bread, wine, words, oil and the laying on of hands as points of contact to provide us with supernatural strength, the grace from God, necessary for our spiritual growth." As Bishop Phillip Zampino said.[101] Prehaps the greatest symbol given to man is Jesus Christ in the incarnation. God became flesh and dwelt among us. *"Therefore the Lord Himself will give you a* **sign:** *Behold the virgin shall conceive and bear a Son and shall call His name Immanuel.[102] This will be a* **sign** *to you: You will find a baby wrapped in cloths and lying in a manger."[103]*

Biblical Contradictions?

My seminary teachers were very patient with me and it seemed that I was the only one who had these questions: "Why do you call your priests *"Father"* when Jesus said "Call no man father?"[104] Look closely at that verse in Matt. 23:9 and notice in the context He says call no man father, or master or servant and yet you do not hesitate to call someone "Mr. So-in-so" without a problem when mister is a form of master. And, he says call no one Rabbi or Teacher and yet you do not hesitate to call someone who instructs in a school, teacher? Do you think this is displeasing to the Lord? I think not. I learned it falls under the category of Biblical understanding called *"hyperbole"*. It is the same principle as when Jesus taught if your hand causes you to sin cut it off and if your eye causes you to sin pluck it out.[105] If people took those verses literally there would be a lot of one eyed one handed people in church. The real reason Protestants adopted their views is twofold: 1. They didn't need to think about it because since the twelfth century they haven't had to call their pastors father. 2. Because they just didn't like Catholics who did use that term.

Most Protestants had adopted Luther's *Sola Scriptora*. *Sola Scriptora* said that everything you need to know about the scripture was taught in the scriptures; otherwise scripture interprets scripture. I was one of them. Every time a new subject or concept was introduced to me I was asking, "Where is that in the Bible?" I must have driven my instructors crazy but they were very patient with me.

Sola Scriptora opens the door to all sorts of problems and no one really believes in it verbatim. If that were the case, then there would be no need of teachers like R. C. Sproul, Timothy Keller or Norman L. Geisler. "The only thing we need is the Bible and nothing else." In my early walk with the Lord, I knew a lot of people who believed that! "Have you read any good books lately?" I'd ask. The answer always came something like, "Yes the Bible, I don't read anything else!" That sounded so pietistic, but the truth is we need our pastors and teachers and that is scriptural,[106] as St. Paul declared. Everyone has a favorite teacher he can point to and say they taught me more than I could have learned on my own. If we started eliminating all human teachers we might find ourselves sitting at home on Sunday not going to Church, which would be unscriptural. [107]

Besides, if all we needed was a Bible, then what did the early church do before the ratification of the canon?[108] What did the believer do before the Bible was made available to the masses?[109] Most of the people in these times were uneducated and were unable to read, what did they do? No, *Sola Scriptora*[110]was the doctrinal result of Luther's reaction to the abuses he determined was in the Church at the time. The Church always saw the scriptures as the primary source of doctrinal authority, but they knew it could not stand alone. Jesus had said he would establish his church and the gates of Hell would not be able to stand against it.[111] He didn't say he would write a *book! The Church is the authority based upon the scripture.* And the reasoning for including a particular writing in the New Testament canon included many considerations: orthodoxy, antiquity, apostolic authenticity and usage by earlier Church Fathers, as verified by existing documents. The canon was sifted out of the over two-thousand documents. The task was daunting to say the least. Now we can understand why those who had no Bible relied on the Church Fathers and the Church leaders for their catechism and why the Lord placed the onus on the Church.

26

Convergence

WHEN I ATTENDED ST. SIMON PETERS IN EASTON, I thought I was going to an Episcopal Church. I thought I had come full circle from where I started with Fr. White at St. Martins in Moses Lake. I had received the Lord Jesus as my Savoir as a direct result of the Jesus People and Steve Anderson directing me to John 14. The result was I became an evangelical carrying my Bible with me wherever I went, evangelizing everyone I met. I had gotten saved outside the Church, but instinctively knew I needed to be a part of a church. I would learn through the community we created at The Way that I was baptized into the mystical body of Christ but I could not nor should not be a "lone bone on my own"! In the Bible I read that Jesus said he would build his Church and the gates of Hell would not prevail[112] against it. I knew according to the Word, the Lord had his elect[113] but where would I find them? As I had searched I came to the Episcopal Church and inadvertently stumbled into the Charismatic / Pentecostal movement. Suddenly I found myself emerged in "Charismatic Conferences" which seemed to be as varied as there were denominations; each had their own charismatic group. The more I moved around the more I realized one group excluded the other! The Evangelicals excluded the Liturgical / Sacramental and the Charismatics / Pentecostals and vice versa. You could be a Liturgical / Sacramental and a Charismatic but you had to do it separately in a "prayer meeting" or "conference" but not in the service. Evangelicals could exclude the Charismatics by pointing out that "the gifts" were not longer for the church. After the last Apostle died and the canon of the Scripture had been established, the gifts died with the "Apostolic Age". The Charismatics disagreed that the gifts had died and had no need of the so called restrictions of the Liturgy. Everyone could and would point to the Bible and pronounce how they were correct and the others wrong when they all had the same Bible. How could they all be right and yet all wrong? So there had to be something else, but where and how was it? Where was the New Testament Church and what did it look like? Would it look the same as it did when it was born or had it grown and developed as it grew?

One Mighty Stream

The CEC was (and is) a Convergence Church. Convergence is not a denomination. It is a move of God toward the identity of the Church as described in the first five hundred years. It is not Episcopalian but it is Liturgical /Sacramental ruled by Bishops[114]. It is not a Baptist church, but it is evangelical and believes the Bible is the highest and final authoritative canonical Word of God by which we judge all things. It is not a Pentecostal / Independent Charismatic Church but it is a Charismatic church which follows the leading of the Holy Spirit

and all the gifts of the Spirit,[115] seeing them function in and
through the Church. Jesus Christ above all is its Lord and
Savior and there is Salvation by no other name. In essence, the
CEC (convergence) is Trinitarian. As God is Father, Son and
Holy Spirit and man is Spirit, Soul and Body, so is the Church:
Spirit / Holy Spirit (Charismatic), Soul / The Son (Evangelical)
and Body / The Father (Liturgical / Sacramental). Each person
of the Trinity plays a part in the expression of the other so that
one cannot exist without the other. Thus the CEC embraces the
whole of the Church and not just a single part as the world has
come to know.

I had had a full understanding of both the Evangelical
and Charismatic but did not understand the Liturgical /
Sacramental – the Catholic. For that I would need further
"Spiritual formation". So after years of Bible College and Grad
school I was learning again. I began to understand what Bob
Mumford had taught that if you think you had arrived you
probably had and then would not go on. I thought I had arrived
and had learned all I needed to know, but there was so much
more. I wanted all the Lord had to give me. Whereas, once I
thought I saw "the end" at the embracing of a diploma and the
laying on of hands. I now saw something different because
I had not arrived and neither would I in this life. I began to
believe what some who had had near death experiences had
said, that in the afterlife one continued his education. I in
fact had an insatiable desire to learn. Let me say it again,
having just completed my PhD the aspect of having to return to
school somewhat exasperated me coupled with an underlining
excitement!

Liturgy is Dead

If liturgy is dead then why dig it up? Liturgy can't be dead or alive. Only people can be dead or alive. Then why did I buy into the dead liturgy hypothesis? It was because of a philosophy I had embraced during my youth. One that said if we were alive in the spirit then all others were dead or not quite as alive as our group. It was a type of spiritual pride and for some it developed into a sect like mantra which grew into a bona fide cult. There is something about thinking your group is the only right group that really gets God's goat. And maybe it is not that you think yours is the only right group, but the *most* right group that gets you in trouble. When leadership starts saying that, in so many words, you can bet the end is near. The Lord withdraws His presence, then his anointing, and then the word dries up. I heard someone say, "You know what is left when there is a famine of the word and the spirit in the church? Asses' heads and doves dung."[116] Asses' heads represent the wisdom of men and doves dung is what is left when the dove has flown away.

The liturgy is not dead. It is the scriptures glaring in your face but many have put a veil over their faces so that it does not blind them with its brilliance. The light it conveys is convicting and piercing but we muffle it with the cares of the world, successes and defeats of selfish ambition. Emotionally isolating ourselves because of our successes and failures and infantile longings for validation and recognition means we intellectually bring death into the church and then blame everyone and anything that doesn't penetrate or challenge our displacement.

A living, breathing expression of Christ in our churches comes with the facets of the Lord to the world. We must cease looking for something to satisfy "my" need and look to find out what His need is. Christ was and is evangelical He came to seek and save the lost.[117] The Great Commission[118] has not changed since he charged the believers on one of His last moments on earth. Christ is Liturgical / Sacramental, Liturgical in so much as He came to do His Fathers will, and He worshiped Him[119] and each of the seven sacraments were instituted by Him.[120] Christ is Charismatic and went about healing and casting out spirits,[121] telling us we must do the same.[122] Christ needs to be expressed in the Evangelical, Liturgical /Sacramental and the Charismatic. This is the Charismatic Episcopal Church and this is how I found myself on my face before the Lord.

Not So Ordinary Ordination

The enemy of my soul was plaguing me with images of my life of failure as I lay face down in front of the Altar. I did not want to be here. He reminded me I did not belong here. I had failed as a son, to my parents a disgrace, a high school dropout, a druggy. I had failed as a soldier. I was a convicted convict. I had failed as a husband to my first wife, and I knew it was only God's grace that Meg hadn't kicked me to the curb. I had failed my children as a father and role model. I had failed to establish a long lasting ministry. I knew as the carpet seared my nose and the pictorial cross I wore bore into my chest[123], and my arms outstretched that I had no good in me to validate me being here. I was a fraud, failure, and faithless.

The accusations weighed so heavy upon me I thought the

weight of them would push me through the floor into hell, where I knew I belonged. It was as despair gripped my heart to the point of crushing it that my peripheral vision caught sight of something walking beside my head. I knew I could not lift up my eyes to see what it was. What I saw was a foot, bare but in a sandal. Could it be? Was it? Tears ran down the bridge of my nose into the carpet as the accusations washed away. I heard a voice in my spirit saying:

"You are forgiven for all your failures, and your pitiful charade as you would see it. Have I not been with you the whole way? Have I not led you through your successes and your failures? When you have stood in the cloud of darkness and under the deluge of tears was I not there with you? When you were so despaired of life you thought to end it, did I let you? How can you take credit for any of the good that has come and remained with you? If you could and would take credit you would not be here. Look again at your life and see where I was not? I was there in your mother's prayers. I was there when your life hung in the balance as you lay in the incubator. I was there when a Bible was given you as a baby. I was there when as a youth you were arrested that Christmas; I was there when you stole a car and drove to Vegas and your father picked you up at the jail. I was there when you got out of the army and went to DC and lived on the streets doing drugs. I was there that night when you lay in the park and the man pulled a gun on you. I was there when you went to the penitentiary in Baltimore. Where have I not been? I was there on the streets in Spokane when you were approached by the Jesus People and something lit within you. I was there when you went into Steve Anderson's room and he handed you John 14. I was there when you said yes. I was there in the living room of your parent's house when you asked to be baptized in the Holy Spirit. I was there at the Way Coffee House when I had to show you your pride in taking credit for my work. I was there at your first marriage and when you came undone and when you had nothing more to hang onto but the knowledge that I am God, all doctrine, formula, and faith slipping through your fingers like sand in a wave. There was nothing left to hold on to. I was there at every doubt and fear and moral failure and I have never left you, nor will I ever. I have brought you here and will keep you, you know now that you can't keep yourself."

The tears passed and what seemed like a life time of refection was only a passing moment ...

"*God and Father of all, we praise you for your infinite love in calling us to be a holy people in the kingdom of your Son Jesus Christ our Lord, who is the image of your eternal and invisible glory, the firstborn among many brethren, and the head of the Church. We thank you that by His death He has overcome death, and having ascended into heaven, has poured His gifts abundantly upon your people, making some pastors and teachers, to equip the saints for the work of the ministry and building up of your body.*"

I was now kneeling as Bishop Phil prayed this prayer and lay hands on my head. He continued:

"*Therefore, Father, through Jesus Christ your Son, give your Holy Spirit to Rob; fill him with grace and power and make him a priest in your Church.*"

He then took the anointing oil, having made the sign of the cross on my head and then pressing it into my palms. He took the Bible and placed it firmly in my hands and said:

"Receive this Bible as a sign of the authority given to you to preach the Word of God and to administer His holy Sacraments. Do not forget the trust committed to you as a priest of the Church of God."

I arose and looked out to a room that had filled to capacity since my face time down on the carpet. I was a new priest, a presbyter with a long history and an even longer adventure ahead!

"Non Nobis Domine!"

Recommended Reading

Peter Gilquest –	Love is Now
	Becoming Orthodox
Watchman Nee –	The Normal Christian Life
	The Spiritual Man
	The Release of the Spirit
Bob Mumford -	Take Another Look at Guidance
	Fifteen Steps Out
	The Agape Road
C.S. Lewis -	Mere Christianity
	The Problem with Pain
	The Great Divorce
Stephen Kaung -	The Splendor of His Ways
Norman Grubb -	Continuous Revival the Secret of
	Victorious Living
	The Deep Things of God
Dennis Bennett -	The Holy Spirit and You
	Nine O'clock in the Morning
David Wilkerson –	The Cross and the Switchblade
John Sherrill -	They Speak With Other Tongues
Jack E. Stiles –	The gift of the Holy Spirit
Dr. William Comfort –	Did Tongues Cease
St. Francis of Assisi –	Little Flowers

Gerard Groote –   The Following of Christ
Justo L Gonzalez –   The History of Christianity
Eusebius –   The Church History
The Twelve Apostles –   The Didache
Andrew Murray –   Absolute Surrender
DeVern F. Fromke –   The Ultimate Intention
                           Unto a Full Statue
Arthur Wallis ·   Radical Christian
St. John of the Cross –   Dark Night of the Soul
St. Teresa of Avila –   Interior Castles
Madam Guyon –   Experiencing the Depths of Christ
Alexander Schmemann –For the Light of the World
                           Historic Road of Eastern Orthodoxy
Kallistos Ware –   The Orthodox Way
Scott Hahn –   The Lambs Supper
                           Lord Have Mercy
Stephen K. Ray –   Crossing the Tiber
Robert Webber –   Evangelicals on Canterbury's Trail
                           Common Roots: the Original Call to
                           an Ancient-Future Faith
                           Worship Old and New
Bishop Phil Weeks –   Non Nobis, Domine!

Endnotes

Chapter 1

1   Loess is a clastic, predominantly silt-sized sediment, which is
    formed by the accumulation of wind-blown dust.
2   Nestled beneath majestic basalt cliffs and rim rock slopes at the
    southern end of the lower Grand Coulee in Eastern Washington
    is a tiny inland sea noted for its mineral rich water and creamy
    black mud. At the turn of the last century, Soap Lake was one
    of the most well known mineral spas in the country. Before the
    development of sulfa drugs and penicillin, Soap Lake and spas
    at Saratoga Springs, New York, White Sulfur, West Virginia and
    Hot Springs, Arkansas were Meccas for the treatment of disease,
    illness and injury.

Chapter 2

3   Wikipedia
4   He did later when I was in my forties and married a second time.
5   I always suspected that if Santa knew if we were "naughty or
    nice" wouldn't he know if we were sleeping or pretending?
6   Mt. Rainer, Mt. St. Helens, Mt. Adams and Mt. Baker in
    Washington's Cascade Range were all "extinct" volcanoes. We
    were told we had nothing to worry about until Mt. St. Helens
    proved them wrong.

7   Basically this was a fan with fiber filler all around it and Dad hooked a hose line up to it and the water ran out over the filler and down the drain on to ground. The fan pulled air across the wet fiber and the damp faucet water cooled the house down. We never worried about "wasting water" there was plenty of it hundreds of feet underground and the city pumped it out and sent it to us.

Chapter 3

8   When Dr. Martin L. King was murdered in Memphis, Tennessee on Thursday, April 4, 1968 crowds began to gather at 14th and U. Stokely Carmichael, who was from Trinidad and Tobago and a Howard University graduate, who had parted with King in 1966, as former head of the Student Nonviolent Coordinating Committee in 1967, led members of the SNCC to stores in the neighborhood demanding that they close out of respect for Dr. King. Although polite at first, the crowd got out of control and began breaking windows, starting fires, and widespread looting which spread to over 30 other cities across the United States.

9   After Woodstock she was hearing voices from her "entities." Eventually they would tell her to move into the woods and make a house out of plastic blown from some construction site somewhere. Years later, I would look for her and find her still in the woods and talk her into staying in an apartment with my wife and I after I had become a Christian and a young pastor. I tried to help her but nothing would sway her. Her voices were "divine"; it was my first encounter with schizophrenia and the realization that not everything strange was a demon. The voices in her head would tell her to leave the safety of the apartment and return to the woods. Her mother would get custody of the baby and Paul would eventually divorce her and remarry. Woodstock is often glamorized as being the place that epitomizes "Peace and Love" but I wonder how many addicts, STDs, and LSD induced mental illness it produced?

Chapter 4

10   My mother called it ESP; she too had a strong sensing like that too. Watchman Nee called it "The Latent Power of the Soul." I now understand it to be what the Bible calls "A Gift of Knowledge", that is when the latent power of the soul gets infused with the Holy Spirit.

Chapter 5

11   The Maryland Penitentiary, authorized in 1804 and opened in 1811, vacillated between the two competing penal philosophies of the times, but was renowned for nearly always being profitable (Resolution no. 15, Acts of 1804). A legislative committee inspected the building under construction in 1807 and reported that the new penitentiary had depositories for raw materials and manufactured goods, nine cells measuring roughly 8 by 16 feet, separate rooms for women, and a chapel. The 1809 law, which specified for what crimes and what terms persons were to be sentenced to confinement in the new penitentiary, merely stipulated that convicts "shall be kept therein at hard labour, or in solitude," and male and female prisoners kept separate (Chapter 138, Acts of 1809). Thus, at its inception, the Maryland Penitentiary operated under neither the Philadelphia system of total isolation nor the Auburn system of moral isolation with its discipline of silence by day and solitary confinement by night, enforced by the whip. Both systems, however, exerted some influence. In 1829, the Directors of the Maryland Penitentiary reported the completion of a new east wing designed for solitary confinement at night. In 1837, the Directors were required to remodel or rebuild the old west wing so that prison discipline based on the Philadelphia plan could be extended to the women's department. Further, "the directors shall pay particular regard to the enforcement of the Philadelphia system, to the fullest extent

of its admissibility, in the new cells, so as to be able to report to the Governor annually, the effects thereof upon the convicts, as a reformatory and punitive confinement, and also upon the financial and manufacturing operations of the Penitentiary, for the purpose of affording a comparative estimate of the merits of the two great systems of punishment now in use in the United States" (Chapter 320, Acts of 1837). The President and Directors of the Maryland Penitentiary noted in 1838, however, that "the experience of the past year has served to test the efficacy of the Auburn system of prison discipline in our Penitentiary, to the introduction of which the new workshops were expressly adapted." By 1841, the Auburn System was definitely in use.

[12]   This is the NKJV which I came to memorize – GNT reads: **1** "Do not be worried and upset," Jesus told them. "Believe in God and believe also in me. **2** There are many rooms in my Father's house, and I am going to prepare a place for you. I would not tell you this if it were not so. **3** And after I go and prepare a place for you, I will come back and take you to myself, so that you will be where I am."

[13]   This would develop into legalism that was hard to shake when confronted with grace.

[14]   The Holy Spirit was hovering over the waters in the beginning of Genesis. The result was the creation of life on the earth Genesis 1:2, He was the breath that was breathed into the clay and caused man to be a living soul Genesis 2:7, He is the source that draws us to the Father Jn.6:44, 15:26, He is the Heavenly Husband of Mary that enabled her to conceive the Christ child Luke 1:35, He reveals the Lord Jesus to us Jn.14:26, He is the power that enables us to share the gospel to the world Luke 24:49, and He is the impetus that enables us to live for Christ and overcome the world, the flesh and the Devil.

[15]   The **Athanasian Creed**, or ***Quicunque Vult*** (also *Quicumque Vult*), is a Christian statement of belief focused on Trinitarian doctrine and Christology. The creed has been used by Christian

churches since the sixth century. It is the first creed in which the equality of the three persons of the Trinity is explicitly stated.

16   Acts 1:5, 2:4

17   Lk. 11:13

18   1 Cor. 12:10

19   Acts 2:4 KJV

20   1 Cor. 13:1

21   Psalm 119:113 KJV

22   What I would soon learn is our Triune God had made man in his image as tripart body, soul and spirit. Our body is our world consciousness, our soul is person (or other) consciousness and our spirit is our God consciousness. Our spirit is where His Spirit dwells within us (2 Cor. 1:21-22 Darby (margin), Rom.8:16) when we invite him to dwell in our heart.

23   1 Cor. 14:14

24   1 Cor. 14:2

25   1 Cor. 14:4

26   Rom. 8:26-27

27   Chuck Smith and Lonnie Frisbee had begun what the press called "The Jesus People". Chuck had been a "Foursquare," minister a church started by Aimee Semple McPherson in LA in 1927. Chuck left the Foursquare church and started the Calvary Chapel Fellowship Churches, at the time of his death, Oct. 3, 2013 there were over 1000 fellowships worldwide.

28   Carl Parks and Linda Meisner were loosely associated. Carl in Spokane with "The Voice of Elijah" newspaper that became the "Truth" papers and Linda was with the Jesus People in Seattle.

29   Parham originated the doctrine of initial evidence—that the baptism of the Holy Spirit is evidenced by speaking in tongues.[1] It was this doctrine that made Pentecostalism distinct from other holiness Christian groups that spoke in tongues or believed in an experience subsequent to salvation and sanctification. In a move criticized by Parham his Apostolic Faith Movement merged with

other Pentecostal groups in 1914 to form the General Council of the Assemblies of God in the United States of America

[30]   I don't remember its actual name and my attempt to find it has not succeeded.

[31]   I Cor. 12:8-9 NAS, the word of knowledge is the ability to know something about someone unknown to the speaker except by the Holy Spirit. A prophetic word is the Mind of God for the moment to a person or a group, many passages of the New Testament were believed to have come from a prophecy given to the church, it is not necessarily a fore telling as a "forth telling."

[32]   **The local churches** is a Christian group whose beliefs and practice are based upon the teachings of Watchman Nee and Witness Lee. Many of the group's ideas, including plural eldership, disavowal of a clergy-laity distinction, as well as worship centered around the Lord's Supper, were first practiced in Europe by the Plymouth Brethren. Nee, however, considered the divisiveness that he observed among the Brethren to be unscriptural. Seeking a New Testament basis for the unity of all believers, Nee developed the teaching that there should only be one church per city. Such a practice would mean that Christians would meet together simply as fellow believers who live in the same city rather than meeting on the basis of any particular doctrine or person. Nee felt this way even considering his own doctrine, The Spiritual Man a three volume book he thought too perfect a work when it was completed and had it withdrawn from the market when it was published.

[33]   Greg, Jim and Clint would later, after I had returned to Maryland and had been living there a while, send me a taped message where they would describe how they felt about me and it was humbling to say the least. They each described how I had been used by the Lord and the impact I had on them in superlatives far exceeding what I had known to be true. I would later reflect on the message and either they thought of me as a saint or dead and this was my eulogy. I would find out it was more the latter than the former when I returned several years later and invited

myself to a prayer meeting they were having, The Way being long closed. They ignored me, not even looking at me when I offered a thought, until I happened to mention The Way fondly. Greg, whose back was turned to me, turned around with the most vicious expression and said, "I couldn't be happier that The Way is closed." It cut me like a knife to the heart.

34 William W. (Bill) Gothard, Jr. (born November 2, 1934) is an American Christian minister, speaker, and writer, and the founder of the Institute in Basic Life Principles (IBLP), notable for his conservative teachings. Among the several strong distinctives of his teaching have been encouragement of Bible memorization, large families, homeschooling, aversion to debt, respect for authority, conservative dress,[1] and extended principles related to identity, family, education, healthcare, music, and finances. At the height of his popularity during the 1970s, the Basic Youth Conflicts seminar with Bill Gothard was regularly filling auditoriums throughout the United States and beyond with attendance figures as large as ten thousand and more for a one-week seminar. In this way, he reached many in the evangelical community from the Baby Boomer generation during their teen years and years of young adulthood. Other seminars during this time included an advanced youth conflicts seminar and as well as seminars for pastors, physicians, and legislators. Wikipedia

35 I had no one but myself to blame, it was a lesson that I just couldn't seem to get straight, the same one the Lord had tried to teach me at The Way. I had forced the relationship into marriage all under the banner of what I knew to be "the Lords will".

36 Eph. 3:16 in order that he may give you according to the riches of his glory, to be strengthened with power by his Spirit in the *inner man*: (mar. "spirit")Darby.

37 **Pelagianism** is the belief that original sin did not taint human nature and that mortal will is still capable of choosing good or evil without special Divine aid. This is still sometimes called Limited Depravity. Thus, in contrast to 1 Corinthians 15:19-22 (especially

verse 22), Adam's sin was "to set a bad example" for his progeny, but his actions did not have the other consequences imputed to original sin. Pelagianism views the role of Jesus as "setting a good example" for the rest of humanity (thus counteracting Adam's bad example) as well as providing an atonement for our sins. In short, humanity has full control, and thus full responsibility, for obeying the Gospel *in addition to* full responsibility for every sin (the latter insisted upon by both proponents and opponents of Pelagianism). According to Pelagian doctrine, because humans are sinners by choice, they are therefore criminals who need the atonement of Jesus Christ. Sinners are not victims, they are criminals who need pardon.

38 This theological theory is named after Pelagius (AD 354 – AD 420/440), although he denied, at least at some point in his life, many of the doctrines associated with his name.

39 Matt. 24:22 "And unless those days were shortened, no flesh would be saved; but for the elect's sake those days will be shortened."

40 1 Tim. 3:4-5 He must manage his own family well and see that his children obey him, and he must do so in a manner worthy of full respect. (If anyone does not know how to manage his own family, how can he take care of God's church?)

41 John Lennon

42 There are many other legends behind Saint Valentine. One is that in the 1st century AD it is said that Valentine, who was a priest, defied the order of the emperor Claudius and secretly married couples so that the husbands wouldn't have to go to war. Soldiers were sparse at this time so this was a big inconvenience to the emperor. Another legend is that Valentine refused to sacrifice to pagan gods. Being imprisoned for this, Valentine gave his testimony in prison and through his prayers healed the jailer's daughter who was suffering from blindness. On the day of his execution he left her a note that was signed "Your Valentine."

43 Eph.5:22,24

44 Eph.6:1

45 I Tim.3:5

46 I am glad he was there for the kids, especially my son who I was especially difficult with (like my Dad was to me). And I wish there hadn't been "completion" going on for their sake. I made so many mistakes that maybe another book is in order "How *not* to act as an adopted Father".

47 We suspected she had been pregnant several times before and lost them early.

48 I today regret having asked him to do this, knowing now what I know about being prolife.

49 Bob Mumford in *Take Another Look at Guidance*, compares discovering God's will with a sea captain's docking procedure: A certain harbor in Italy can be reached only by sailing up a narrow channel between dangerous rocks and shoals. Over the years, many ships have been wrecked, and navigation is hazardous. To guide the ships safely into port, three lights have been mounted on three huge poles in the harbor. When the three lights are perfectly lined up and seen as one, the ship can safely proceed up the narrow channel. If the pilot sees two or three lights, he knows he's off course and in danger. - Gregory Asimakoupoulos (Bible.org)

50 A variation of a quote by Eldridge Cleaver: "You're either part of the solution or you're part of the problem."

51 I wasn't the only one who prayed for those with cancer that were healed.

52 He didn't us the biblical term but rather described it in derogatory terms.

53 The way it worked in New Covenant was that when a Church grew to a certain size as determined by the Pastor and elders it would divide into a new church with those involved in the growth taking the leadership.

54 Oxford Graduate School, Dayton, Tennessee

55 The Mysterious Seed – Bob Mumford P.18 pg.1

56 Genesis 50:20

57   I Tim. 2:12

58   **Aglow International** is an interdenominational organization of Christian women and men. Formerly known as **Women's Aglow Fellowship**, it has more than 200,000 members meeting together each month through local Aglow groups in 171 nations. More than 21,000 Aglow leaders worldwide minister in their communities. An estimated 17 million people each year are ministered to through over 1,250 community, neighborhood and workplace groups in the US, as well as 3,101 local groups internationally. The organization was born in 1967 out of the charismatic movement that swept the US in the 1960s.

59   I Tim. 3:1-2 This is a true saying, If a man desire the office of a bishop, he desires a good work. A bishop then must be blameless, the husband of one wife, vigilant, sober, of good behavior, given to hospitality, apt to teach. Many in the evangelical church have tried to change the meaning to be a local Pastor to fit in to what they practice rather than seek to understand the purpose in the historic church, which evolved from being only a local pastor to being one over an area of churches with each church having their own Elder (presbitorous – Greek from which we get our English word Priest (see New World Origins of English Words).

60   International Communion of Charismatic Episcopal Churches

61   Short for ICCEC

62   Surrounding the back of the medal are the letters V R S N S M V - S M Q L I V B, in reference to *Vade retro satana: Vade retro Satana! Nunquam suade mihi vana! Sunt mala quae libas. Ipse venena bibas!* ("Begone Satan! Never tempt me with your vanities! What you offer me is evil. Drink the poison yourself!")

63   They have different last names now I believe, forgive me for not knowing them.

64   **Non nobis** is a short Latin hymn used as a prayer of thanksgiving and expression of humility. The Latin text derives from Psalm 113:9 (according to the Vulgate numbering), which corresponds to Psalm 115:1 in the King James Version.

65   Built in 1921 and then in 1934, the Schine Chain Theatres purchased the Avalon and renovated it with an art deco theme. It would become one of the most famous movie houses in the area, hosting three world premieres. Eastern Shore movie-goers saw Clark Gable's first screen kiss, Bette Davis' first psychotic role, and Roy Rogers' first gunfight at the Avalon. Three world premieres took place at the Avalon including "The First Kiss" starring Gary Cooper and Fay Rae, which was filmed in Easton and St. Michaels. The theater eventually fell into disrepair and closed its doors in 1985. In 1989, it was restored as a performing arts center and then purchased in 1992 by the town of Easton. The Avalon is currently operated by The Avalon Foundation, a non-profit organization. The Avalon has since become a major music venue and center for community events in the area.

66   St. Timothy's in Catonsville, MD

67   ECUSA eventually closed the church and an Anglican church took over, that joined in fellowship with the Catholic Church.

68   Kathryn Johanna Kuhlman (May 9, 1907 – February 20, 1976) was an American faith healer and evangelist.

69   I also have nothing but respect and love for Bishop Phil and for those who lived and served there I love you all and have nothing but fond memories of how the Lord used you and your devotion to the Lord, I cannot share your disgruntle because I was not involved and cannot take up anyone's offence.

70   The name is derived from the three last psalms of the Psalter (148, 149, 150), the Laudate psalms, which in former versions of the Lauds of the Roman Rite occurred every day, and in all of which the word *laudate* is repeated frequently, and to such an extent that originally the word Lauds designated not, as it does nowadays, the whole office, but only the end, that is to say, these three psalms with the conclusion.

71   In western Catholicism, canonical hours may also be called *offices*, since they refer to the official set of prayer of the Roman Catholic Church that is known variously as the *Divine Office* (from the

Latin *officium divinum* meaning "divine service" or "divine duty"), and the *Opus Dei* (meaning in Latin, "Work of God"). The current official version of the hours in the Roman Rite of the Roman Catholic Church is called the **Liturgy of the Hours** (Latin: *Liturgia horarum*) in North America or **Divine Office** in Ireland and Britain. In the Anglican tradition, they are often known as the **Daily Office** (or Divine Office), to distinguish them from the other 'Offices' of the Church, i.e. Holy Communion, Baptism, etc. They are made up Lauds – morning prayer, Terce - midmorning prayer, Sext – mid-day prayer, None – mid-afternoon prayer, Vespers – Evening prayer, and Compine – before bed prayer.

[72] Dipping our fingers in the fount is to remind ourselves of our baptism into the faith from the world leaving the world outside and entering into the house of worship. It is also a symbol of washing off the world and any evil spirits that may have attached themselves to us while there since they like water-less places. Matt.12:43

[73] The sign of the cross is outlining our head, heart and breath (lungs) in the Name of the Father, Son and Holy Spirit with the shape of the cross reminding ourselves that we are crucified with Christ Gal. 2:20, 21. *"Go throughout the City of Jerusalem and put a **mark** (tau= T) on the foreheads…" Ezekiel 9:4.* Around the year 200, Tertullian says: "We Christians mark our foreheads with the sign of the cross". Today we also make the small sign of the cross on our head, our lips and heart before the Gospel is read as a prayer to ask the Lord to place this reading in my mind, on my lips and write it upon my heart.

[74] Nave is the root word from which we get our word *Navy* meaning boat, the part of the church building where the people in the parish sits is called a Nave because the church is an ark like Noah's Ark washing in baptism us from the flood of the flesh 1 Peter 3:20, 21.

[75] II Corinthians 2:8 "See to it that no one takes you captive through philosophy and empty deception, according to the tradition of

men, according to the elementary principles of the world, rather than according to Christ." The key to this verse is not to let anyone displace Christ by philosophy, deception, or traditions based upon worldly principles. There are Christian traditions and worldly ones we need to avoid the one and embrace the other.

[76] 1 Corinthians 3:12

[77] 77 · Saul and Barnabas taught the Antiochian Church how to worship see Acts 11:22, 25, 26

[78] Sources of the Western Tradition, Justin Martin, (On the Liturgy of the Church) Vol. 1

[79] Synagogue worship was started during the Babylonian exile, during the time of Ezra and Nehemiah when they could not worship at the Temple. Their eagerness to return to Jerusalem and restore the Temple worship places its importance to them over the Synagogue. But after the captivity they would retain both, even as it was at the time of Jesus and the birth of the Church.

[80] The word *remembrance* in 1 Cor. 11:22 is the Greek word *anamnesis* and it means more than remembering where you left your keys. Its connotation is to make "present the past". When Jesus died on the cross time and space were stripped away, and his sacrifice became present for all time. When John wrote: "So Jesus said to them, "Truly, truly, I say to you, unless you eat the flesh of the Son of Man and drink his blood, you have no life in you." Jn. 6:53. It says: "After this many of his disciples turned back and no longer walked with him." Vs.66 Jesus didn't run after them and say, "Wait a minute guys I didn't mean that literally, this is a metaphor." No, he didn't try to stop them that is because he said what he meant. At the last supper he took bread and broke it and gave it and said take eat this is my body given up for you." He didn't say this is sort of like my body nope *"this is my body"*. So during the second part of the service we see Jesus crucified for all time giving up his life for us and the bread becomes the body of Christ and the wine becomes the blood of Christ. Not a

resacrifice, but what Jesus did **2000** years ago is made present as time and space is stripped away and eternity is left in its place.

81   New believers not yet baptized.

82   Didache 9:5 "But let none eat or drink of your Eucharist except those who have been baptized in the Lord's Name. For concerning this also did the Lord says, "Give not that which is holy to the dogs.""

83   The English word "sacrament" is derived indirectly from the Ecclesiastical Latin *sacrāmentum*, from Latin *sacrō* ("hallow, consecrate"), from *sacer* ("sacred, holy"). In Ancient Rome, the term meant a soldier's oath of allegiance, and also a sacred rite. Tertullian, a third-century Christian writer, suggested that just as the soldier's oath was a sign of the beginning of a new life, so too was initiation into the Christian community through baptism and Eucharist.

84   It is interesting to me that a lot of protestant churches have altar calls calling for people to come to the rail to receive the Lord when in the Sacramental Churches all the faithful come forward to receive the Lord in the Eucharist and a recommitment of their faith every week.

85   http://www.ctlibrary.com/ch/1994/issue43/4322.html

86   2 Thess. 2:15 "So then, brothers and sisters, stand firm and hold fast to the teachings we passed on to you, whether by **word of mouth or by letter.**" Act. 2:42, Eph. 2:20

87   Or a combination of teachers we like; whether it is Joel Osteen or R.C. Sproul they become the magisterium we look to.

88   1Cor.11:2 "hold fast to the traditions, just as I hand them to you." 2 Thess. 2:15 "hold fast...traditions that you were taught... by oral statement...or by letter." 2 Thess. 3:6, 2 Tim. 2:2

89   The Historic **Avalon Theatre** is a beautifully restored art-deco **theater built in 1921.** Visually spectacular, its detail included leaded glass doors at every theater entrance, an 18-foot dome with 148 lights, a **300** pipe electric-pneumatic organ, an electric player piano, and a ballroom on the second floor.

90 **90** Holy Water is water that has been prayed over and used much like Holy Oil in prayer. There is nothing magic about. It works with faith as with the waters of baptism. Matt.12:43 "Now when the unclean spirit goes out of a man, it passes through waterless places seeking rest, and does not find *it*. NASB Mark 5:13. The swine dived into the sea rather than live and inhabit demons. Suggested reading: "*Making Visible the Void"*by Austin Randolph Adler

91 This is of course is a silly question proposed by medieval seminaries; it falls into the same category of "How many angels can dance on the head of a pin". The question has also been linked to the fall of Constantinople, with the imagery of scholars debating about minutiae while the Turkish besieged the city. In modern usage, it therefore has been used as a metaphor for wasting time debating topics of no practical value, or questions whose answers hold no intellectual consequence, while more urgent concerns pile up. Wikipedia

92 Jn.9:3; Phil. 2:7-8

93 Mal.1:11 "For from the rising of the sun to its going down, My Name shall be great among the Gentiles; in every place incense shall be offered to My Name."

94 Rev.8:3

95 Matt. 16:24

96 Rom. 10:15 "And how can anyone preach unless they are sent? As it is written: "How beautiful are the feet of those who bring good news!"

97 Mk.9:25

98 The origin of our English word "Priest" is from the German *Priester* based on the Latin *presbyter* 'elder". The Oxford Dictionary of Word Histories.

99 Isa. 1:18, Rev.4:4 "Surrounding the throne were twenty-four other thrones, and seated on them were twenty-four elders. They were dressed in white..."

100   The Golden Tread of Liturgy that holds together the apocalyptic pearls of the book of Revelation. See The Lamb's Supper (Doubleday Publishers) p.119 By Scott Hahn

101   Life in Jesus News Letter.

102   Isaiah 7:14

103   Luke 2:12

104   Matt. 23:8-10 "But be not ye called Rabbi: for one is your Master, *even* Christ; and all ye are brethren. And call no *man* your father upon the earth: for one is your Father, which is in heaven. Neither be ye called masters: for one is your Master, *even* Christ." KJV

105   Matt.18:8-9 "If your hand or your foot causes you to stumble, cut it off and throw it from you; it is better for you to enter life crippled or lame, than to have two hands or two feet and be cast into the eternal fire. If your eye causes you to stumble, pluck it out and throw it from you. It is better for you to enter life with one eye, than to have two eyes and be cast into the fiery hell."

106   "for which I was appointed a preacher and apostle and teacher." 2 Tim. 1:11

107   *"... not forsaking the assembling of ourselves together, as is the manner of some, but exhorting one another, and so much the more as you see the Day approaching." Hebrews 10:25 (NKJV)*

108   Thus, some claim that, from the 4th century, there existed unanimity in the West concerning the New Testament canon and that, by the 5th century, the Eastern Church, with a few exceptions, had come to accept the Book of Revelation and thus had come into harmony on the matter of the canon. Nonetheless, full dogmatic articulations of the canon were not made until the Canon of Trent of 1546 for Roman Catholicism, the Gallic Confession of Faith of 1559 for Calvinism, the Thirty-Nine Articles of 1563 for the Church of England, and the Synod of Jerusalem of 1672 for the Greek Orthodox.

109   The Bible was printed at Mainz, Germany by *Johannes Gutenberg* from 1452-1455.

[110] *Sola scriptura* - scripture alone, is one of the five *solas, sola fide* – faith alone, *sola gratis* – grace alone, *solus Christus* – Christ alone, *Soli Deo Gloria* – to God be the glory, considered by some Protestant groups to be the theological pillars of the Reformation. But sola scriptura is an unscriptural concept 1 Corth. 11:2; It is the highest authority, the final authority but not the *"only"* which is what "alone" means. There are the Churches traditions and teachers as well both spoken and written handed down to us. "So then, brothers, stand firm and hold to the traditions that you were taught by us, either by our spoken word or by our letter." 2 Thess. 2:15 ESV

[111] 111 "And I say also unto thee, That thou art Peter, and upon this rock I will build my church; and the **gates of hell** shall not prevail against it." Matthew 16:18

[112] Matt. 16:18 KJV

[113] Matt. 24:22, 24; Titus 1:1 KJV

[114] Titus 1:6-8

[115] 1 Corinthians 12:1-11

[116] 2 Kings 6:25 "And there was a great famine in Samaria, as they besieged it, until a donkey's head was sold for eighty shekels of silver, and the fourth part of a kab of dove's dung for five shekels of silver."

[117] "For the Son of Man came to seek and to save the lost." Lk.19:10

[118] "And he said to them, "Go into all the world and proclaim the gospel to the whole creation." Mk 16:15

[119] "I glorified you on earth, having accomplished the work that you gave me to do" Jn. 17:4

[120] "Go therefore and make disciples of all nations, *baptizing* them in the name of the Father and of the Son and of the Holy Spirit, *teaching them to observe all that I have commanded you.* And behold, I am with you always, to the end of the age." Matt.28:19 -20 "If you forgive the sins of any, they are forgiven them; if you withhold forgiveness from any, it is withheld." Jn.20:23The

Sacrament are Gracelets designed to help us to succeed. "For the law was given through Moses; grace and truth came through Jesus Christ." Jn.1:17.

121 "And when Jesus entered Peter's house, he saw his mother-in-law lying sick with a fever. He touched her hand, and the fever left her, and she rose and began to serve him. That evening they brought to him many who were oppressed by demons, and he cast out the spirits with a word and healed all who were sick. This was to fulfill what was spoken by the prophet Isaiah: "He took our illnesses and bore our diseases." Matt. 8:14-17

122 "And these signs will accompany those who believe: in my name they will cast out demons; they will speak in new tongues; they will pick up serpents with their hands; and if they drink any deadly poison, it will not hurt them; they will lay their hands on the sick, and they will recover."Mk. 16:17-18

123 Fr. Dennis had warned us about wearing them during ordination.

For more information on the Charismatic
Episcopal Church go to: www.iccec.org

Printed in the United States
By Bookmasters